BROKEN DREAMS

BROKEN DREAMS

Vanity, Greed and
the Souring of
British Football

TOM BOWER

POCKET
BOOKS

LONDON · SYDNEY · NEW YORK · TOKYO · SINGAPORE · TORONTO

First published in Great Britain by Simon & Schuster UK Ltd, 2003
This edition published by Pocket Books, 2003
An imprint of Simon & Schuster UK Ltd
A Viacom Company

1 3 5 7 9 10 8 6 4 2

Simon & Schuster UK Ltd
Africa House
64–78 Kingsway
London WC2B 6AH

www.simonsays.co.uk

Simon & Schuster Australia
Sydney

A CIP catalogue record for this book is available from the British Library

ISBN 0 7434 4033 1

Typeset by M Rules
Printed and bound in Great Britain by Cox & Wyman Ltd, Reading, Berkshire

To Alexander and Oliver,
and to the memory of
George G. Bower

Contents

1

INTRODUCTION

A Snapshot on 13 March 2002

In the uneven light, the complacency was suffocating. Football's apparatchiks were celebrating a funeral. On 13 March 2002 at West Ham's new stadium in east London, a hundred people witnessed the entombment of a valiant campaign for honesty in English football.

They were gathered for the launch of the Independent Football Commission, originally proposed to combat corruption in English football. On a raised dais in the middle of a long reception room beamed Professor Derek Fraser, the new Commission's chairman. Fraser's principal qualification seemed to be his obscurity. Until his appointment, the historian and vice-chancellor of the University of Teeside was unknown in public life beyond three inconsequential committees in Middlesbrough. In the distant past, Fraser had occasionally bought a ticket to watch football matches from the terraces. Chairmanship of the Independent Football Commission promised him enhanced status, association with a collection of marginal Westminster personalities and a guaranteed seat in every stadium across England and Wales.

During his introduction Professor Fraser did not minimize his impotence. He explained that the Commission could advise but not impose its opinions. 'I think the IFC can work,' said Fraser, emphasizing the word 'think', and continued, 'I can't promise it will work.' His own priority was to examine ticketing and merchandising – 'issues at the heart of football', he said – although he lacked any significant experience of investigation or regulation. Football fans would dispute his priorities. Many active supporters were irritated by individual clubs exploiting their life-long support, but the majority were more troubled by the developing financial crisis that endangered their club's survival. That peril was being aggravated by the drain of money towards spiralling wages, foreign clubs and unscrupulous agents. Fraser appeared oblivious to the fears of insolvency and widespread suspicions of dishonesty. 'I'm unaware of any corruption in football,' he announced, 'but there was a lecture at my university about corruption in public life. I was surprised about it.'

In the audience, Richard Scudamore, the pugnacious chief executive of the Premier League since October 1999, smiled with satisfaction. Over the previous three years, Scudamore, a former executive at Yellow Pages, and paid a salary of £653,495 by the Premier League, had opposed a proposal by the Labour government to create an effective regulator empowered to investigate any wrongdoing and enforce probity in football. That afternoon he chortled, 'I got what I wanted.' In his emphatic manner Scudamore insisted, 'There's no corruption in football.' The promoters of football's new gospel, especially the twenty chairmen of the Premier League clubs, habitually sneered at the orthodox fans who challenged those profiting from the game's glamour and passion. Football was no longer 'a working man's game' but an entertainment business. The Premier League had wilfully challenged and minimized the authority of the Football Association. Regulation was disliked by the mavericks, tycoons and opportunists attracted to football. United by their egoism and passion, they were accustomed to and even relished the harshness of their game, as shown by the selection of players and their violent clashes on the pitch. In summary, they disliked controls. 'Football is not a business but a sport dependent on excitement and speculation,' explained Scudamore breathlessly. 'The game's finances have always been precarious. Clubs have always spent more than they earned. Teams have always been on the verge of bankruptcy. And there'll always be rich men ready to pour more money into clubs just to be part of the game.'

The swirl of money from the Sky television bonanza had transformed English football. Premier League clubs employed some of the world's greatest players and their matches ranked among the best for any audience. Bravado mesmerized the English game. The slaughter at the Hillsborough and Heysel stadiums had been overshadowed by the new profiteering, attracting the incompetent and the dishonest. Old fans were appalled by the new culture. In the opinion of Scudamore's paymasters, however, any investigation of football's money trail was undesirable, unless compelling reasons arose.

On the platform, Richard Scudamore's triumphalism was endorsed by Adam Crozier, the chief executive of the FA. The image-conscious former advertising salesman, bearing a striking resemblance to Peter Mandelson, had once acknowledged the cancer of corruption in football. At a Lancing College old boys' dinner in March 2001, Crozier had identified specific transfers of foreign players, suggesting that millions of pounds had disappeared in 'bungs' – secret payments by agents to managers of clubs. Crozier's indiscretion had caused uproar among members of the FA. He had chosen never to repeat the truth publicly, preferring to categorize his revelation as 'tongue in cheek'. Thereafter, the aspiring modernizer emphasized the success of football's 'wide and extensive regulation'. At the launch of the Commission, Crozier praised the FA's imposition of 'best financial practice' on clubs, and spoke about the importance of 'accountability and transparency'. In self-justification he added, 'We, the FA, are the regulator.' If Crozier's self-praise was accurate, and football was well regulated by his staff, then the creation of the new Commission was unnecessary, but Crozier felt compelled to utter an admission. 'I can see that a lot in the running of football has not been right,' he conceded, and that justified the Commission's purpose to 'change football's culture, how it is managed and developed'. This was a marketing man lacking passionate affection for football or the confrontational manner to take on the combative chairmen of the Premier League clubs. He glanced nervously at Richard Caborn, the bearded minister of sport, sharing the platform.

The junior minister had discredited himself shortly after his appointment in June 2001 by revealing on radio his ignorance about sport. Creating the Commission had been delayed by two years, admitted Caborn apologetically, appealing to his audience to ignore 'earlier mistakes'. The word 'mistakes' was a guarded reference to the dispute during 1999 between those proposing the regulator – including Downing Street and members of the Labour government's 'Football Task Force' – and the Premier League and Football Association. The scars and anger had not disappeared. Caborn's endorsement of the Commission as 'the last piece of the jigsaw to be put into reality' rang hollow for those disappointed by the creation of a feckless committee rather than the establishment of an independent regulator. His speech also highlighted the irony of celebrating the victory of Richard Scudamore creating a toothless regulator at West Ham's stadium; an irony to which Professor Fraser and Richard Caborn were oblivious.

One year earlier, Harry Redknapp, West Ham's robust manager, had been dismissed. During seven turbulent years, Redknapp had bought and sold 134 players, an extraordinary number for any club. His hyperactivity had alarmed Terry Brown, West Ham's taciturn chairman. 'What is Harry up to?' Brown had occasionally asked Peter Storrie, the club's managing director. Storrie reassured Brown that there was no evidence of any dishonesty by Redknapp, just unease about his close relationships with agents and his own advice, 'You should make the bucks while you can.' Terry Brown's worries caused little concern to Richard Scudamore. The financial mysteries bedevilling the Premier League, the fatal imbalance between the clubs' precarious solvency and the multimillion pound earnings of their celebrity stars evoked limited distress. Football, like show business, in Scudamore's opinion, did not warrant the same intrusive supervision as imposed upon banks, Lloyds insurance and international corporations in the City of London. Passing football's 'fit and proper test', Scudamore believed, should not depend upon the financial record of football's executives but on the criterion of all sports: survival of the fittest, threatening the weakest with extinction.

This philosophy ignored football's status as the national sport, central to England's way of life and a microcosm of the nation's successes and failures. That football should be free of any suggestion of corruption and conflicts of interest was considered to be essential by outsiders who cast doubt over the game's probity. Those doubts were rejected by football's owners, managers and administrators. In their frantic bid to prosper, football's participants had been preoccupied by the events on the pitch, scornful about any debates concerning the morality of their methods in achieving that success. The romance conjured up about 'the beautiful game' by the book *Fever Pitch* escalated the passions and softened the doubts among football's new middle-class fans and the media. Even those club owners and executives who harboured suspicions about dishonesty in rival clubs, and occasionally feared duplicity by their own managers, preferred to overlook the financial chicanery surrounding the trade in players. Obtaining incriminating evidence about questionable relationships between managers and the players' agents was difficult even if the suspicions of wrongdoing were compelling.

Duplicity in the smaller clubs was serious but the scandals unearthed during the previous decade at Tottenham, Arsenal and Nottingham Forest had become notorious. The legacy was ceaseless gossip made far worse after Sky television paid £1.3 billion in 2001 for the exclusive rights over three years to the Premier League's matches. The new fortune had flowed swiftly through the clubs to footballers and their agents, often abroad. All were enriching themselves by charging millions of pounds to organize and approve the transfers of players. The more disreputable agents were suspected to be secretly paying club managers a portion of their commissions as bribes for buying their players. Dishonest managers, some club chairmen were convinced, were even purchasing unqualified players just to receive the secret payments, or 'bungs', from the agents. The trade in people was diverting precious money out of English football, especially from the clubs struggling in the lower divisions. England's football, the purists complained, was being strangled by greed.

Football's tacit endorsement of sleaze is emblazoned on the stadium at Nottingham Forest's ground. Huge red letters on the roof pronounce 'The Brian Clough Stand'. Brian Clough, the club's famous former manager, was condemned in 1998 for his dishonesty but he remained a hero for his team's victories in Europe. Financial irregularities off the pitch were deemed by Clough's many admirers to be irrelevant. The remedy proposed by the critics was an independent regulator but the reaction by football's executives to accountability was emphatic. 'Get rid of any idea of an independent regulator,' David Dein, the successful vice-chairman of Arsenal and aspirant to become the chairman of the Football Association, had told Richard Scudamore.

Dein's gospel of non-interference mirrored that of the old guard in the City of London during the 1980s. Just as the unscrupulousness of a minority threatened football, the City of London's reputation and fortunes had been harmed by similar behaviour. Self-regulation, the City of London players had repeatedly preached, was essential for their continued prosperity. But successive scandals, destroying the credibility and value of traditional City institutions, demolished the resistance to independent regulation. Numerous greedy, incompetent, blinkered English players in the City were ousted, casualties of their own self-interest. Many of England's prestigious financial institutions vanished without a trace. Their successors were dynamic and efficient, but mostly foreign-owned. Richard Scudamore, David Dein and others in the Premier League denied that the same fate threatened English football. Stubbornly, the sport's scions preached that the problems of football's ethics and morality would be resolved by those involved in the game. It was different from the City, they argued; their sport was not a business but an infatuation. Yet their self-interest was short-sighted.

In public, the clubs' directors took a sentimental view of football's survival and spoke of old values, but at the same time they swaggered like modern business tycoons, preoccupied by money and promoting superstars. The message was confusing. Emotion had not been the sentiment displayed by Richard Scudamore's members during the flotation of their clubs on London's stock exchange during the 1990s, or in their quest for £1 billion of loans. Football, the chairmen had boasted to the bankers, was a mature, money-making machine. Then, deluded by their self-promotion, the clubs' chairmen had recklessly wasted their millions.

In 1992, there were eleven foreign players employed by English clubs. In 1999, there were over 200 foreign players and, out of the £150 million spent on players during that summer, £125 million was earned by overseas clubs. The money was lost to British football. In 2002, nearly half the 896 players registered by Premier League clubs were not British, despite the lower wages which British players expected. Managers, owing no life-long loyalty to the clubs' chairmen, and knowing that managers were rarely fired for spending too much money, had been buying in a bid for glory. The wages paid by clubs were exceeding their income. Some chairmen, employing players on contracts beyond the expiry of the Sky agreement and struggling to repay loans, feared their finances were unsustainable. Only the sale of players could cover their trading losses. Vulnerable chairmen turned to Richard Scudamore to judge the odds in their gamble with financial reality. 'We can stay bullish,' said Scudamore. 'We've got a good product.'

Investors disagreed. During 2001 football clubs' share prices collapsed. The clubs had become financial pygmies. The national sport revealed its dependence on external funding, private and governmental. Few protested that public money was supporting the country's richest sport, although football's commercial naivety threatened self-destruction. Like the City of London, the clubs could contemplate consolidation to avoid poverty, disintegration and disaster, but in the process the harmonious equality of England's football tradition would disappear. While the Premier League clubs could prosper, the gulf between the giants and the rest would ruin football and an inherent quality of English culture. That scenario was refuted by Richard Scudamore and his principal supporters in the Premier League. The extinction of football clubs, unlike England's former major industries – coal, shipbuilding, heavy machinery and electronics – was impossible, Scudamore argued, thanks to the wallets of publicity-seeking millionaires eager to replace a sinking chairman.

Becoming the owner of a Premier League club was the dream of countless businessmen eager to emerge from obscurity to mix with celebrities and enjoy the spotlight. The lure attracting aspiring chairmen was the eruption of roars of excitement in their own stadiums. Sitting in the centre of the front row, their self-importance was fed by the idea that they could grant the wishes of the fans. Even so, their pleasure was often offset by the pain of threats and abuse from fans whose lives were dedicated to their clubs. Any failure to deliver an optimistic prediction threatened a chairman's reputation. To avoid that fate, they bowed to irrational pressure that the club's money should never be conserved but spent on new players. The reality of the business of football was spending at whatever cost to sustain popularity among those besotted by the game, to avoid the risk of losing a reputation.

Public humiliation troubled the twenty chairmen of the Premier League clubs. Embarrassment was familiar in their trade. Players were debunked by their managers; managers, fearing dismissal, were chastened by the clubs' chairmen; and the chairmen were abused by shareholders and disgruntled fans, especially those executives vaingloriously seeking applause by appearing on the pitch. Those emotions were evident at the Premier League's regular meetings held every three months, either at the League's headquarters near Hyde Park or at the Landmark Hotel, near Marylebone in central London.

To suggest equality, the chairmen sat in the alphabetical order of their clubs, but in their medieval court there was no sense of democracy. The Big Five – Rick Parry of Liverpool, Peter Kenyon of Manchester United, Peter Ridsdale of Leeds, David Dein of Arsenal and Ken Bates of Chelsea – were tenacious combatants, often trying to price the other fifteen chairmen out of the market. In their battle to win the championships, the Big Five's expenditure depressed their smaller neighbours and enhanced their self-esteem, which was also regularly massaged by their appearance on the back pages of the tabloid newspapers, and by their salaries. Ridsdale earned £645,000 per annum, Kenyon £563,000, Parry £457,000, Dein about £500,000, while Ken Bates's complete income remained a mystery. Their new fame, spread beyond their small fiefdoms, encouraged cynicism, not least among themselves. Amusingly, the same men who constantly discussed and determined the fate and public reputations of professional footballers, displayed extreme sensitivity about the public portrayal of their own status.

Ken Bates and David Dein epitomized the exceptional vanities. The bearded chairman of Chelsea, having completed the reconstruction of his stadium within the aspiring Chelsea Village complex, was convinced that his team would win immortal glory. Few among his peers shared that optimism, not least because his abrasive manner weakened his credibility. Although Bates often spoke sense and won applause – 'Oh Peter, why don't you piss off out of the Premier League,' he memorably cursed Peter Kenyon for advocating a European super league – his vulgarity and tiresome pontification about every subject undermined his audience's trust. The frequent banter between Bates and David Dein provided hilarity but little sense. Whatever Dein said always sparked a venomous tease from Bates, whom he taunted as 'an evil man with too much influence'.

David Dein attracted respect but also wariness. Even among that select clan, the ambition and outspokenness of the suave vice-chairman of Arsenal were exceptional. His acknowledged passion for his club – he was the architect of Arsenal's success and a modernizing influence on English football – was said by his critics to equal his passion for himself. Few doubted that his ultimate target was to become the chairman of the Football Association. Opinion about the likelihood of his success was divided, but rivals hinted at his weakened personal finances and the strain of his relationships with other Arsenal directors. Twice he had been embarrassed by Bates during those meetings: first, for his forlorn attempt between 1991 and 1992 to forge an alliance with ITV rather than the more profitable Sky; and second, after other Arsenal directors were revealed as secretly negotiating to buy

Wembley stadium for the club while the FA was simultaneously committing itself to a redevelopment scheme.
Dein asserted complete ignorance about these negotiations. Gleefully, Bates trumpeted Dein's distress;
although in retaliation Bates was reminded about the
£105,000 fine imposed in January 1991 on Chelsea by
the Football League for irregular payments to players.

These personality clashes amused Peter Ridsdale, the
dedicated chairman of Leeds since 1997. The profile of
the amiable former human resources director, and managing director of Top Man, carefully nurtured as
everyone's friend, especially among his team's supporters,
was overshadowed by the violence among his players and
their fans. The club had also borrowed £60 million from
Lazards to buy players and win the championship. The
unkind among his peers recited Ridsdale's alleged rheto-
ric: 'I don't know whether to stand for election as the
chairman of the FA or for the House of Commons.' His
support for Bates, and against Dein, especially for the
reconstruction of Wembley, placed him as a trusted
insider, and another favourite to chair the FA.

Regardless of those differences, the three – Dein, Bates
and Ridsdale – were united in public to protect their
mutual interests. Disciplinary proceedings against
Premier League clubs were avoided and any mention of
irregularities was smothered. The three felt they could
rely on Rick Parry of Liverpool not to protest. The
respected former chief executive of the Premier League
was accustomed to backstabbing among the twenty chairmen and admired the rough-edged, swashbuckling style
of the old guard still lusting for success. Reluctant to perform as a main player, Parry was pleased to praise Bates's
altruism for saving Chelsea and the commitment of Doug
Ellis of Aston Villa to the game.

'Deadly' Doug Ellis, seated between Dein and Bates, was the unfashionable face of the Premier League. 'I'm a frustrated footballer who had to buy a football club,' he said about Aston Villa, where the game was first played in 1874 to keep workers warm. With the millions he had earned from nineteen businesses including hotels, holiday tours, telephones, a brewery, house building and land speculation, Ellis indulged his vanity. His bright-red Rolls Royce, registration number AV1, was parked prominently by the stadium and, on match days, whenever he raised his eyes from the pitch, he gazed at the gigantic red letters on the roof of the new stand opposite spelling 'The Doug Ellis Stand'. 'They insisted on the name,' explained the chairman about his fellow directors, although over the years he had repeated, 'The best committee is one person.'

A less pleasing sight for the chairman on match days was the substitutes sitting idly on benches, each earning over £20,000 per week. 'My God,' he cursed, calculating their cost at £20 million, contributing to the club's pre-tax losses of £400,000 in 2002, a distressing reversal from £22 million profits in 1998. His rivals, Ellis believed, would be crippled by their loans to buy players. Those who dreamt of profits from football relying on the crude arithmetic that a 42,000 crowd on match days produced an income of £540,000 were misled. A good result on the pitch spawned an illusion of financial success. Success in the Premier League cost a fortune, Ellis calculated, and the debts were suicidal. 'I never borrow money which I can't afford to pay back,' he preached. The consequence was a team which never won trophies, unfilled seats in the stadium and the hostility of Villa's supporters towards the chairman's financial prudence. 'I'll not call them yobbos,' Ellis told critics. 'They are my customers.

But my duty is to look after the shareholders' interests.'
The major shareholder was Ellis himself, who had
bought a 47 per cent stake in Aston Villa in 1982 for
£425,000 and kept 33 per cent of the shares on flotation
in 1997, valuing his stake at the time at £42 million. By
the end of 2002, his shares were worth £4.3 million.

Ellis had a strange affection for Bates. 'His ego gets in
the way of his club,' mused Ellis. 'He's a man who
believes in his own eternity and suffers from self-inflicted
love bites.' Ellis had never forgotten Bates's gripe after
chartering his yacht in the Mediterranean. 'The cook was
no good,' Bates complained on his return. Bates was similarly carping about Ellis: he was old, offered nothing for
the future, he was surrounded by no talent and his team
attracted poor crowds.

As the founding chief executive of the Premier
League, Rick Parry, a sober accountant, had witnessed
the influence of the new millions paid by television upon
his nineteen colleagues. Greed, egoism and rivalry had
contaminated their relationships. At the outset, he had
been staggered. 'It's a nightmare. Horrific,' he complained to a friend. 'They're knifing each other.
Practically hitting each other. They even send me newspaper cuttings to support their allegations of
wrongdoing.' The roots of their hostility were traced
back to David Dein's coup in 1988 in forging a deal on
behalf of the First Division with ITV. In 1992, the
supporters of ITV's bid opposed any proposal by Sky's
supporters, and vice-versa. 'I can't get a two-thirds
majority for anything,' Parry had confessed. The crunch
was the proposal that the Premier League should accept
the sponsorship of Carling beer. Automatically, seven
supporters of ITV's bid voted against. 'That's it,'
hollered Ron Noades, the combative chairman of Crystal

Palace. 'I'm fed up with all of this. It's a complete shambles. I'm off.' To the astonishment of David Dein,
Noades stomped out of the room and was followed by
twelve other chairmen. Parry gazed at the remaining six.
Dein looked sheepish. 'I think the meeting's come to an
end,' said Parry teasingly. 'There's no quorum,' agreed
Sir John Quinton, the chairman, 'so that's the end.' Dein,
a man with a carefully cultivated reputation, blushed.
Erasing the memory of that embarrassment had been
Parry's task while touring the country to negotiate a permanent truce. Even so, the mood was changing. The
unexpected value of Sky's bid would transform their
clubs. Continuing the arguments would impede their
opportunity to maximize profits. So the seven capitulated
and outright warfare ceased.

Eight years later, managing the permanent rivalry at
the quarterly meetings was the responsibility of Dave
Richards, the former chairman of Sheffield Wednesday.
Moderate and shy of the media, Richards was tolerated as
chairman because, unlike Sir John Quinton, his predecessor, he understood the business idiosyncrasies of the
clubs. In the football world Richards was still considered
to be financially savvy although his company, Three Star
Engineering, had slid towards insolvency. In 1997, he sold
36 per cent of Sheffield Wednesday for £15.6 million to
Charterhouse, a merchant bank, who expected to take a
profit after the club reached the top of the Premier
League. Instead, the club was relegated to the First
Division and the bank was marooned with huge debts.
Charterhouse would sell its interest in 2000 for £2 million. Richards's appointment as chairman, with the
support of Ken Bates, was not applauded by Joe Ashton,
the local Sheffield MP: 'It's like the captain of the *Titanic*
being appointed First Lord of the Admiralty.'

Even among their peers in the conference room, more than half of the chairmen, titans in their home towns, were too nervous to speak. Freddie Shepherd of Newcastle was silent; Bill Kenwright of Everton, hailed as a 'lovely man' but deemed to be 'out of his depth', paying excessive wages and transfer fees on the orders of his executives, sat passively; and Terry Brown, the solid chairman of West Ham, watched with disdain the clash of vanities. Daniel Levy, the Cambridge-educated chairman of Tottenham, observed the propriety of a newcomer, listening to a group of men who shared basic courtesies but wilfully abandoned loyalties to score an advantage.

Between the clamorous and the silent were the tolerated minnows. Rupert Lowe, the decent chairman of Southampton, won some kudos for realism. 'We've bobbed and diced with death for twenty-three years,' he conceded, but he was scathing about those espousing the 'That's the way we've always done it' mentality. Opposite Lowe was Richard Murray, the sensible saviour of Charlton Athletic. For ten years Murray had toiled, watching two-thirds of his financial investment disappear. 'Football is a charity not a business,' he lamented. Only Liverpool, Arsenal and Manchester United, exploiting global brands, could be certain of profits. Murray's consolation was to participate in the world's richest football game while dismissing, like the other chairmen, any notion of distributing their new wealth around the remaining clubs of the Football League.

David Sheepshanks, an Old Etonian and the erratic chairman of Ipswich, recently promoted to the Premier League, sought to spearhead greater modernization. In 1999 he hired Lord Bell, the publicist, to promote his bid to succeed Keith Wiseman as chairman of the FA. Bitter that the Premier League had preferred to support Geoff

Thompson's candidacy, Sheepshanks sought to recover from his defeat by campaigning to replace either Ellis or Bates on the FA's board in 2002. 'A man with a huge ego who should think about his own club,' murmured Ellis about Sheepshanks, the sage bemused by the conceit of a self-publicist. 'To have an ego in football without the gravitas is dangerous. He sets himself up as a champion of all clubs, but here it's dog-eats-dog.'

None of the club chairmen was prepared to allow outside monitoring of finances. Nearly all opposed the idea of signing undertakings that their directors had not made secret payments to agents or players. 'There's overwhelming opposition to regulation,' admitted David Davies, an executive on the FA. Few chairmen cared to trust the FA.

At the end of every meeting, the twenty representatives departed to continue their fight among themselves. Football, they were content to reassert, remained a law unto itself – even in the event of financial catastrophe or intolerable dishonesty.

1

THE SOLITARY INVESTIGATOR

The investigator was frustrated. Four years after his appointment as football's 'sleaze-buster', Graham Bean was unloved and faintly ridiculed. Malpractice and even allegations of corruption were rife in the Premier League, but the tycoons owning and controlling the game appeared unconcerned by the defiance of the rules and regulations.

Graham Bean's appointment in November 1998 by the FA as football's 'compliance officer' had been dismissed as tokenism by most of the twenty chairmen of the Premier League, who ranked among the world's richest football owners. The notion of a 37-year-old detective constable from Yorkshire singlehandedly eradicating corruption in the national sport, they scoffed, was fatuous. His nomination served only to placate public opinion and the Labour government. To many of those self-important tycoons, revelling in power and publicity, the 'sleaze-buster's' anticipated failure was reassuring. As far as they were concerned, interference in their business was unwelcome.

By chance Bean had heard the telephone ring at his home, a terraced house in Cudworth, near Barnsley, at

9.30 a.m. as he passed on his patrol around the village.
After eighteen years as a policeman – smashing violent
gangs and securing dozens of convictions – Bean had welcomed the news as a stepping stone to something better.
Fortunately his credentials had appealed to the FA. The
detective was the representative of the Football Supporters
Association and was participating in the Labour government's Football Task Force. On the morning of his
appointment, the passionate football fan was proud about
the FA's courage and honesty. As the regulator of the
sport's integrity in the country's 43,000 clubs, the organization was empowered to supervise the game's finances,
protect clubs from property developers stripping out the
assets and root out corruption. 'FIFA don't have someone
like me,' he noted about football's international governing
authority, 'because they're so corrupt.'

Four years later, Bean had become disillusioned with
the FA and with the chairmen of the football clubs, especially those in the Premier League. 'English football is
bent,' the 'sleaze-buster' confided to friends. Bungs,
bribes, frauds and a flood of cash had besmirched his
beloved sport. Corruption, he concluded, was endemic.
His task, he lamented, was physically impossible for one
man. He had visited every club to discover and appoint a
single informant but under pressure from the clubs'
chairmen, the FA was 'backing down too quickly' after
his reports of irregularities. The FA's priorities, he
believed, were 'wrong'.

Some blamed in particular Nic Coward, the FA's secretary, for failing to enforce the rules. The 34-year-old
grey-haired lawyer trained at Freshfields, a major solicitors' partnership in the City, was unaccustomed to
complicated investigations and to any distasteful repercussions. Some criticized Coward's lack of leadership, his

preference for rugby rather than football, and his inclina-
tion to mask problems. To some occupants of the FA's
new headquarters in Soho Square, Bean's exposure of
twelve months of corruption at Hull and Chesterfield
football clubs in 2000 had elicited few congratulations.
Even the imprisonment in 1999 of Ken Richardson, the
owner of Doncaster Rovers, for conspiring to burn down
the stadium of the 120-year-old club had not aroused the
FA to impose any fine, not least because the process would
have publicized the decision in 1984 to ban Richardson for
twenty-five years from horse racing. Some FA officials
sensed Coward's lack of support and a nervous antagonism towards Bean's investigations. The evidence was
Coward's attitude after the criticism of Paul Scally, the
chairman of Gillingham FC. Scally had been criticized for
allegedly betting on football games and the club was under
investigation for alleged financial irregularities. Eventually
Coward acted against Gillingham although his hesitation
could be criticized as apparent indifference. 'What's happening?' asked Bean some months later. 'I know I've got a
decision to make on Gillingham,' replied Coward. As the
official responsible for the FA's regulations, Coward was
criticized as a reluctant enforcer who vocally rejected any
responsibility for vetting. Eventually, Scally paid, but
Coward's apparent hesitation reflected the indifference
among the FA's senior personalities.

Bean was the sole guardian against that indifference
but the twenty chief executives attending the quarterly
meeting of the Premier League at the Landmark Hotel
on 12 December 2001 were scathing about him. 'A lone
police constable isn't going to solve anything,' Rick Parry
had told his competitors. 'What hope has he got?' agreed
another of football's warlords. 'Just another sergeant,'
said David Sheepshanks dismissively about 'Constable

Bean'. 'A bloody compliance officer pursuing newspaper tips,' scoffed Ken Bates with his customary venom. The abrasive property developer had protested to the FA about Bean, even mentioning court action to avoid Bean's intrusion. Some chairmen appeared to approve the dictum 'First you get on, then you get rich, then you get honest'.

Their contempt towards Graham Bean mirrored their irritation towards the agents who represented their employees. Control of the agents – condemned as rogues – was a familiar topic among the chairmen, despite their disagreement about retaliation. 'I don't want any controls over agents,' said Bates. Although they may have had mixed feelings towards Ken Bates, many chairmen shared his resentment towards any interference in their negotiations to sign players. In their view, so long as the buyer and seller were satisfied, financial chicanery was irrelevant.

That detachment towards uncontrolled agents troubled David Dein. He suggested a code of conduct, insisting that agents were paid over the length of a player's contract to discourage any incentive to move players constantly and earn extra commissions. 'Crap,' snarled Ken Bates. As usual, the discussion ended in stalemate, although eventually Bates and the FA accepted Dein's idea. It would have marginal influence. Their paperless business, brokered in secretive conversations between men committed to discretion, was impenetrable to outsiders. In many cases the financial arrangements between the clubs and agents were unverifiable. Payments were occasionally either deposited in anonymous offshore companies established to conceal the identity of the beneficiaries, or given in cash. In this atmosphere, there was little sympathy for Graham Bean.

Richard Murray, a representative of the less wealthy clubs, ranked among Bean's few supporters. 'There are some dubious people involved in management and agencies,' he said, 'and we need to do something.' Corruption, Murray thought, helped the bigger clubs at the expense of the smaller clubs. With less money, some minor clubs would disappear and honest people would be deterred from involvement. The rebuttal was swift. 'As long as they don't stand on my toes,' snapped a voice down the table, 'I don't care. I won't go out of my way to investigate.'

There was an uncomfortable silence until Rupert Lowe suggested that agents' fees should be controlled through the PAYE income tax system. Lowe, who had angrily spurned the offer of money by an agent during a train journey to Lille, was supported by David Sheepshanks. The Old Etonian's refusal earlier that year to pay agents had proved harmful: agents, Sheepshanks discovered, had refused to offer his club any players. Reluctantly, he had agreed to pay 5 per cent commission, but he wanted the Premier League clubs to agree that all payments should be declared. The silent expressions of rejection by Parry, Bates, Dein and Martin Edwards and Peter Kenyon of Manchester United terminated the debate. Richard Scudamore, deftly presenting himself as all things to all men, understood the Big Five's requirement to dictate the outcome of critical issues. Little had changed since Peter Leaver QC, his predecessor, had concluded, 'the clubs whinge about agents all the time but don't want to do anything. They don't even want to register their fees.'

Regulations are anathema to mavericks, especially types like Ken Bates, the architect of Chelsea's revival, whose business history appeared to test the assurances

by Adam Crozier and Richard Scudamore that the game
and its finances were properly regulated to ensure that
only those passing the 'fit and proper' test would be
accepted by the Premier League and FA. 'An unwelcom-
ing club,' Bean had reported to Nic Coward, referring to
Chelsea. Even Arsenal was immune to Bean's scrutiny.
'Investigating anything at Arsenal is more than my job's
worth,' confessed Bean. The relationship between the
Premier League clubs and agents would not be investigated. Scudamore nodded towards Rick Parry to voice
the conclusion. 'We need to compete with Real Madrid
and other European clubs,' said Parry. 'We can't control
the agents alone. We've got to leave it to FIFA.'

Relying on FIFA, the international football regulator,
was futile. The organization's past investigations of
alleged irregularities involving agents had been incom-
plete, filed and forgotten. In its Zürich headquarters,
Sepp Blatter, the president, was under attack for corruption. Millions of pounds were said to be unaccounted for
and there were stories about Blatter's payments of cash to
African delegates in 1998 to secure their votes for his
election. Corruption in football was firmly established at
the sport's summit. Few doubted that the sport, awash
with billions of pounds, was defiled by 'bungs'. Graham
Bean's struggle to produce evidence of dishonesty satisfied outsiders and reassured the guilty. Football's history
over the previous thirty years proved the existence of dishonesty and confirmed the impossibility of its cure.

Hard-drinking, foul-mouthed and popular, Tommy
Docherty, the coach of Manchester United from 1972
until 1977, personified the lovable debauchery and irresistible intoxication of football. Born in Glasgow's
Gorbals, the footballer had been the darling of his fellow
professionals and the media. He personified the game's

habit of giving enormous pleasure but also inflicting terrible destruction during a managerial career before the dramatic change in football's finances.

In Docherty's era, BBC Television annually paid less than £50,000 for the rights to film all of the First Division's matches, and the club owners profited from cheap labour. Contractually, players were the possession of the clubs, unable to move freely; they always risked an abrupt termination of their careers by injuries. Bobby Charlton, Denis Law and George Best – all football legends in their lifetimes – were earning between £250 and £350 per week. Apart from Stanley Matthews and other unblemished heroes, football players were treated with limited respect. In a revolutionary change in 1978, the Football League allowed players to be transferred on free contracts to determine their own fate and the transfer fees rose. Some club managers sought to benefit from the new, lucrative trade.

Greed was Tommy Docherty's ruin. In 1977, he was dismissed by Manchester United. His fame was transformed into notoriety. Away from the spotlight, gossips spoke about his affair with the wife of the club's physiotherapist and his avarice. In November 1978, he was suspended by Derby for admitting in a libel trial that he had told 'a pack of lies'. He was also accused by the club of taking a £1,000 bribe for allowing George Best to play a match in 1973 for Dunstable. His nemesis came when he was arrested by Detective Superintendent Jim Reddington of the local police concerning three suspicious transfers valued at £2 million. With remarkable speed, the players had arrived at Derby and left soon after, arousing the suggestion that Docherty had received 'bungs' from the transactions. After his exhaustive inquiry Reddington decided not to prosecute Docherty and, untroubled, the manager departed from Derby in April 1979 for Queens Park Rangers. Docherty remained unashamed of the allegations. 'I've always said there's a place for the press,' he said after the storm of publicity, 'but they haven't dug it yet.' In a lunchtime speech to the Football Writers Association, the manager was candid about his morality. 'Lots of times,' laughed Docherty, 'managers have to be cheats and conmen. People say we tell lies. Of course we tell lies. We are the biggest hypocrites. We cheat. In our business the morals are all different. The only way to survive is by cheating. And there's no way that can be changed. That's our life, that's the law of our life.'

Docherty's confession aroused little surprise. In that era, at least one turnstile on every football ground was said to belong to the club's chairman, to provide cash for bungs and his lifestyle. 'Folding doesn't tell stories,' was the maxim mentioned by players, stuffing brown envelopes in their pockets and laughing over the apocryphal story describing a gust of wind blowing their manager's cash dividend across a beach. Docherty, insiders knew, was unexceptional. Sir Denis Follows, the general secretary of the FA, was renowned for his collection of emeralds and the acceptance of gold cuff-links as presents for casting his vote. His confidants at the FA were familiar with Follows's complaint that Stanley Rous, his predecessor and the president of FIFA, had informed the representatives of other nations about his gratitude for contributions to his collection of gold watches. Rous, it was said with some laughter, had lost his position in 1974, after twelve years, to the challenger Joao Havelange because the Brazilian had actually given the gold watches to African delegates casting their vote for him. Rous's greed influenced Ted Croker, the FA's general secretary in the 1970s. Croker was fond of charging his suits, haircuts and holiday golf trips to his expenses. His income, it was said, was supplemented by supplying black market tickets for key matches to Flashman, a notorious character. In 1977, allegations were made about the corruption of Don Revie, the admired but neurotic manager of England's team, and renowned for encouraging the Leeds United team to play violently.

Don Revie's appointment as England's manager had surprised those who remembered his corruption during the 1960s as the manager of Leeds. Eyewitnesses recalled five occasions on which Revie had offered cash to opposing players to 'go easy' and let Leeds win or score more goals. Among those who refused was Bob Stokoe, the player-manager of Bury, who rejected Revie's offer of £500. Revie also offered illegal payments to attract players to Leeds. Other eyewitnesses recalled that Revie in 1971 had ordered his subordinates to enter the dressing rooms and offer players money to throw a match allowing Leeds to win. In 1972, he had repeated the offer to get 'the right result' against Wolves, when Leeds needed one point to win the Double. The offer was rejected, and Leeds lost 2–1. Rigging match results in English football was not unknown. In 1963, three had been jailed for such a conspiracy on behalf of Sheffield Wednesday; but that had not been orchestrated by a lauded manager of the England team.

In 1977, the *Daily Mirror* threatened to expose Don Revie. To avoid embarrassment England's manager suddenly abandoned the national team without any public explanation and accepted a two year contract with Abu Dhabi's Football Association. Revie assumed (correctly) that while he was away he could stymie the FA's investigation of the *Mirror*'s dossier. Ted Croker, the FA's

general secretary, had assembled a five-man committee,
but they were content to remain paralysed until Revie
returned to Britain four years later. To Croker's satisfaction, when Revie returned to Britain the *Mirror*'s
allegations were suppressed by Revie serving a writ for
libel on the newspaper and claiming that the rules of '*sub
judice*' prevented him answering the FA's questions.

Croker's behaviour showed that the football family
cared for its own kind; the 'guardians' of football would
resist outsiders imposing any restrictions upon their
heroes. Although a judge subsequently condemned
Revie's behaviour as 'deceitful and greedy', Croker continued to remain silent and quietly assisted Revie's
masquerade. Croker's memoirs, published in 1987, con-
jure a false scenario for Revie's unexpected resignation in
1977. Revie, Croker wrote, threatened to resign unless
he was paid £100,000. Croker described the FA's refusal
to pay as the provocation for Revie's departure and effectively concealed the anticipated revelation of Revie's
corruption as the reason for the manager's resignation.
The truth only emerged after Revie's death in 1989, and
even then the FA maintained its silence. Some simply
blamed an encrusted regulator, but insiders understood
that Revie's corrupt methods had developed deep roots.
Insiders were even suspicious that some players at
Manchester United may have also been involved in a conspiracy to fix certain matches between 1960 and 1962.
Harry Gregg, United's goalkeeper, claimed publicly that
he had been offered money to allow goals through.

The personification of football's culture of dishonesty
was Brian Clough, the hero of Nottingham Forest.
Drunken, outspoken and flamboyant, Clough, who managed Nottingham Forest between 1975 and 1993, was
praised by fans and commentators for winning the

League and twice winning the European Cup, in 1979
and 1980. The price was Clough's apparent belief that
success had bequeathed a licence for a secret income.
Between April 1987 and April 1993, Clough masterminded fifty-eight transfers worth £19.5 million and he
allegedly pocketed about £1 million in cash paid back to
him by grateful agents and managers. Provocatively, in
1980, Clough created a company called Sting Ltd.
Eventually he would pay the Inland Revenue £600,000
for unpaid taxes. Clough's dishonesty passed unchecked,
partly because he generously ensured that others benefited from his deceit, and partly because no one in
football's family deemed it proper to interfere.

Some of the players at Forest were paid cash paid out
through the club's community scheme and the catering
business; some scouts were rewarded with huge sums of
cash in brown envelopes, and a favoured few were alleged
to have received signing-on fees in Guernsey accounts.
Even the club's accountant, Andrew Plumb, was convicted of stealing money. During the Clough era Plumb
stole £70,000 from the club for personal expenses, possibly from cash received at the turnstiles for tickets. The
club never complained to the police, and even after
Plumb's conviction the club declined an independent
examination of its accounts.

In spite of the restrictions on football agents, the FA
showed little concern whether the rules were followed. 'I
don't trust any agent,' said Doug Ellis, who had reluctantly collaborated with rogue agents over the previous
thirty-three years – he saw them as necessary evils to sustain his dream. In 1993, Ellis had sought to buy Mark
Bosnich, an Australian goalkeeper who had been forced
by British immigration laws to resign from Manchester
United and return home. In order to play for Aston Villa,

Bosnich would need to become a British citizen. A plan to
change Bosnich's nationality was encouraged by Graham
Smith, the director of First Wave, an agency. By marry-
ing Lisa Hall, an English woman, suggested Smith, the
Australian would automatically receive British citizenship. 'I suggested a marriage,' said Ellis, although Lisa
Hall would angrily deny that the marriage was 'arranged',
albeit that six months later the couple parted. Graham
Smith's fee from Ellis for arranging a transfer was an
immediate payment of £150,000 and a promise of a further £150,000 after Bosnich had made 150 first-team
appearances. As a member of the FA's international and
finance committees, Ellis knew that his use of an agent
was a breach of the FA's rules.

Graham Smith denied acting as an agent for Bosnich.
'Everything we do is absolutely 100 per cent above
board,' Smith declared. 'If I put a price on a player it's
not a transfer fee. It's a consultancy fee.' Few believed the
explanation. Aston Villa was fined £20,000 by the FA for
irregular dealings with an agent, but Ellis remained on
the FA's committees. 'I only broke the rules slightly,' said
Ellis, adding that only 'very few' managers took 'bungs'
from agents. The chairman of Aston Villa showed himself to be a canny businessman with a special talent for
sniffing out dubious relationships.

The leaders of English football consoled themselves
that corruption in other countries appeared to be far
worse. In Brazil, Renata Alves, a secretary employed by
the national coach, admitted that he left meetings with a
briefcase stuffed with dollars from commissions for selling players; while Wanderley Luxemburgo, a Brazilian
coach, admitted that players were included in the national
team at the request of unnamed agents to increase their
value. In Italy, Paolo Rossi, a sprightly forward, was

accused of throwing matches in return for bribes but was acquitted in a trial on the grounds that 'sporting fraud is not a crime'. In Portugal, referees were convicted of accepting money, furs, holidays and prostitutes from clubs for fixing matches. In France, a six year investigation of Olympique Marseille's defeat of AC Milan in 1993 for the European Cup established that teams and players had been bribed to ease Marseille's path to the championship. In Switzerland, Kurt Roethlisberger, an international referee, was banned for life after offering a Swiss club to fix a match for 100,000 Swiss francs. The condemnation of Roethlisberger triggered off other accounts about referees and stories of whole teams across Europe and South America wilfully throwing matches in return for bribes. In the Greek and Italian championships the final positions at the end of the season were notoriously price-sensitive.

English football appeared immune from that level of corruption until in November 1994 the *Sun* newspaper published allegations that Bruce Grobbelaar, an unorthodox and theatrical goalkeeper, had taken a bribe of £40,000 in 1993 while playing for Liverpool to allow Newcastle to score and win. Grobbelaar was also accused of being offered £175,000 to 'miss' saves in two matches and that he had lost a £125,000 bribe by mistakenly saving a goal. The evidence against Grobbelaar appeared damning. He had been secretly filmed in a hotel room discussing the bribes with a friend from Zimbabwe. The revelations cast a mood that English football had 'lost its soul' in 'a season of scandal'. But the comments of Rick Parry, the first chief executive of the Premier League, suggested scepticism: 'None of us want to believe it, and I don't by the way, because that would be betraying the game more than any single act I could think of.'

Grobbelaar and others were arrested on 14 March 1995.
Two years later, a jury failed to reach a verdict. At the end
of the second trial in August 1997, Grobbelaar and his co-
defendants were acquitted. Grobbelaar's innocence
appeared to be finally established by a jury awarding him
damages of £85,000 in a libel case against the *Sun*. But
the two juries who had declared his innocence were
refuted by the Court of Appeal in January 2001. Three
judges upheld an appeal by the *Sun* and declared that
Grobbelaar had confessed to match-fixing in the secret
tape, a decision in large measure confirmed by the House
of Lords who awarded Grobbelaar contemptible damages
of £1 on the basis that although there was evidence of his
taking money, it was not proved that he was fixing match
results. Six years after the original allegations Grobbelaar
was declared to be guilty. By then, any shock had evaporated. The only punishment he suffered was a fine of
£10,000 and a ban on playing for six months imposed by
the FA for admitting he forecast the result of matches to
a Far East betting syndicate. Grobbelaar had become an
unmentioned sideshow to more serious chicanery.

   In the House of Commons, on 30 January 1995, Kate
Hoey, the feisty Labour MP with a special interest in
sport, had demanded that the Conservative government
intervene to deal with 'the variety of allegations, scandals
and corrupt practices which have surrounded the game in
recent years'. Hoey, an active football supporter, used the
protection of parliamentary privilege to accuse a clutch of
football's heroes of dishonesty. Among her cast list were
Brian Clough, George Graham, Ron Atkinson, Terry
Venables and an infamous agent, Eric Hall. 'Millions of
pounds,' she alleged, were 'siphoned off from the game in
backhanders, bungs and fixes.' Some personalities, she
alleged, had breached the 1906 Corruption Act; and one

was renowned for asking, 'Is there a sweetie in it for me?' Conservative ministers, she shrilled angrily, refused to treat football seriously. Shrugging off Eric Hall's insistence that 'football is monster clean' and the 'patronizing' denial of sleaze in football by Doug Ellis, she demanded an independent inquiry to expose how the taxpayer was being 'ripped off'. 'This government,' she lamented, 'is refusing to step in and bring to book the arrogant men who run our national sport.'

Hoey's passionate plea was rejected by the Conservatives. Ian Sproat, the minister of sport, believed that football should regulate itself. Rather than government control, he preferred to rely on the assurances of Howard Wilkinson, the manager of Leeds United and of the League Managers Association. However, in February 1995 Wilkinson conceded that 'strong action needs to be taken' to end the sleaze in football. If the business was to prosper, said Wilkinson, the sport's regulators were required to investigate the allegations of corruption. Since then, without government pressure, little had been done. Football's critics were invited to vanish. The game belonged to its admirers and heroes, and few more heroic than Terry Venables, who represented the genius, the fun and the worship of the game. His admirers preferred to ignore his unscrupulousness.

2

THE HERO:
TERRY VENABLES

Lying is common among the football fraternity and Terry Venables was a flawless practitioner of the art. On 21 June 1991, the purpose of his lies was special. The location of his deception was Henry Ansbacher's, a small merchant bank in the City of London. And here Venables was to consummate a union with Alan Sugar, the founder of Amstrad, the computer and electronics company. In what was blessed as 'a football marriage made in heaven', the two men were to become the joint owners of Tottenham Hotspur.

Even Alan Sugar, a crude streetfighter glowering with suspicion, was deceived by the camouflage. El Tel's wise-cracks, his scruffy clothes and the universal acclaim from being Tottenham's football coach obscured his greed for money. Venables's eccentricities diverted any doubts. His habit of publicly holding court in hotel lobbies – alternating between the Royal Garden in Kensington, the Carlton Tower in Belgravia and the Royal Lancaster in Bayswater – rather than using a conventional office, aroused amusement. Terry, everyone knew, hated solitude and lusted for strangers' recognition while guffawing with his admirers. Even his recent purchase of Scribes, a bankrupt nightclub in Kensington, evoked smiles. The image of Terry hosting a continuous party in a gloomy basement – pouring champagne and leading raucous karaoke sing-songs – was endearing. No one speculated that the cheeky chappie, ambitious and desperate, had blatantly lied to fulfil his dream of buying Tottenham.

Irving Scholar, the seller, was departing reluctantly. Magnetized by football like so many of his breed, Scholar was an eccentric whose chairmanship of the football club had become notably unimpressive. In Venables's opinion the property developer, living as a tax exile in Monaco, had failed to understand that football belonged to the fans not the shareholders. As one of the club's business managers, Scholar had also failed. Tottenham's debts to the Midland Bank were £11 million and, to Scholar's embarrassment, the bank had appointed David Buchler, an insolvency expert, to the board after the stock exchange suspended the company's shares.

Requiring help to fund the club's debts, Scholar had searched for saviours, finally choosing Robert Maxwell. On the night Scholar was due to sell the club to Sugar and Venables, Robert Maxwell attempted to frustrate the deal. 'Oi, you,' Sugar screamed down the telephone at Maxwell in front of a room full of bankers and lawyers summoned to complete his purchase, 'this is my fucking deal. What the fuck do you think you're doing? Eh?' Sugar had paused for Maxwell's reply. 'Don't even think about lousing up my fucking deal, or me and you will fall out in a fucking big way.' Sentiment never encroached on Sugar's business dealings. By nature he kept his distance, disdaining any attempt to glad-hand or indulge in frivolities. For him there was more than a football club at stake. He had been enticed into the deal by Rupert Murdoch, who was

anxious to sabotage Maxwell's bid. Murdoch feared that if
Maxwell owned Tottenham the new Premier League
would sell their television rights to ITV and not to Sky.
Sugar would favour Sky's bid because he would be contracted to manufacture the broadcaster's satellite dishes.
Accordingly, after trashing Maxwell, Sugar had an incentive to cajole the professionals in the room into completing
the sale to the 'dream-team'.

Sugar appeared to be Venables's ideal partner. Both
were rough diamonds from the east of London and both
appreciated money. To Venables's misfortune, his new
partner was infinitely more successful in accumulating
the riches that remained the footballer's dream. To
Venables's good fortune, Sugar had said nothing in the
bank when the football manager had failed to produce his
down payment of £750,000 for the shares. Without a blink,
Sugar's brief telephone call had conjured the required
money and Venables's ambition had materialized.

No one suspected Venables's plight as he boldly signed
the formal document pledging that £2.25 million, out of a
total of £3 million, for his purchase of Tottenham shares
was 'from his own resources'. His dearth of money was
unknown to Alan Sugar and his bankers. Despite the millions of pounds Venables had earned over the previous
fifteen years, excelling as a footballer and manager of four
clubs, including Barcelona, he had invested badly and
spent freely. To buy the shares Venables had secretly borrowed £2,150,000 from Norfina, a fringe bank, and
£250,000 was advanced from Yawetz, another lender. The
loans were negotiated by Eddie Ashby, a businessman
Venables had appointed as his adviser and manager. Ashby,
an apparently innocuous businessman, understood
Venables's weakness. 'Venables didn't need help,' Ashby
would later explain, 'he needed protection from himself

and those around him.' Like Sugar and Scholar, Venables was immune to any self-doubt. The football manager with a low attention span believed that he knew as much about money as football but was nevertheless grateful for Ashby's assistance. 'There is no doubt that the Venables–Sugar takeover of Tottenham,' said Ashby, 'would not have happened without me. I knew that I had saved Tottenham.' But the subsequent judgement by DTI investigators would be that Venables was the least naive person in that room and that he had preferred to indulge in a 'charade' and 'a piece of window dressing designed to deceive'.

Terry Venables's dream was to build a successful club. Alan Sugar's dream was to earn profits and glory. Venables regarded his arrangement with Sugar as remarkably convenient. Accustomed to docile chairmen willing to pay out millions of pounds without expecting any influence over its expenditure, Venables hoped that Sugar would adopt the chairman's traditional role, as an invisible presence while the management of the team was entrusted to the chief executive. Sugar's unusually benign tone misled Venables to assume his right to spend Sugar's money without question. 'Just sit in the corner and shut up while I stand amid adoring crowds,' was Sugar's subsequent interpretation of Venables's attitude. While Venables trained the team and enjoyed himself, his commercial duties as chief executive of the club were given over to Eddie Ashby. In Ashby's recollection, Venables's reason for delegating these duties was explicit: 'I ain't got a fuckin' clue where to start. It's running the fuckin' business side that's scaring the shit out of me.' Ashby's version was never contested: 'I acted as Terry's alter ego for everything except football.'

Compared with the bizarre range of rough diamonds and *nouveaux riches* attracted to football, Eddie Ashby

appeared excessively conventional. He had earned some
wealth in his twenties as a contractor jointly providing
cleaning services with Michael Ashcroft, later rewarded
with a peerage by the Conservative party. Their relationship ended in acrimony. More recently Ashby had been
the director of forty-three companies which were either
in receivership, in liquidation or struck off. To some it
appeared that he had assiduously sought to avoid the
attention of the Inland Revenue and Customs and Excise.
On 18 June 1991, just as Ashby assumed the title 'personal assistant to the Chief Executive Officer of
Tottenham' and delighted about 'a dream come true', he
was declared bankrupt. Venables's general manager was
forbidden by law to undertake any duties controlling any
company, and especially Tottenham, a public company.
'I'm a bankrupt,' Ashby told Venables, fearing immediate
dismissal. 'This bankruptcy thing, it ain't a problem,'
replied Venables, apparently fearless about that. Ashby
assumed that Venables was unwilling to abandon his co-
conspirator in his lies about the finance for his
Tottenham shares. To avoid benefiting his creditors,
Ashby's salary and expenses were paid to a company
owned by his wife and son.

Terry Venables had always been reluctant to allow the
normal rules to interfere with his ambitions or habits, not
least after attaining his new status. Any consultations, he
assumed, especially about the expenditure of money, were
unnecessary. Alan Sugar became aware of his partner's
caprice while on holiday in Sardinia. Tottenham
announced the purchase of Gordon Durie, a Scottish forward, for £2.4 million. Sugar exploded in anger. Not only
did he expect to be consulted about expenditure, but
Venables had recklessly broken the pledge to the club's
bank not to increase the company's debts. 'I'm in charge

of money,' Sugar screamed. 'What's going on?' In Venables's life, irate chairmen were unexceptional and easily ignored, but Sugar appeared to be more obsessed with money than most. The clash of two men, both criticized as 'control freaks', was a pertinent omen. Venables's calculated indifference was brutal: 'Are we a fucking success if we make £5 million and get relegated or are we a success if we win the League and lose fucking money?' Their differences were irreconcilable. Venables wanted money to buy players while Sugar wanted money as a profit on his investment. The contest was between Sugar, the abrasive but disciplined businessman, and Venables, the winsome chancer. The rift conditioned their individual reactions to the unexpected disclosures about the mismanagement of Tottenham's finances.

The keeper of the secrets was Peter Barnes, the club secretary. Soon after the sale, in July 1991, Barnes handed an internal file to Eddie Ashby containing some unconventional contracts concluded during the years before Sugar's arrival. 'This has got all the secret deals in it,' was Ashby's colourful version of his conversation with Barnes. The secrets concerned payments to players and agents.

One series of secret payments had been made to Ossie Ardiles, a formidable Argentinian midfielder. 'This reeks of commercial immorality and impropriety,' asserted Jonathan Crystal, a barrister, a director of Tottenham and a friend of Venables. 'The situation . . . is disgraceful. There has been a consistent pattern of improper arrangements and schemes designed to pay money to Mr Ardiles without any regard for the tax consequences or the regulations of the Football League.' Other unannounced arrangements highlighted in the file were 'loans' approved by Tottenham's management to Paul

Gascoigne and Chris Waddle, both star footballers, for house purchases and a BMW car for Gascoigne's father, which were not declared to the Inland Revenue.

The file also contained records of unusual payments to agents. In an informal arrangement, Tottenham had paid £25,000 to Eric 'Monster' Hall, a former music business hustler who had spotted the potential wealth in football transfers. 'I'm not a one-man-band,' puffed the extravagant cigar smoker, 'I'm a one-man-orchestra.' Those payments breached the FA's rules prohibiting agents receiving any money for transfers. Until 1995, the FA had forbidden players to be represented by agents. Tottenham's unauthorized relationship with Hall had encouraged a culture of impropriety in the club.

The serious revelation in the secretary's file was the apparent financial loss to other football clubs in the sale of three players – Paul Allen, Mitchell Thomas and Bobby Mimms – to Tottenham. In common with other football clubs, Tottenham had persuaded the players to transfer to White Hart Lane by secretly offering money or cars. Under FA rules, all those payments were to be recorded on the printed contracts. Tottenham had failed in several transfers to fulfil that obligation. This uncomplicated deception influenced the permanent tribunal established by the FA to fix fair prices for the players' transfers. The tribunal's decision was determined by the amount of the player's wages that would be paid by the buying club. Tottenham's habit had been to present to the tribunal a contract showing a false, lower income. The false contract reduced the transfer fee which the selling clubs would receive from Tottenham. The players did not suffer; under the valid but secret contract, the players were guaranteed 'loans' in excess of £400,000 and tax-free payments which would not be repaid. Luton FC had lost

£200,000 in the sale of Mitchell Thomas, while West Ham had lost £250,000 in the sale of Paul Allen. Both players were represented by Eric Hall.

Eric Hall's relationship with Tottenham was remarkably close. A majority of the club's players were represented by the agent on a handshake. The absence of written agreements was not a sign of trust but rather to avoid providing any incriminating evidence for the FA. Hall epitomized the proactive agent, acting often in his own interest. With some aggression, he used his inside knowledge and influence to stir up deals, instigating transfers by inserting stories into newspapers. 'Eric's a deal maker,' Venables told Sugar without revealing that his friend had been allowed to issue false invoices to Tottenham to conceal his activities, encouraging conflicts of interest to flourish. In the negotiation of a new contract for Justin Edinburgh with Tottenham, Hall demanded £5,000 from both Tottenham and Edinburgh. The player claimed to have paid his fee in cash from his hospital bed after a visit by Hall, although the agent denied the allegation.

After reading the file, Eddie Ashby self-interestedly concluded, 'This is the way some football clubs are run. You can't survive unless you fiddle.' Tottenham's conduct, although contravening the FA's regulations, had not been unusual among English football clubs. After all, Venables had received £50,000 just for signing his contract.

Hiding money offshore and paying cash from wodges of banknotes pulled from his trousers, Venables epitomized the football aficionado. The source of Venables's wodge was a mystery even for Ashby, although he suspected that it came from Venables's father, a publican in Chingford. 'Untangling Terry's wealth,' said Ashby,

'would be a mammoth task.' In the chaos he discovered
unpaid taxes, unpaid domestic bills, and Venables pro-
fessing ignorance about his own assets and loans. The
chaos was reflected in Venables's lifestyle; the new chief
executive of a public company shunned any desk, preferring to spend his time at the training ground, in hotel
lobbies, or at Scribes, a drinking club.

Scribes in Kensington satisfied Venables's lust for
occupying the centre of attention. His parties attracted
on one spectacular night Bill Wyman, Adam Faith, Kenny
Lynch, Dennis Wise, Vinnie Jones, Denis Law and Paul
Gascoigne, all gyrating on a wooden dance floor taken
without payment from White Hart Lane. In the background sat 'Mad' Frankie Fraser, the retired murderer,
surrounded by journalists prepared to sing their host's
praises in return for access to personalities and exclusive
stories. Few were aware that under Venables's management the club had lost over £100,000 and, unable to pay
its debts or honour its cheques, had received writs, sum-
monses and judgements from its creditors. 'We were
stretching it out as long as we could,' admitted Venables,
who used his creditors' money to pay himself £32,000
and finance his entertainment. For the enjoyment of that
rollercoaster Venables thanked Ashby. 'What you did with
Scribes was brilliant,' Venables told Ashby, who agreed to
manage Scribes and Tottenham even though he was a
bankrupt. This was against the law and unsuspected by
Alan Sugar on his arrival at White Hart Lane on 21 June
1991 for the first board meeting. At the top of the agenda
was the sale of Paul Gascoigne to Lazio of Italy. The sale
of the club's best player had been reluctantly agreed by
Irving Scholar to repay the club's debts.

Negotiating the sale had been assigned by Scholar to
Dennis Roach, a north London agent who would be

closely involved with Tottenham for over thirty years, and with many other major British clubs, in an extraordinary career which established him as football's principal agent.

Adroitly, Roach, alias 'The Cockroach', a former minor football player, had become expert at inserting himself into the trade of players between clubs. Transfers often depended upon his paid participation, and his notoriety appeared to encourage Roach's sense of invincibility. He knew the football regulators in Britain were ineffective and compromised; their officials were answerable to the same club owners who traded with him and tolerated the conflicts of interest and cash-payment culture. In the intensifying search by managers for foreign players, many relied upon Roach despite his astronomic fees and a reputation splattered by controversy and enmity.

Dennis Roach was part of the so-called 'St Albans mafia', an unusual group of football enthusiasts – including Tony Berry of Blue Arrow, a recruitment company, and a director of Tottenham – who grew up as wartime children around the north-western fringes of London. Like many working-class boys, Roach sought his escape from poverty through football, although he was unblessed with the necessary ability to become a top player. He was born on 3 April 1940 in Bushey; Roach's father, Frederick, was a council employee. After an enjoyable but academically disappointing passage through a local grammar school, he played as a professional for Bedford, Hillingdon and Barnet. Roach would mention that his signing-on fee to Bedford as an apprentice paid for his wedding, but Roach was twenty-eight years old when he married Janet Lovegrove, a hairdresser, in a Catholic church on 5 June 1968, long after his football career ended, partly due to an injury. That slight mistake was not an aberration; in later years, Roach presented colourful stories about his career. The varying accounts were constructed on one truth: football was his passion but money was even more important.

In parallel to his frustrated football career, Roach was selling fitted kitchens and carpets with his brother from a shop in north London. His good fortune during that period was to establish a relationship with a Saudi businessman who in turn secured a contract to provide carpets 'for six hundred houses in Saudi Arabia'. Although in later years Roach did not protest when reports described his customer as 'a Saudi prince', in reality the sale was to Saudi Airlines.

His second piece of good fortune was to meet, on a Portuguese beach in 1972, Johan Cruyff, the outstanding Dutch forward. To the famed international footballer, Roach resembled an Irish wide-boy, speaking eloquently, intently and with humour – the qualities which encouraged many to invite the agent, frequently described as 'my best friend', to be the guest speaker at weddings and birthday parties. Roach decided to attach himself to Cruyff and break into the football business. Unlike the carpet trade, trading footballers would be lucrative and fun and, with no risk of unsaleable stock, there were limited overheads. Few players, Roach recognized, were able to exploit their commercial value in negotiations with the clubs' owners and most were naive about finance. They would tolerate agents' fees so long as there was no cost for themselves. Another attraction was that little in the business was recorded on paper, creating possibilities to avoid taxation.

Dennis Roach's version of what followed is impressive. Cruyff, says Roach, hired him to act as his personal agent.

Efficiently, says Roach, he negotiated an agreement with
Nabisco for Cruyff to promote Shredded Wheat and,
impressed by that success, Cruyff arranged Roach's
appointment as the Dutch national team's media manager
during the 1974 World Cup in West Germany.

That version is partially inaccurate. In reality, Roach
attached himself to Cruyff as a groupie, at first in hotel
lobbies, and later at parties. He negotiated Cruyff's commercial contracts but admits that his services to the
Dutch national team were unpaid: 'I paid for my own
hotel room and got money from the television networks
for arranging interviews with Cruyff and the other star
players.' Two years later, Roach was described in an
English newspaper as Cruyff's agent.

The witness to Roach's subsequent ingratiation with
Cruyff's entourage was Michel Basilevitch, a Frenchman
later employed by Cruyff as his executive agent. 'Roach
was obsessed to be involved in football,' recalled
Basilevitch, 'but by then I looked after Cruyff with his
father-in-law.' Basilevitch had met Cruyff in Spain,
where the Dutchman played for Barcelona. Basilevitch
manufactured the club's sportswear. 'Come and work for
me,' said Cruyff to the Frenchman. Thereafter,
Basilevitch did not allow Roach to work for Cruyff and
describes himself as the eyewitness to the foundation of
Roach's increased fortunes.

In 1978, fearing death threats, Cruyff refused to travel
to Argentina for the World Cup. On the day of the final
between Argentina and Holland, Brian Moore, the ITV
presenter, invited the footballer and his agent to appear in
the studio in London. The two arrived with an entourage
including Roach. In the hospitality suite they met Prince
Mohamed bin Abdul Aziz from Saudi Arabia. Roach
spotted an opportunity. The world's most powerful and

rich men lust to meet football stars. To the prince's delight, Roach arranged that the famous Cruyff would visit the Saudi's home in Park Lane the following day.

Using his friendships with Cruyff and Basilevitch, Roach cultivated relationships with key Dutch players – including Ruud Krol and Johan Neeskens – and identified the best young English players whose prospective careers could earn his own fortune. In particular, Roach targeted Glenn Hoddle, whose father he knew as a footballer playing for Barnet; and he offered his services to Trevor Francis, famous for becoming England's first £1 million transfer, when he moved to Nottingham Forest. Francis's agent was an accountant. 'You should have me as your agent,' Roach told Francis. 'I know about football. I can get more money for you.' Roach's self-promotion was successful, although his employment as an agent was still forbidden by the FA.

To circumvent the FA's prohibition on agents representing players, Roach described himself as a 'sports entrepreneur'. There was a lucrative income, he realized, in copying the agents representing UEFA, the European football association, and FIFA, the supreme international regulator of the sport, and arranging tours for famous English football teams to other continents. Over the following years, he arranged for Nottingham Forest to play in South America, Manchester United and Tottenham to tour Australia, and Chelsea to play in the Far East. The climax was a football tour of South Africa, organized by Roach despite the international sanctions against the apartheid regime and South Africa's expulsion from FIFA in 1976. His partner was Richard Tessel, a South African who shared his certainty of profits to be made by circumventing sanctions. Roach impressed Tessel as a man who could 'sell ice in the middle of the winter to the

Eskimos. He's just got the gift of the gab.' An ingredient
of Roach's salesmanship was his boast that he owned the
'Kingston Royals', a basketball team which, he told journalists, would win the 'inevitably successful' British
basketball league.

In July 1982, in cooperation with Richard Tessel,
Roach recruited Ossie Ardiles and other British football
stars for his tour of South Africa, underwritten by a hotel
chain, and led by John Barwell and Jimmy Hill. The tour
was a baptism of fire, displaying Roach's energy and
ethics. Star Sports, the company organizing the tour, was
registered in the Channel Islands, and Roach received
£260,000 in cash from the sponsors. Many of the players
were paid in cash. After three games the tour was cancelled, allegedly after Roach refused to pay a black South
African official a bribe of £50,000 for 'protection'. His
problems were aggravated after a boycott by South
African players and a threat by FIFA to ban for life any
player continuing to participate. Key players, including
Ardiles, abandoned the tour, but Roach returned home
carrying profits and a reputation with Tessel that 'there's
not a time that Dennis doesn't try to do a dodgy deal'.
Roach's admirers would denounce that criticism as an
unwarranted exaggeration derived from his repeated
attraction of controversy.

The experience emboldened Roach. Not only were
the profits good, but the tours introduced him to the
heart of English football. During those journeys, he suggested to the best players in First Division clubs that he
could offer 'a bit of legal and financial advice' and
pathfinder sponsorships by a football boot manufacturer.
Roach was unusually reassuring. Unlike the dictatorial
club managers and the distant chairmen, Roach was a
kindred spirit, sympathizing with the footballer's plight

in familiar language. Simultaneously, he established close relations with the clubs' executives to guarantee immediate acceptance of his telephone calls. Brokering those relationships triggered another profitable tour. During two weeks in Swaziland in 1983, Tottenham, Liverpool and Manchester United played three games against local teams. Roach and Star Sports received £800,000 for the tour and paid each club £100,000. Proud about his new wealth, Roach bought a large house on the best road in St Albans and soon after moved to an eighteenth-century house in Mudeford, Dorset, with a two-acre garden where he would subsequently build a swimming pool and tennis court.

Roach had created a unique position. Unlike the majority of parochial English managers and footballers, Roach spoke French fluently after living for one year as a teenager in Paris. Aggressively, he said, 'I put myself about, making myself known in Europe, getting people to like me so they would call me if they needed something.' Among the first to call was the manager of the German club Bayern Munich.

Bayern had appointed Roach as its representative to buy Alan McInally from Aston Villa. Graham Taylor, the manager, wanted to sell McInally but knew that the fans would be outraged. 'Just get it done,' Taylor told Roach over lunch to agree the transfer. To Roach's surprise, the following day's newspapers reported Taylor's 'anger' that he was under pressure to sell McInally and described his frustrated impotence in being compelled to deal with a dreadful, aggressive agent. In his public reply Roach justified the new phenomenon: 'His club must deal with people like me'. In private, he accused Taylor of being 'not straightforward' about McInally's desire to leave. Taylor concluded the public spat: 'I don't deal with agents,' he snapped naively, unwilling to consider his limited choice in arranging the transfer, which was completed soon after.

Roach understood the new era. Increased income from television was helping England's leading clubs to match the wages paid by their European rivals. Roach offered the convenience of bearing the financial risk to find foreign buyers or bring them to Britain for inspection. Similarly, British footballers playing in Europe were grateful for an agent helping their return to England. Two Englishmen employed by Monaco – Glenn Hoddle, the former Tottenham player, and Mark Hateley – asked Roach to broker transfers. He negotiated Mark Hateley's transfer to Glasgow Rangers; and he later earned a fee of £400,000 for negotiating with Ken Bates the appointment of Glenn Hoddle as player-manager of Chelsea after a brief period at Swindon. Roach offered the two players additional benefits: they were sold identical houses in a new development in Oxford Gate, a quiet cul-de-sac in west London. Each cost £325,000. A third house was allocated by Roach to Martin Edwards of Manchester United, and a fourth to Mark Hughes, after his transfer in 1988 to Manchester United, and a fifth in February 1988 to Terry Venables, another close associate of the agent.

Roach would subsequently explain that he bought houses for his friends and clients because he possessed money allocated to them. Venables's accounts showed that Roach had personally paid the £30,000 deposit. The transaction was unusual but Roach was prepared to accommodate any requirement. His income continued to grow. One reward was a new eighty-foot yacht moored in Poole, near his new home, financed, it was said, from his account in Monaco.

By force of personality and guile, Roach was auda-
ciously participating in lucrative and unsupervised
foreign transfers. 'I'd insert myself into any deal if it was
good money,' he volunteered. David Pleat, the manager of
Tottenham, was among football's traditionalists to complain about Roach's methods and his consequent wealth.
'Things are getting out of hand,' said Pleat, irritated by
Roach's attempt to sell Clive Allen, a striker, to Torino
without the authority of either the player or the club.
'Allen's my client,' insisted Roach, who negotiated the
player's sale to Bordeaux. By contrast, other managers
were attracted to Roach's manner. Brian Clough was an
active trader of players whose transactions were unchal-
lenged by Fred Reacher, the club's chairman. Clough,
admitted Reacher, was 'pretty much the law on playing
matters'. Among the transfers Roach brokered for
Clough was Lee Chapman's from Niort of France to
Nottingham Forest. The transfer price recorded in
Nottingham Forest's internal accounts was £378,000 plus
£135,000 commission to Roach. Detailed accounts subsequently compiled by Price Waterhouse, the auditors,
recorded the payment to Roach as £65,000. Clough and
Ronnie Fenton, his assistant, would be criticized by a
subsequent Premier League investigation for benefiting
from 'fraudulent' arrangements by recording different
transfer fees in Nottingham Forest accounts compared
with those lodged with the FA.

Roach had not acted illegally. He was simply amenable
to the requirements of club managers. Clough's arrangements appeared to be routine. On 8 August 1989,
unfettered by the club's owner, the FA or the law, Clough
negotiated the purchase of two young players from
Leicester City for £15,000. After the usual negotiations,
the official contract stipulated that the transfer fee was

£40,875 and Fenton was dispatched to the Leicester Forest service station on the M1 motorway. 'Is that my money in the envelope?' Fenton asked a familiar face. The parcel was handed over. In the midst of another transfer in March 1993, Ronnie Fenton visited Southend United and agreed to buy Stan Collymore, a rising star, for £1.75 million, to satisfy Nottingham Forest's need of a striker to avoid relegation. Fenton's requirements were understood. To complete the deal, Vic Jobson, Southend's chairman, was told, 'You'll have to give Fenton a bung of about £50,000.' Initially, Jobson refused but agreed after Nottingham Forest were relegated to the First Division. Collymore was sold for £2 million in July 1993.

Roach, like most others immersed in the football world, would never have betrayed Clough by calling him dishonest. To belong to the fraternity required an acceptance of the special rules. 'Clough was always a gentleman,' said Roach. 'They should build a statue for him.' After fifteen years as an agent, Roach's expertise and his willingness to obey the gospel were proven despite Clough's condemnation: 'Agents,' Clough railed, 'put things into players' heads which weren't there already.' If not in the head, it was inserted on paper. During an investigation of Roach's business by the Inland Revenue, an official showed Roach two different but equally 'valid' contracts negotiated by himself for the same player's transfer to Spain. 'So what?' replied Roach. Roach and his company, PRO International, acted fearlessly.

The sale by Tottenham in 1989 of Chris Waddle, a winger, was a template of Roach's operation over the following decade. Chris Waddle's sale was initiated by Irving Scholar to pay for a new stand at White Hart Lane. Waddle had been represented for many years by

Mel Stein, a solicitor, but Glenn Hoddle advised his friend to switch agents. 'Use Dennis, he's good,' urged Hoddle, who regarded Roach as a father figure. Waddle agreed and encouraged Stein to cooperate with Roach. 'It's all rubbish,' commented Roach about Stein's previous negotiations. 'I'll do it better.' Although Stein might have expected some respect because he also represented two other stars – Paul Gascoigne and Alan Shearer – he was cowed by Roach.

Shortly after, Scholar telephoned Stein. Marseille, he said, had made 'a good offer' for Waddle. 'It's a lot of money and I won't stand in his way,' added Scholar encouragingly. The only obstacle, said Scholar, was the club's reluctance to deal with Roach, who was coincidentally on holiday. Stein began negotiating and was on the verge of concluding the deal when Roach returned. 'What the fuck are you doing with my client?' he shouted, and arranged for Waddle to travel with him to Marseille.

At midnight on 13 July 1989, Waddle telephoned Stein from Marseille. 'I've got a contract in front of me. Shall I sign?' After reviewing the contract faxed to his home, Stein agreed that Roach had done well. The transfer would produce a record £4.25 million. Roach also provided help to avoid taxation. 'You've got a good signing-on fee,' Roach told Waddle. 'Let me invest it for you through Toranco, my company in Monaco. Don't worry. I'll look after it for you.' Stein made supplementary arrangements to avoid tax by suggesting that the footballer spend seven days in Jersey, a tax haven.

Waddle began playing for Marseille but became a victim of the club's perilous finances. To resolve the problem, Stein and Roach travelled to Marseille, but Roach soon departed for Bordeaux. In his absence, Stein negotiated with Alain La Roche, the club's manager.

During their conversation, Roach telephoned and over the loudspeaker was heard saying to La Roche, 'The lawyer does not know about the 2 million francs. That's between you and me.' 'What's the 2 million francs?' Stein asked Waddle. 'I don't know,' replied the footballer. 'Do yourself a favour,' said Stein, who possessed a tape recording of Roach's request. After hearing the tape, Roach agreed to return the money to Waddle from Monaco.

Roach felt no embarrassment. Those dealing with the agent were attracted to his tenacity rather than his ethics. Mel Stein himself was being questioned by the French police on a separate issue. Integrity was often compromised to secure the transfer of a player and earn the commission. Roach's scrupulousness was as irrelevant as the morals of the owners of many football clubs. By 1988, Roach had become a valuable ally to many executives in leading clubs, who called upon his expertise to facilitate their dealings. Ron Atkinson, just fired from Manchester United, was grateful that Roach asked Richard Tessel in California to arrange a month's job 'with the local American football association' for a $50,000 fee plus expenses. Despite the FA's prohibition scavenging traders were welcomed by the chairmen of England's football clubs. Like Roach, even Maurice Watkins, a director of Manchester United, ignored the rules.

In 1988, Roach was paid £25,000 by Manchester United for negotiating the transfer of Mark Hughes, a Welsh forward, from Barcelona for £1.8 million. The payment broke the FA's rules. After Roach's participation emerged, Watkins insisted that Roach's fee was for 'promotional work' and not for the transfer. Reluctantly, Graham Kelly, the FA's chief executive, agreed to investigate the payment. Watkins emphatically denied the

allegation. Kelly relented and closed the investigation.
'C'est la vie,' the timid official sighed. 'It was impossible
for me to refute Watkins's denial,' he subsequently
explained. 'I was keen to enforce rules but no one was
keen to stop agents getting commission although it was a
breach of the rules. There was no point in taking it further.' With hindsight, Kelly admitted his error. 'At the
time,' he conceded, 'I didn't see the sums of money escalating to suggest corruption.' Kelly's explanation was
self-delusory; football was already tainted by increasing
sums of money which the FA preferred to ignore. Kelly
was universally acknowledged to be powerless to enforce
rules if football's scions, the participants in the deception,
did not protest about the skulduggery and preferred to
operate beyond the FA's control. In Roach's opinion the
solution was to legitimize agents as acknowledged parties
to the players' contracts. Until then, he could take advantage of an 'open market' lacking any regulations. 'It's a
very complicated business, this,' he admitted, 'and quite
honestly you tended to get your commission from where
you could.'

In early 1991, Scholar asked Roach, at the request of
the club's board of directors, to find a buyer for Paul
Gascoigne who ranked among Britain's most valuable
footballers. Commercially it was wiser, Scholar decided, to
use Roach rather than personally offering the player.
Direct approaches by Scholar to other chairmen would
give the impression of desperation, undermining
Gascoigne's value. In contrast, Roach guaranteed discretion and deniability. Scholar's agreement with Roach for
Gascoigne's sale stipulated that the agent would receive
£10,000 in advance, £55,000 once the sale had been completed and 1 per cent of any transfer fee. That commission
was in addition to the £64,400 he would receive during

that year from the club. Mel Stein, Gascoigne's agent, would also expect a fee of £400,000 for his services.

In Roach's version, he received a tip from Italy that Lazio were interested in Gascoigne and he told Scholar. Roach denied expecting any additional payment from Lazio, but some evidence suggested that Roach also expected to receive payment from the Italian club, which was a breach of every rule. But Lazio would not be behaving unethically to pay Roach – and he denied payment from both sides.

After a series of telephone calls Roach secured a bid of £6.7 million from the lawyers representing Lazio, who also agreed that Roach's own success fee, paid by Lazio, would be £37,500. Despite the huge fees, Roach's attitude towards Gascoigne was ungenerous. In a conversation, he told Richard Tessel laughingly, 'When he plays at Wembley, as you put your clothes up on the peg, he craps in your socks. That's the mentality of the boy. He's pig ignorant.' The true story was that, as a joke, Gascoigne's team-mates at Tottenham had cut the toes off his socks. In revenge Gascoigne had defecated into their socks in the changing room. That behaviour was hardly likely to endear Gascoigne to Roach, whose principal concern was, 'How much will I make on the deal?' Controlling a player's destiny was the source of his profit. In May 1991, on the eve of the deal's completion and the receipt of considerable income, a disaster struck. At the FA Cup Final, Gascoigne was seriously injured. The transfer was postponed, plunging Scholar into a financial crisis compelling his sale of Tottenham and, in turn, exposing a crippling sickness within English football.

Despite Gascoigne's injury, Lazio continued the negotiations. On 20 June 1991, their representatives in London sent a letter directly to Tottenham offering £5.5

million for the injured midfielder. The following day, Tottenham was sold by Scholar to Sugar and Venables. On arriving at his first board meeting Sugar was unaware of Lazio's latest offer. Venables would assert similar ignorance. Since Venables boasted of his prowess at negotiating and was a friend of Dennis Roach, his neighbour, his innocence was questionable.

Six days later, on 26 June, Venables and Tony Berry, a director of Tottenham under investigation by the DTI for his controversial management of Blue Arrow, met Lazio's representatives at the Hyde Park Hotel. Also present was Gino Santin, an Italian restaurateur and friend of Venables, introduced to act as a translator. Lazio's offer for Gascoigne was reduced to £4.825 million. In Sugar's name, Berry was keen to accept. As Sugar later confirmed: 'We're talking about a fucking geezer with one leg.'

The first to veto Sugar's acceptance was Venables: 'I've been transferrin' players for years and I'm a fuckin' maestro at it.' On Venables's initiative, Gino Santin was asked to act as an intermediary with Lazio. Sugar agreed. With surprising naivety, the businessman believed that football transactions were similar to normal commerce. Unsuspecting, he was introduced to the erratic world where unknown parties inserted themselves into transactions to earn spectacular sums merely by nodding their approval of a transfer. Or casting a veto.

At a board meeting in July 1991, Tottenham's directors agreed to pay the restaurateur a 5 per cent commission, with a maximum of £150,000, if he proved successful. A third person involved was Mel Stein who was to receive £400,000 on completion of the transfer. 'Are you being fuckin' serious or are you pullin' my pissa?' snapped Venables when told about Stein's potential income from the deal. (Soon after, Stein was charged with perpetrating a fraud in America and was named in a French arrest warrant for fraud in totally unrelated matters. He was acquitted on both charges.)

Scholar had retained Roach to sell Gascoigne, but once Santin and Mel Stein became involved Roach accepted £27,500 in compensation and withdrew. By then, unknown to some directors of Spurs, Lazio's directors had agreed to pay Roach £75,000 for 'making the deal work'. Although Tottenham's new board, during an eight-hour meeting, noted 'Lazio may also be paying Roach in connection with the Gascoigne sale – this is illegal both under the Football League and FIFA regulations', no action was taken after Roach denied receiving any money. Yet his exclusion from the big prize rankled. 'How Alan Sugar ever got to be the managing director of a public company,' Roach resentfully complained, 'I'll never know. He's so uncouth. Every other word he uses is a swear word.' Roach was especially troubled by Sugar's scrupulous attitude to money, 'He's so careful. He treats every pound note like a dead body.'

In late July 1991, Venables reported that Santin had negotiated the sale of Gascoigne to Lazio for £5.5 million. The offer was accepted on 1 August 1991. The following year, Santin demanded his commission of £200,000. The invoice provoked Sugar to scream 'outrage' and spit at Venables, 'I thought you said he'd do it for a fucking drink?' Venables spat back, 'Yeah, but that was as a translator. He put it all together.' Still unaware that Santin's negotiations had produced the same deal which Lazio had offered just before the takeover, Sugar signed a cheque for £200,000 plus VAT on 7 September 1992 payable to Santin's company, the Anglo European Market Research and Consulting Company, registered in Switzerland. Curious that Santin, apparently a resident in

the UK, should use a Swiss company, Sugar also began
wondering if Venables would secretly share that commission. An official inquiry found no evidence whatsoever of
an agreement that any part of Santin's fee was paid back
to Venables. But, as an entirely separate issue, no one
knew that in 1987 Venables had opened an offshore
NatWest account in Jersey where he had accumulated at
least £71,000.

The unusual circumstances surrounding Gascoigne's
sale influenced Tottenham's new directors at their meeting on 7 August 1991. For the first time, they became
aware of the 'Barnes file', the secret arrangements during
Irving Scholar's management. The contents, they agreed,
were 'a very sensitive area'. Five weeks later, on 12
September 1991, the directors decided, 'Mr Sugar is very
clear that a report must be sent to the appropriate authorities.' To understand the legal consequences, on 10
October 1991, Eddie Ashby and others consulted
Anthony Grabiner QC, an eminent lawyer and a
Tottenham supporter. Grabiner's advice was unequivocal: 'AG suggested that Alan Sugar and Venables should
arrange to meet with representatives of Football League
to explain our position rather than have any letters written.' Sugar's solicitor, Brian Fugler, added, 'it is of the
utmost importance' and 'imperative that . . . immediate
action is taken'. On 24 October 1991, the board agreed
that Sugar and Venables should report the issue to the
Football League.

Over the following weeks, Sugar and other directors
reconsidered their attitude. Some suggested, especially
Venables, that disclosure might be unwise. More advice, it
was agreed, should be sought from Peter Leaver QC, a
former director of Tottenham. To the relief of the directors, Leaver appeared less insistent on disclosure and

instead recommended taking action against Scholar for 'misfeasance'. For the moment, the crisis appeared to have passed.

Alan Sugar, however, was beginning to realize that his experience in the East End and the City bore little comparison to the unorthodox jungle of the football business. Even the trade in players usually appeared to produce losses. Bought at the top of the market, most players were subsequently sold as a diminishing asset. Every decision 'to refresh my squad' appeared to be solely based upon Terry's instinct. For the computer manufacturer accustomed to fixed costs and written records, Venables's unwillingness to record anything in writing, despite the requirements of a public company, and his habit of trading players, was irritating. 'It's all in me 'ead,' smiled Venables emerging from another endless session watching videos of football players. Gordon Durie, bought in such haste, had proved to be a failure. Venables showed no remorse for the costly mistake.

Sugar was intolerant of chaos. For his part, Venables feared the threat of Sugar's financial muscle. Amid increasing tension, the footballer believed that his failure to match Sugar's investment would demean his status and weaken his influence. This sentiment was aggravated by his ignorance concerning finance. In particular, Venables appeared unable to grasp that Tottenham's debts and the suspension of its shares on the stock exchange could best be resolved by the directors investing more money in the club to repay the bank loans. Sugar suggested that the two partners issue more shares to refinance the club, costing £800,000 each. Venables's reaction, fuelled by Ashby, was antagonistic. He feared that Sugar was dismantling the 'dream-team' by placing himself under financial pressure, and altering the partnership from equality to 47/23

per cent in Sugar's favour. To avoid that imbalance
Venables signed an agreement with Sugar at the
Grosvenor House Hotel on 21 November 1991 pledging
money to buy the shares which he did not possess. That
signature confirmed Venables's recklessness; finding the
additional money for the shares, he knew, would be difficult. His saviour was Ted Ball of Landhurst Leasing, an
unorthodox finance company.

To secure the loan of £1 million from Landhurst,
Venables pledged on behalf of Edennote, the company
which contracted Venables's services to Tottenham, four
public houses and their contents. That pledge, signed by
Venables, was dishonest. One public house in Cardiff did
not exist and he did not own the three others or their contents. In Venables's favour, some would suggest that Ashby
was responsible for the 'exotic' deal, an allegation which
the bankrupt denied. The document which undermined
Venables's protestations of innocence was a personal guarantee to Landhurst signed by Venables, based upon the
'sham sale and leaseback' of assets which Venables falsely
claimed to own. Subsequently, Venables denied signing
the personal guarantee. Exacerbating his dishonesty,
Edennote was trading while permanently insolvent but the
secret was protected by accounts which, DTI inspectors
later concluded, were contrived to give 'a misleadingly
favourable impression' and concealed a loan of £500,000 to
Venables. Sugar was unaware of that subterfuge, which
Ashby would describe as 'Terry's crucifixion'.

Ostensibly, Venables's partnership with Sugar
remained solid. While Venables struggled to win prizes
for Tottenham, Sugar watched from the chairman's seat
in the directors' box at White Hart Lane, enjoying the
glamour of 36,000 fans roaring their support for his team.
The chairman ruefully reflected that those thousands

were utterly uninterested in the shenanigans among the club's directors, although football constantly threw up bombshells.

The worm turned at Easter 1992. The multi-millionnaire Michael Ashcroft regretted his partnership with Eddie Ashby in the cleaning business. Their recriminations were mutual. Ashcroft remained suspicious of Ashby who, as Tottenham's 'general manager', had become the football club's central organizer. Ashcroft telephoned Tony Berry, a director of Tottenham and similarly a former cleaning contractor. Berry took the call in his kitchen in Boca Raton, Florida. 'Your man Ashby,' said Ashcroft, 'is a bankrupt, officially bankrupt.' Berry was stunned. As a bankrupt, Ashby was forbidden to act as Tottenham's 'general manager'. Sugar was told about Ashby's impropriety on the same day. 'We can't have these crooks around,' snapped Sugar. He urged Venables to fire his adviser but Venables refused. The embarrassment was disclosed in May 1992 to the *Independent* newspaper.

Sugar was ensnared by football's sleaze and by his dependence upon Venables. Like all club chairmen, his choices were limited: Venables could either be fired or supported. Fearful of the fans if Venables was dismissed, Sugar reluctantly agreed that Ashby could continue to attend board meetings. Although his entanglements were accumulating, the board's minutes recorded that Sugar envisaged 'no problems with Mr Ashby's bankruptcy per se'. Dismissing Ashby had become complicated by his familiarity with the circumstances surrounding the purchase of Teddy Sheringham from Nottingham Forest.

In the Tottenham boardroom after a match in early summer 1992, Venables had discussed with Sugar the purchase of the striker Teddy Sheringham from

Nottingham Forest. One surmountable problem, explained Venables, was the unusual demand of Brian Clough, the club's manager. 'Cloughie likes a bung,' explained Venables. Sheringham's transfer would depend on Clough receiving a large, secret payment, in cash. 'Well, just forget it,' Sugar replied spontaneously, refusing to authorize a procurement fraud. Bribes were completely out of the question. 'I had never heard anything like this before,' commented Sugar. Subsequently, Venables described how Clough, following another transfer, had received a 'bag full of money' in a motorway café. Sugar became convinced that the negotiations between Venables and Clough were 'an aggravation' because of Clough's demand for a bung. His interpretation was supported by Tony Berry. During a lunch with Venables at Langan's, a fashionable London restaurant, Venables had received a call on Berry's mobile telephone. Berry was convinced that the call concerned the payment of a bung to Clough, despite Venables's denials. Nevertheless, at the end of August 1992, Sugar finally approved Sheringham's transfer.

Since Venables and Clough could not settle the deal directly, Frank McLintock was asked to help as an intermediary. McLintock, a former Arsenal player, was the co-owner of First Wave, a football agency. Venables agreed that McLintock would be paid for his work. On 27 August 1992, Sheringham, accompanied by McLintock, arrived at Tottenham's training ground and signed his transfer for an announced fee of £2.15 million. Forest's accounts, however, would only show the receipt of £2.1 million. No one could subsequently explain the missing £50,000.

The same afternoon at White Hart Lane, McLintock was paid £58,750 in cash by Tottenham's finance director.

The invoice was marked, 'For attention of E. Ashby'. The payment was approved in writing by Sugar in the belief that the cash – £50,000 plus VAT – was a payment to an agent. That evening, McLintock and Sheringham met Ronnie Fenton, Clough's assistant, at the Posthouse Hotel in Luton, off the M1 motorway. A box containing the money from Tottenham was handed over to Fenton.

Over the following days trusted members of staff at the Forest ground received envelopes from Fenton containing between £200 and £250. The gossip rippled through the club that £50,000 had been handed over 'somewhere on the motorway' to the assistant manager who, while drunk, had admitted to Alan Hill, the chief scout, that the £50,000 had been split between himself and Clough. By then £8,750 had been returned to Tottenham because it had been wrongly added as VAT. The confusion aggravated the tense relationship within the club.

Alan Sugar's frustration was palpable. The abrasive businessman proudly dominated Britain's computer market but was apparently powerless to control a mere north London football club. Screaming obscenities at Korean suppliers for failing to deliver acceptable parts for his computers produced results, but ranting at Darren Anderton and the other players, he was warned by Venables, would prove unproductive. Sugar resented the footballers' criticism that he was 'paranoid that he was being ripped off'. He could not tolerate any criticism, especially accurate comments; but he feared the compromises demanded by football's heroes, who ignored the requirements of a public company. Terry Venables suspected the real reason was that Tottenham was Terry's 'blue and white army' and not Alan's. Sugar, Venables believed, was incandescent that the fans chanted for

Terry and not for himself as the 'The Saviour'. Denied that weekly adulation, Sugar, Venables convinced himself, was seeking to exploit his partner's vulnerabilities.

Eddie Ashby's continued employment as 'general manager' was one of Venables's weaknesses, compounded by the continuing failure to inform the Football League about the 'Barnes file'. Helpfully, on 25 June 1992, Jonathan Crystal and Brian Fugler – two lawyers close to Tottenham – had received advice from Peter Leaver that since the club had recently come under the jurisdiction of the Premier League rather than the Football League, the requirement to disclose the file had disappeared. But that relief did not cure Sugar's dislike of Ashby and Venables. His predicament was partly resolved by finally forbidding Ashby to attend board meetings, although the bankrupt continued to manage the club on Venables's behalf. Venables himself was, for Sugar, another dilemma.

Sugar believed that the chief executive and manager was using Tottenham as his private piggy bank to pay for holidays, extra motor cars and his father's medical bills. Dennis Roach was secretly recorded commenting, 'Terry doesn't trust anybody. Go to him with a deal and he thinks he can do it better. But he wasn't exactly intelligent by giving his daughter a job at Tottenham for forty-five grand when the previous girl earned fifteen grand.' In Sugar's opinion, Venables and Ashby were always 'at the edge'. Ashby's original appearance of reasonableness had become suspicious. Mistrust had ruined Venables's relationship with Sugar, and Venables resisted attempts to broker a truce. His stubbornness was shortsighted. Sugar began to plan for his partner's removal.

The headline charge against Venables was carefully crafted by Sugar to highlight the footballer's managerial incompetence and alleged dishonesty. In his draft affidavit, Sugar mentioned Venables's disclosure concerning the transfer of Teddy Sheringham from Nottingham Forest to Tottenham. The single disclosure – 'Cloughie likes a bung' – was calculated to cause a sensation. Despite Venables's vehement denials, insiders recognized the truth. The only uncertainty was whether adequate evidence could be produced to prove Clough's receipt of a bung for Sheringham's transfer.

Alan Sugar calculated the odds to be in his favour. On 6 May 1993, he chaired a tense board meeting at White Hart Lane, waiting for the moment to move in for the kill. 'Like a volcano,' John Ireland, the company secretary, described later, 'we were always waiting for him to erupt and when he blew we were paralysed.' In Sugar's mission to crucify, he initially targeted Jonathan Crystal, the barrister, for criticizing Tottenham's purchase of Amstrad computer equipment. 'We ain't spunking money on fucking lawyers. You ain't going to spunk any more of my money up the wall,' Sugar began, shouting at Crystal mercilessly. In Sugar's harsh judgement, Crystal was little more than a gaunt, unhappy and insecure Rottweiler always yapping around Venables's feet. 'You fucking cunt, you fucking cunt, you fucking arse-licking cunt,' Sugar burst out in a rage at the lawyer. While Crystal feared a physical attack as punishment for uncritically supporting Venables, Sugar launched an equally violent attack against Venables himself. Emptying his briefcase on the boardroom table, he threw a letter at the startled manager. 'You'd better read this,' spat Sugar, so overwhelmed by the excitement that he uncharacteristically omitted to utter a swear word. The ultimatum had been carefully crafted by his lawyers. Sugar demanded Venables's resignation in return for accepting £2.8 million for his shares and compensation for his remaining three-year contract.

Shortly after Sugar stormed out, Tony Berry took Venables down to the Oak Room. Previously a fan, Berry had become disillusioned by Venables's misuse of money. Vulnerable to the DTI's continuing investigation of his own business record, Berry had swung to support Sugar's complaints. 'Take the money and get out of trouble,' Berry told Venables. 'There's so much against you. It's a generous offer. It's the market price. You'll pay off your debts and can stay on as coach, leaving Sugar to manage the money.'

'You just want to back the winning side,' replied Venables, unable to calculate that Sugar's 47 per cent stake and Berry's 2 per cent plus an additional director's vote were sufficient to force his removal. Tottenham had been valued by Coopers Lybrand, said Venables, at £30 million, pricing his own shares at £8 million, rather than the £2.8 million offered by Sugar, and its value was rising. Eventually, Tottenham would be worth £160 million. Venables failed to understand that the only valid price at that moment was Sugar's. 'It'll only end in tears,' urged Berry who, after seventy hours of grilling by DTI inspectors, understood the perils of running foul of corporate law. 'Terry, there's been stealing. Things have gone.' 'Nah, you don't know the whole story,' scoffed Venables. Bluster, bullying and a revolt by the fans, Venables believed, pitting the supporters against the shareholders, could smother Sugar, whose image was bad. Unwittingly, the two street fighters were set to reveal the reality of English football.

Since Venables refused to resign, Sugar required a majority of the directors to approve the manager's dismissal. His method was unorthodox. At Highbury on 11

May 1993, during a match against Arsenal, Sugar convened a 'board meeting' of directors without telling Venables and Jonathan Crystal. 'I was at the match and I'm the company secretary,' said John Ireland later, 'and I didn't know there was a board meeting.' Tony Berry was only told about the board meeting after arriving at Highbury. 'It seemed the right thing to do at the time,' he told a friend. The board minutes circulated the following day recorded that Venables's dismissal had been approved. After Ireland protested, a proper board meeting was convened and Venables's dismissal was ratified.

The violence after the news of Venables's dismissal was spontaneous; he was loved by Tottenham's supporters. Fans stormed Sugar's home, car and the man himself. Under siege, Sugar plotted to destroy Venables and his supporters. 'They're all fucking crooks,' he ranted, consciously cutting corners to dislodge Venables.

In June 1993, Sugar published his affidavit denouncing Clough and his fondness for bungs. The conspirators were alarmed. Nearly one year after the Sheringham transfer, McLintock sent a new invoice dated 27 August 1992 for £50,000 to Tottenham. McLintock's invoice described the payment as 'assistance in arranging a distribution and merchandising network on behalf of Tottenham Hotspur'. Simultaneously, First Wave, his company, made a voluntary disclosure to Customs and Excise admitting its failure to declare the VAT for the £50,000 fee. The paperwork, explained the directors, was missing.

Venables's counter-attack against Alan Sugar was suffocated by aggressive legal tactics. A petition was presented to the court by Sugar's lawyers demanding that Venables deliver security for costs, which Sugar anticipated Venables would find impossible to fulfil. Another petition requested the winding up of Edennote, his private company, to prevent him suing Tottenham for wrongful dismissal. Stymied, Venables reluctantly sold his Tottenham shares and resigned as coach, but he was unwilling to surrender. Football was his life's passion, not an agent for his destruction; he was a fighter, even when the cause appeared to be lost. Unlike Sugar, Venables understood that football's potentates detested narks.

3

THE RELUCTANT
INVESTIGATORS

'Cloughie likes a bung' was too raw for football's regulators. Neither Graham Kelly, the modest chief executive of the FA, nor Rick Parry, the Premier League's chief executive, wanted to believe Sugar's megaphone denunciation of football's corruption. Unfortunately, his affidavit condemning Venables was too explicit to ignore.

Reluctantly, Kelly and Parry visited Sugar at Amstrad's headquarters in Brentwood. Their encounter was fraught. The visitors shared little in common with their host, a disliked outsider, unwilling to dissemble the truth and embrace football's gospel. Sugar had prepared his case but, to his irritation, Kelly only stayed briefly and departed for another engagement. Proudly 'open-minded', Kelly had arrived without suspicions about Clough and Venables and departed without suspicions about Clough and Venables. Kelly was instinctively unreceptive. Morality was irrelevant. 'I was too remote to hear about "bungs" and I didn't go looking for evidence,' he said later. In Kelly's opinion, the dispute concerning 'bungs' was more a clash of personalities between Sugar and Venables than anything else.

Rick Parry remained in Sugar's office to glance through the files; he realized that the documents and numbers of people involved could not be buried internally. The evidence and Sugar's attitude required a formal, legal inquiry. Unlike most people in football Parry was prepared to draw a sharp distinction between Venables as the outstanding football coach and his non-field activities which, he told friends, 'stank'.

Days later Rick Parry listened to Graham Kelly's scepticism. 'Sugar,' Kelly mumbled, 'couldn't have been so pure and innocent. Why did he wait for over one year before telling anyone?' Sugar's bellicose manner, Kelly thought, made it hard to be sympathetic. Others in football's fraternity were right, continued Kelly, that it was 'bizarre that Sugar did not know why Venables wanted £58,750 in cash for the agents'. Parry agreed. Sugar promoted himself as a brash street-fighter but was suddenly pleading naivety. But, sensitive to public pressure incited by the intense media battle between Sugar and Venables, the Premier League, he declared, could not ignore the evidence. Kelly remained unconvinced but nevertheless, without enthusiasm, agreed to lunch with Sugar. Afterwards, Kelly remained unsympathetic but bowed to the inevitable inquiry.

On 13 June 1993, the Premier League announced a panel to inquire into all the financial arrangements between Premier League clubs, players and agents with the power to demand documents and attendance for interview of those under the FA's control. The three appointed to undertake the inquiry were Rick Parry, Robert Reid QC, an independent expert in sports law, and Steve Coppell, who had recently resigned after nine years as manager of Crystal Palace. Like Kelly, Coppell was sceptical that bungs had been paid. Parry was neutral. Robert

Reid was suspicious, demanding that the subordinates as well as their managers should be investigated. Those disagreements were concealed at the public launch of the inquiry four months later at the Hilton Hotel in Park Lane. A definitive report, promised Parry, would be delivered in 'double quick time'. Parry was optimistic. None of the three panellists had foreseen problems in discovering the truth about bungs. Yet in a business conducted orally, without a paper trail, unearthing incriminating evidence was difficult. Compounding the problems was the continuing public feud between Terry Venables and Alan Sugar.

The destruction of Venables in the media had been orchestrated by Nick Hewer, an astute public relations expert retained by Sugar. 'Alan wants Venables blown out of the water,' Hewer told Tony Yorke, one of many journalists Hewer cultivated to wage Sugar's war. Initially, Yorke appeared to be sympathetic but gradually the journalist became disillusioned and switched sides, accepting Venables's contention that Irving Scholar had masterminded the secret payments, leaving Venables to bear the blame. Yorke's conversion alarmed Hewer. 'Take Yorke off the fucking story,' Sugar screamed at the editor of the *People* newspaper. Sugar's abuse convinced the newspaper's editor that Yorke's instincts were sound. In the continuing dogfight, Hewer's success was to secure other journalists, including Harry Harris of the *Daily Mirror*, to support Sugar. The revenge against Hewer was the publication of his memorandum to Sugar, which boasted that he was controlling the production of a television documentary denigrating Venables. This was broadcast on the *Dispatches* programme by Channel 4. Hewer's application for an injunction to prevent publication of his memorandum failed, but securing two major television documentaries to demonize Venables was his master-stroke.

Producers of the television rivals *Panorama* and *Dispatches* had simultaneously obtained documents which had been purloined by a disgruntled former employee of Eddie Ashby. The documents proved Venables's secret loan of £1 million to purchase Tottenham's shares from Landhurst, the finance company, on the basis of a false declaration of his assets. After seeing the documents, Tony Berry had said, 'This might solve a few problems.'

The principal document was a photocopy of Venables's signed personal guarantee for the £1 million loan from Landhurst. The original had disappeared from Landhurst's safe on the day the company was declared insolvent. Venables disowned the photocopy. 'That's not my signature,' he would exclaim. 'It's a forgery.' Subsequent examination of the signature on the photocopy by G. G. Jenkinson, a forensic scientist employed as a government chemist, contradicted Venables's denials. The signature, Jenkinson reported to BBC Television, was 'full positive'. Since his signature was apparently irrefutable, Venables's duplicity was confirmed. Venables nevertheless believed that he could outface his accusers. 'He's like nailing jelly to the wall,' said an admirer, preferring to believe in common with many that Venables was naive or too trusting rather than dishonest. Under the ruthless onslaught of Sugar's denigration, Venables and his allies counter-attacked.

Gino Santin sued BBC Television for *Panorama*'s defamatory accusation that he unjustly earned £200,000 from Tottenham for Gascoigne's transfer and won £150,000 in damages; and Eddie Ashby gave the 'Barnes file' to Tony Yorke for publication in the *People* and to Granada TV's *World in Action*. On 26 November 1993, Alan Sugar was interviewed by Granada TV about Tottenham's secret payments, undisclosed by Tottenham since the takeover two years earlier. The embarrassment for Sugar was painful. Before the programme was transmitted, Sugar formally told the Premier League about the payments.

The public exposure of the 'Barnes file' coincided with the completion of a fifteen-month investigation of Tottenham's finances by Paul Kendrew of the Inland Revenue's Special Office. The Inland Revenue agreed to accept £500,000 in unpaid taxes from Tottenham for the undisclosed 'loans' to players; at this time the Revenue's demand had not yet been formally disclosed to the club's shareholders. The satisfaction of stoking up embarrassment was only a respite for Venables.

The *Panorama* programme in September 1993 sparked a further investigation by Paul Kendrew into Venables's personal finances and his decision to allow Ashby, a bankrupt, to manage his companies. The investigator was helped by Sugar, providing information about Venables's false declarations in order to raise money to buy the Tottenham shares. Venables's vulnerability was aggravated by his failure to submit tax returns since 1990 and Kendrew's discovery of a letter from Venables dated 22 January 1993 asking to be paid for an after-dinner speech in cash. Challenged by Kendrew, Venables told him that he never used cash, a surprise to those who recalled Venables pulling wodges of banknotes out of his pocket because he had lost his credit card. Unwilling to provide any evidence to the Inland Revenue about the source of his cash, Venables sought salvation by ignoring Kendrew's requests for information. The official's response was polite. 'I am bitterly disappointed,' complained Kendrew, 'not to have received any kind of written progress report in this matter as repeatedly promised.' Venables's predicament was aggravated by a financially ruinous battle in the courts. In early 1994, he was engaged in six libel actions, eight further trials in the High Court, six official inquiries and four police investigations. In consolation, he could smile that Sugar's declaration of war against him had triggered retaliation by the Inland Revenue against football.

Paul Kendrew and other Inland Revenue investigators suspected football's finances to be dishonest. Using their draconian powers, Revenue officers had hoovered up club records and quoted the results as confirmation of their suspicions. Few of the major clubs possessed organized files. Their sloppy records and reliance on back-dating aggravated the distrust. Every transfer was, in the investigators' opinion, probably corrupt, and they were suspicious also of the clubs' pension schemes. Uncritically, the officers believed the rash of newspaper stories about transfer prices and 'bungs' and threatened to raid every English football club. The widening investigation was in danger of overwhelming the Revenue's resources. Internally, their task was described as 'a nightmare'. To overcome their limitations and persuade clubs to 'come clean', the Inland Revenue's press office began disclosing their suspicions and discoveries to trusted journalists. In return, each article was scrutinized by the Revenue before publication. To the officials' satisfaction, newspaper headlines pronounced 'Millions Missing' from Britain's major football clubs. 'This is very painful for football,' complained Rick Parry. The Revenue was undoubtedly a powerful force for change, he protested to the Treasury, but their investigators were 'naive. Back-dating is not criminal. The leaks to the press are outrageous.' In justification of their tactics the Revenue's investigators exclaimed, 'There's £20 million in unpaid taxes.'

Reform of the club's financial auditing depended upon the FA and in particular Graham Kelly. During a visit by Roger Bonas, a Revenue investigator, Kelly was told, 'football's finances are a shambles. There's no control over the cash.' Kelly, a former bank clerk, was alarmed. 'I wanted to know the details about the shady deals. It was just what I wanted to know.' Kelly ordered Nic Coward to draft letters asking Rick Parry and the Premier League clubs to provide details of their transgressions and settlements with the Inland Revenue. 'It was the ideal opportunity to clean up,' explained Kelly. The letter could only be dispatched with the assent of the FA's Executive Committee. Keith Wiseman, a representative of the Premier League on the FA Council, and senior members of the FA's board including David Dein, refused that permission. Rick Parry, the chief executive of the Premier League, confirmed that the clubs would not voluntarily disclose the information to prejudiced Revenue officers. Skilfully, he had persuaded the Treasury that encroaching upon the sovereignty of England's major football clubs was perilous and pointless. The Treasury ordered the Revenue to cease their guerrilla war. The national sport and its participants appeared to be immune from parliament's laws. 'There was never a conclusion,' lamented Kelly. 'Those around the FA table did not want to create waves. No one wanted the ultimate argument and to dig that far. No one in the FA wanted to rock the boat.'

That conclusion surprised Alan Sugar. In football's freemasonry, he discovered, Terry Venables was prized and protected while he, as the outsider, was condemned. At the FA's headquarters, Sugar's dispute with Venables was treated with disdain. Graham Kelly's search for a new coach for the England team had focused on Venables as the outstanding candidate to save the nation's reputation. The allegations of Venables's dishonesty would not, Kelly resolved, be allowed to interfere in the selection. 'I led the consensus to appoint the best man and ignore Venables's business dodginess,' he proudly asserted. 'I hadn't seen any evidence to disqualify him as coach. Terry contested *Panorama*'s allegations and I was happy to accept his assurances.' Sugar's opposition and his long letters, which Kelly found 'frightening', encouraged Kelly's prejudice. To prevent Sugar's threat to undermine Venables's appointment, Kelly agreed to meet Sugar at Herbert Smith's, the solicitors, to agree a settlement. By the end of the second long meeting, Kelly complained, 'It's like negotiating with Genghis Khan.' Entrenched, Sugar was determined to defeat Venables. 'I've never met anyone like Sugar before,' Kelly told his staff, his antagonism inflamed. 'He doesn't love football. I don't know why he's in football. We're in for a long, hard fight.' Venables's appointment, despite Sugar, was supported by Rick Parry. Neither Venables's role in the Sheringham transfer, nor the allegations of dishonesty regarding his purchase of Tottenham in the second *Panorama* programme, would be allowed to hinder his appointment in England's interest.

In a final salvo, Sugar hoped that an authoritative description of Venables's misconduct written by Mark Killick and Martin Bashir, both responsible for the *Panorama* programme, to be published in the *Financial Times* on Monday 25 January 1994, would dissuade the FA from the appointment. Sugar was disappointed. An article by Tony Yorke on the previous day in the *Sunday Mirror*, endorsing Venables as England's ideal coach, persuaded Bert Millichip, the FA's narcissistic chairman, to support Venables. The appointment was announced on

25 January 1994. 'I never had any doubts,' Kelly insisted. 'Venables was protected by Kelly,' Sugar protested. Kelly agreed; in his opinion Sugar was the villain and Tottenham should be punished.

In a display of disdain for Tottenham and Alan Sugar, the FA's penalty for Tottenham's failure to disclose all the club payments to its players was a fine against the club of £600,000, the deduction of twelve points from the club's total in the Premier League and the exclusion of Tottenham for one season from the FA Cup. Sugar's curses were unprintable. Wilfully, the FA had tarnished Sugar with the crime. Despite his confession to the Premier League of the sins committed by the previous owners, Sugar had not anticipated the FA's venom. The businessman's outrage pleased Kelly. 'Tottenham was a big club with a history of misdemeanours,' explained Kelly. 'Sugar thought the punishment was vindictive but I was comfortable with the penalty.' Critics were reminded by Kelly that in 1990 Swindon had been demoted from the First to the Third Division and lost eleven points for offering secret inducements to players. 'No one complained that was harsh,' recalled Kelly inaccurately.

The atmosphere among the football community appeared to be bitter. Football's chiefs, seemingly embarrassed by the public recrimination, spoke about searching for culprits and invoking remedies. The image of a business tortured by self-examination and self-criticism was, however, false. Graham Kelly, Keith Wiseman, Rick Parry and the executives of England's major clubs resented criticism and interference by outsiders in their affairs. Among many in the football fraternity, there was no sense of shame or blame, but a singular desire to enjoy their sport and its social life. Ever since the creation of the

Premier League, the senior members of the FA, a combination of professionals and amateurs, had floundered uncertainly without any vision. Graham Kelly, a decent administrator promoted beyond his abilities, appeared to reinforce his organization's impotence. He echoed the popular opinion that Clough, Venables and Tottenham were not scandals impugning the integrity of their business but were merely mavericks who had generated unfortunate publicity. 'The beautiful game has become a vehicle for intruders,' commented Rob Hughes in *The Times*, identifying the agents as vultures. In Kelly's interpretation, the vulture was Alan Sugar.

Graham Kelly preferred to ignore the events which followed the arrival on 15 March 1994 of Ronnie Fenton of Nottingham Forest at the Royal Lancaster Hotel in London to meet Rune Hauge, a Norwegian agent. Shortly after Terry Venables had been appointed as the England coach and occupied an office at the FA's headquarters, Fenton and Hauge discussed a secret commission payment of £45,000 to the assistant manager of Nottingham Forest for transfers of players to the club. At the end of their meeting, Hauge directed Lisa Davey, his representative of a trust company in Guernsey, to 'find the best practical way for [Fenton] to receive the funds and send him a letter with your proposal'. Eventually, during Fenton's holiday in France, £30,000 would be transferred to a bank in St Tropez and the remainder was paid in other tranches.

That payment concluded a succession of agreements between Fenton, Hauge and Brian Clough concerning the transfer of Scandinavian players to Nottingham Forest. Their relationship had started in the early 1990s. Ambitious to break into the British market, Hauge offered his services to Clough. The manager confessed to hating agents because 'they were making too much money out of it' but he recognized that the Norwegian was particularly skilled in identifying potential excellence among young Scandinavian players. Clough arranged introductions for the Norwegian to several British football personalities including Alex Ferguson. Both sides were ignorant of the true costs. Scandinavian clubs were unaware how much British clubs were prepared to pay for players, while the English were unaware that Scandinavian footballers were cheap. Hauge profited from that collective ignorance and offered a share of those profits to managers. Hauge had perfected his methods. In 1992, he negotiated the sale of Torben Piechnik from FC Copenhagen to Liverpool for £550,000, but Copenhagen only received £250,000. Hauge received the remainder. Piechnik proved to be a disappointment. After seventeen appearances, he was released by Liverpool without any transfer fee.

In October 1992, Ronnie Fenton asked Hauge to investigate the signing of Alf-Inge Haaland, who played for Bryne of Norway. Like most uneducated British foot-ball managers, Fenton found negotiating with foreign clubs difficult, and Hauge was accommodating. Bryne agreed to Haaland's sale for £150,000 and promised Hauge any money received over that amount. Hauge quoted Clough £250,000 as the transfer price, but Clough told Fred Reacher, Nottingham Forest's chairman, that the price was £350,000. Bryne sold the player for £150,000. Hauge's profit was £200,000 plus 20 per cent of any higher price if the player was resold by Nottingham Forest. Fenton clearly expected a share of those profits from Hauge. A few weeks later, after the transfer of Thorvaldur Orlygsson from an Icelandic club to Forest, Fenton collected £45,000 sent in cash by Hauge from a trawler visiting Hull.

Those payments remained unknown until George
Graham, the Scottish manager of Arsenal for eight years,
requested in August 1994 to speak to his club's directors.
'I've got a bit of a problem with taxes,' the club's 50-
year-old, dark-haired idol told Peter Hill-Wood, the
Etonian chairman of Arsenal, and David Dein, the club's
vice-chairman. 'Could we keep it between the three of
us?' Arsenal's directors nodded in agreement. Over the
previous weeks, inspectors employed by the Inland
Revenue had complained that some of Arsenal's employees had not declared all their income. The club's directors
had been puzzled. Clearly, Graham's request for a meeting identified him as one culprit. They imagined that the
discrepancy concerned a few thousand pounds. At their
next meeting, Graham arrived with his accountant and
explained that he had deposited some money in a trust in
Jersey for his children and he was now obliged to declare it.
'How much?' he was asked. '£425,000,' replied Graham.
Both directors were astounded. 'That's much more than
we imagined,' quavered Hill-Wood. 'I wonder whether you
can help me explain it to the Revenue?' asked Graham. The
directors remained uncommitted: 'Give us more information and we'll see what we can do,' said Hill-Wood
innocently. As the club's star, Graham could expect the
directors' help. He had previously played as a stylish midfielder for the club and under his tutelage Arsenal had won
the League, the FA Cup, the League Cup and the European
Cup Winners' Cup – no less than six trophies in eight years.
Graham was capitalizing on that deep reservoir of gratitude
and goodwill, but had slim hopes that the truth would not
emerge.

Five months earlier, in March 1994, Henrik Madsen, a
Danish television documentary reporter, had filmed an
interview with George Graham on Arsenal's training

ground. 'Didn't you receive a secret payment on the Jensen transfer?' asked Madsen unexpectedly, referring to Arsenal's purchase in 1992 of John Jensen, a midfielder from Brondby, a Danish club. Graham was nonplussed: 'Me, take money? Hey, you'd better be careful, that's a serious accusation.' Graham's lie and his threat were a footballer's normal reaction to the truth. By summer 1994, after a tip-off from Norwegian tax officials pursuing Hauge, the British Inland Revenue began investigating Graham. During eight years of management, George Graham had negotiated the trade of players worth £36 million, most apparently concluded without Arsenal's business managers scrutinizing any details.

George Graham and Rune Hauge had negotiated together Arsenal's purchase of John Jensen in July 1992. Acting on Graham's directive, Arsenal had transferred £1.57 million to Brondby but the Danish club had only retained about £900,000. The remaining £739,433 had been re-transferred to Interclub, Hauge's company registered in Guernsey. Soon after Hauge had secretly deposited £285,000 into Graham's personal bank account in Guernsey. Inexplicably, Arsenal recorded the transfer fee in their handbook as £1.1 million.

During September 1994, Arsenal's directors heard about the payment from Inland Revenue officials and from reports about Henrik Madsen's journalism, but did nothing until October. Coincidentally, Arsenal were playing Brondby in Denmark and after the match David Dein asked Brondby's directors how much they had received for Jensen. The reply, '£900,000', would have been more astonishing if Arsenal's directors had not been forewarned.

On the team's return to England, Hill-Wood and Dein confronted Graham. The manager's confession was prepared. 'It was an unsolicited gift,' Graham said in a reply contrived by his advisers. He offered to repay the full amount plus interest to the club. At an emergency board meeting the directors admitted their horror and considered their strategy. Unlike most other clubs the board of Arsenal was artfully balanced between David Dein and his friend Danny Fiszman who together owned 40 per cent of the shares, and the Carr family who owned 25 per cent. The Carrs owned hotels and had controlled the *News of the World*. Peter Hill-Wood, the chairman, owned about 1 per cent and the remainder of the shares were owned by outsiders represented on the board by non-executive directors. No single director could dictate the club's policy. Their discussion concerning George Graham ended in unanimity and an unconventional decision. Instead of instantly dismissing the manager and summoning the police, the Arsenal directors initially appeared to be as anxious as their manager to preserve the secret. Graham was too successful and the directors too conservative to desire a confrontation. Their intention was to appear unvindictive. At a board meeting on 18 November 1994, they finalized an irresistible offer to Graham. Towards the end of the season in 1995, the club and manager would announce, with mutual pleasantries, that the manager had decided to retire and seek new challenges. In return for repaying the bribes and for the remaining two years of his contract, Graham would receive some compensation. The sum of £750,000 was mentioned but nothing was agreed. Graham accepted a verbal offer and, in the meantime, the lips of both sides were sealed.

David Dein would reject that critical interpretation. To avoid an action for wrongful dismissal, Dein explained recently, the directors summoned 'a leading employment lawyer to assist them in a very delicate process of what to do based on such information as became available to them. The matter was handed over for investigation to the Premier League, who passed their report to the FA to deal with any disciplinary aspects. We acted on the best legal advice and took the appropriate action.' That considered explanation overlooked important sensitivities and the timetable.

Arsenal's directors considered Graham's dishonesty as a football matter and the football community sought to keep everything within the family. The etiquette of the business, properly and subtly, was not to wash the dirty linen in public. Initially, the club's procedures for dealing with Graham remained unclear other than that they were intended to culminate in Graham's unsensational resignation. Unexpected events destroyed that satisfactory scenario hastening Graham's departure, and also exposing the dirty linen, compelling Arsenal to hand over responsibility for deciding Graham's fate to the FA.

Dishonesty at Arsenal was not confined to George Graham. In 1989, two years before Steve Burtenshaw joined Arsenal as the club's chief scout, he had signed an exclusive agreement with Hauge. Burtenshaw was to receive 25 per cent of all the business he introduced to Hauge and expenses, but that sum would be reduced 'according to the number of "paybacks" which are involved'. The term 'paybacks', Burtenshaw knew, meant 'palm greasers'. Over the next two years, Burtenshaw introduced at least twenty-four managers, coaches and chief scouts to Hauge, which the Norwegian agreed 'was absolutely essential for us as an introduction to the market'.

In July 1991, to Hauge's disappointment, Burtenshaw cancelled the agreement to avoid a conflict of interest with his new employer, Arsenal. But Burtenshaw soon overcame his reticence. He was secretly paid £35,000 for

aiding Jensen's transfer, and Hauge deposited a further
£32,242, as payment for Burtenshaw's other assistance, in
a Dublin bank account. The payments would be discovered during the Inland Revenue's investigation of Arsenal.
The exposure of Burtenshaw's dishonesty had not
encouraged Arsenal's directors to launch their own investigation. Rather, the revelation of the circumstances
behind Arsenal's purchase of Pal Lyderson of IK Start, a
Norwegian club, proved to be the final straw.

George Graham had flown on 10 September 1991 to
Oslo where Hauge was waiting for him. Before departing
the fee agreed for Pal Lyderson by Arsenal's directors
was £215,000. The following day, Graham telephoned
Ken Friar, Arsenal's chief executive in London, and said
the fee had increased to £500,000. Friar trusted Graham
and Arsenal's directors approved the increase seemingly
without question. The Norwegians were unaware of that
conversation and were surprised when the contract
appeared on 6 November 1991 showing the £500,000
transfer price. Hauge was asked by the Norwegians for
clarification. The agent explained that the higher sum
was necessary to obtain Lyderson's work permit. Arsenal,
claimed the agent, would be reimbursed with £285,000.
Days later, Arsenal transferred £500,000 to Hauge's
account in Guernsey. After paying the Norwegian club
and making other provisions, the remaining £285,000 was
divided between Hauge, who kept £145,000, and George
Graham. In December 1991, over a drink at the bar of
the Park Lane Hotel in Piccadilly, ironically owned by
the Carr family, Arsenal's major shareholders, Hauge
handed Graham a bag containing £140,000 in used £50
notes. Graham deposited the cash in a Dublin bank. 'We
all like a drink,' commented a sage later, 'but George
wanted a whole brewery.'

During his discussions with Arsenal's directors in October 1994, Graham suggested that his disclosure had been prompted by his accountant's insistence that the offshore bank deposits would have to be declared to the Inland Revenue. In truth, Graham knew he had been endangered by Henrik Madsen's book *Men from Brondby*. On page 257, Madsen had recorded Graham's personal enrichment from the Jensen transfer. Graham's further profit from the Lyderson deal emerged from the exposure of Burtenshaw's dishonesty. The revelation of his corruption, George Graham realized, was as embarrassing to Arsenal and the FA as to himself. Everyone had hoped that 'Cloughie's bung' was an isolated incident.

Three weeks after Graham and the club had agreed their settlement, their secret was exposed. On 11 December 1994, Simon Greenberg and Lawrence Lever reported Graham's dishonesty in the *Mail on Sunday*. The immediate reaction by Arsenal's spokesman was defiant: 'We will not sack George Graham.' Taking bungs was apparently acceptable to Arsenal's directors if the manager was successful on the pitch.

Rick Parry and Robert Reid immediately extended their inquiry into the irrefutable circumstances that when Graham had negotiated Pal Lyderson's transfer he had doubled the price and had received a 'bung' from Hauge. Despite these seemingly undeniable facts, Graham explained to the inquiry panel that no conspiracy had existed between himself and Hauge. The £140,000, said Graham, was an 'unsolicited gift'. Deftly, he was supported by Hauge: 'I gave George Graham the money but he didn't ask for it,' said the agent; adding without remorse, 'So what's wrong?' On 17 February 1995, George Graham was shown the inquiry's conclusions about his dishonesty but, on legal advice, refused 'to

answer any substantive questions'. Four days later,
Graham returned from a jog to his Hampstead home and
was summoned by Peter Hill-Wood to Highbury. 'You're
fired,' said Hill-Wood, who favoured short executions.
'What about my compensation?' stuttered Graham, obvi-
ously surprised. 'Forget it,' snapped Hill-Wood. The
club's public statement explained Graham's dismissal for
'not acting in the best interests of the club'. Graham was
defiant. 'The allegations,' he pronounced, 'are nonsense.
I have made no money from transfers.' His emphatic lies
were normal for football's mavericks. Ronnie Fenton,
Brian Clough and Terry Venables also uniformly
ridiculed any evidence and accusations. 'The payments,'
Graham said, 'were not expected and not asked for. I have
never ever benefited from any transfer.' Not one of
Arsenal's directors publicly denounced their former manager as a liar or asked the police to investigate whether a
crime had been committed. On the contrary, the directors
agreed to avoid wasting time and money pursuing
Graham through the courts. 'We wanted to do the best
for Arsenal FC,' explained Dein. 'We acted on the best
advice and that was to let it go no further.'

Sir John Quinton, a banker and the chairman of the
Premier League, was anxious not to annoy his members.
In at least ten recent transfers Hauge had acted for many
of those attending the meeting of the Premier League
chairmen and chief executives on 23 February 1995.
Although the report by Robert Reid and Rick Parry
established Graham's dishonesty, the twenty men agreed
not to embarrass Arsenal's directors, nor to condemn
Hauge. Graham's portrayal of himself as a scapegoat
matched their own interests. The twenty agreed to
endorse Arsenal's decision to dismiss Graham but
ordered Quinton to announce that the manager had not

been found 'guilty of any offence'. Their rationale was flawless. The inquiry had been conducted to collect facts, not to pass judgement. Any disciplinary consequences were the FA's responsibility. Nothing more would be done by the Premier League. Passing the buck avoided the danger of George Graham revealing embarrassing information and, to protect Arsenal's directors from further humiliation, only an abbreviated version of the report was published.

Senior officials at the FA were sympathetic to George Graham's plea that he had not requested the bribe. Graham, they persuaded themselves, was guilty of 'receiving' but innocent of 'soliciting' the money. Piously, David Davies, directing the FA's publicity, announced, 'The responsibility of the FA as always is to seek the highest standards of integrity in the national sport. We will meet that responsibility.' Graham was fined £50,000 and banned for one year. The equivocation was sufficient for the manager to portray himself as 'the sacrificial lamb offered up to ease football's conscience'. In a corridor in the FA's headquarters, Peter Leaver, the Premier League's chief executive, encountered Graham Kelly. 'You've been lenient,' he commented. 'Oh, this is difficult,' replied Kelly. 'Our lawyers have warned us to be careful about restraint of trade.' Leaver, a QC, nodded. The Premier League's representative was not in a position to criticize the FA. Both gave the appearance of preferring not to dig too deep.

In public, the famous sprang to George Graham's defence and placed the blame on Hauge and agents. Gary Lineker pleaded that the manager was 'a very likeable and successful man' who had been subjected to 'grossly unfair' treatment and was a 'scapegoat for every manager who's ever had a backhander'. In a revealing exposition of football's morality, Lineker wrote, 'The bung, it seems, has long been commonplace . . . It was almost considered to be an acceptable perk for men who are treated so shabbily by their employers . . . The majority of players are, I'm sure, not partial to the odd paper bag.' This theme was reflected during the inquiry. In one exchange Rick Parry asked Graham Smith, the agent, about the Sheringham transfer: 'Who were you representing in the deal?' The question implied there was a choice between Nottingham Forest, Sheringham or Tottenham. Smith gazed nonplussed. 'Well, me, of course,' replied the agent. That brazenness helped them to heap the blame on the agents. 'It is easy to see,' they reported, 'how the imposition of agents and intermediaries can create opportunities for financial irregularities, particularly where payment is made other than directly to the selling club.' Hauge was punished by a life's ban by FIFA but the sentence was reduced on appeal to two years. Rick Parry was exasperated. 'Why,' he asked Bobby Charlton, 'do the managers take bungs?' 'Because,' replied Charlton, 'managers get abused; they'll be unfairly dismissed; and so they'll take while they have the chance.'

Those accusing Hauge of exercising a corrupting influence ignored the dilemma for some British football executives. Even honest managers were bound to deal with Hauge if he represented a desirable player. For those involved in football, there appeared to be no escape from sharp dealers. Surviving in the football business excluded any other possibility, as even Alan Sugar discovered.

During that same year, 1994, Ossie Ardiles, Tottenham's new manager, asked Sugar to buy Ilie Dumitrescu, a Romanian player, from Steaua Bucharest. Representatives from Padua and Cologne football teams were in Bucharest already bidding. By then, Sugar had

learnt that his sole concern ought to be only the final sum
paid by his club for a player, not the amount any agent
received. Trying to establish the ultimate destination of
his purchase money for any player after its transfer to a
bank account was pointless. Anxious to secure
Dumitrescu and lacking any experience in Romania,
Sugar asked Dennis Roach, Ardiles's friend, to undertake the negotiations.

Sugar harboured reservations about Roach. Roach had
offered to negotiate a friendly match against PSV
Eindhoven and had asked both sides for a fee of £30,000.
Sugar visited Eindhoven and challenged Roach. 'I did
try,' the agent laughed. Conflicts of interest appeared to
be customary in a sport accustomed to disappearing millions. But Roach resisted any involvement in Sugar's
battle with Venables. He had refused to speak to the television producer who called daily for three weeks. 'Do you
fancy ten years in a cell?' he asked his friends. That discretion appealed to Sugar. In his bid for Ilie Dumitrescu,
Sugar was only concerned about the final price. Roach
reported that he had flown to Bucharest and that, over
lunch with Cornel Otelea, Steaua's president, he won the
bid at £2.6 million ($4.3 million). On Roach's advice, the
money was transferred to account number Q5727620 at a
Swiss bank in Lugano. Unknown to Sugar, Steaua only
received £1.4 million. Ilie Dumitrescu received £625,000
and the remaining £625,000 was paid in commissions
among four people.

'Money was paid to other people out of the $4.3 mil-
lion,' admitted Colonel Constantin Matei, Steaua's
director of public relations. 'This is a confidential sum. It
is normal for people who help sell a player to be paid.
That is our business.' Subsequently, Cornel Otelea was
accused of embezzling the club's funds. In the trial, Ilie

Dumitrescu testified, 'Mr Roach is the only person who knows more about where the money went.' Roach expressed his ignorance. The curiosity of the missing million was magnified by Dumitrescu's poor performance. After just fifteen appearances, Dumitrescu was loaned to Seville, who also declared the player had failed to make a good impression. Ardiles's judgement was proven to be questionable. Alan Sugar added to the mystery by later alleging that Roach had conducted the negotiations from Monaco rather than in Bucharest, an allegation which Roach strongly denied.

Alan Sugar was in truth perplexed by a fundamental conundrum. There appeared to be no answer to the question: why were football clubs purchasing dud players? At the FA's headquarters, few showed any appetite to pursue the second question. Dutifully, Graham Kelly had again proposed a compliance unit to scrutinize transfer agreements but Keith Wiseman had been mandated by the Premier League clubs to oppose the proposal. Wiseman acquiesced. He too preferred to gloss over the problem and avoid tackling suspected irregularities. Lamely, Kelly withdrew his suggestion. The only continuing investigation of corruption was being undertaken by the Premier League's inquiry into 'Clough's bung'.

In public, Rick Parry declared after one year, 'As a result of our efforts things are definitely cleaner.' He considered that the Inland Revenue investigation into areas where there had been 'room for abuse' had resolved some chicanery. In private, however, he complained, 'We have a bag of money and 183 different stories about where it went.' The investigation had ballooned into a nightmare. Parry had anticipated a report that would be completed within weeks. None of the three members of the panel had contemplated a full-time inquiry which clashed with their professional careers. Provable facts, however, eluded the trio; the football clubs were worse than reluctant witnesses. Unknown to the FA, in 1994 the management of Manchester United had accepted from Alex Ferguson a brown parcel containing £40,000 in cash, given to Ferguson by Grigory Essaoulenko, the vice-president of Spartak Moscow, at the end of transfer talks about Andrei Kanchelskis, a forward. The money was placed in the club's safe. In the atmosphere of the 'bungs' inquiry, the club's managers preferred not to disclose the 'gift' to the FA, as required by the rules. The uproar could have been catastrophic. After one year the parcel was quietly returned. By then, the criticism had diminished.

Kate Hoey's damnation of Venables's dishonesty in the House of Commons had attracted considerable criticism but she had been unable to produce any incriminating evidence, and the football group among Labour MPs refused to offer any support. The BBC, she decided, appeared to be more concerned to avoid annoying football's executives than pursuing her allegations. A visit to her office in the Commons by David Davies, the FA's director of public affairs, and Mike Lee representing the Premier League, further undermined her credibility. Davies reported that Kate Hoey possessed no evidence and lacked a proper understanding of football. Hoey was unsurprised by Davies's antipathy. Terry Venables was a fellow employee of the FA and Graham Kelly had declared that Venables's business affairs were of no concern.

That lack of interest demonstrated the obstacles for Robert Reid's inquiry. After interviewing club officials Reid had dispatched specialists to examine the accounts of several clubs, including Tottenham, Arsenal and Nottingham Forest. The disappearance of money, they reported, was blatant. 'Clearly money has gone,' repeated Rick Parry, 'but we don't know where.' Postdated invoices had been inserted into records months after transactions. 'A lot of the evidence doesn't stack up,' Reid said. And allegations of corruption, he agreed, however, 'on examination evaporated without substantiation'. Detectives were hired by Reid to trace money transferred from the football clubs to offshore accounts but the identities of the account holders were withheld by the banks. After several payments of extra fees to the detectives had produced no evidence they were fired.

The inquiry's salvation was the provision by the Norwegian tax authorities of Rune Hauge's records, seized from his office, but this awakened their taste for more. The best source of new information would have been the football agents, but since they were unauthorized and unregulated, they were unwilling to reveal their accounts. Neither the Premier League nor the FA could compel them to testify. Frank McLintock gave one unsatisfactory interview and then refused further cooperation, and Hauge refused after the first interview to continue providing evidence. Other interviews, often separated by two or three months, in London, Liverpool, Manchester, Oslo and Malta often ended in frustration. Brian Clough withdrew his cooperation after suffering memory lapses on crucial questions; Fenton admitted that Clough had once received £8,000 at a motorway service station, but Fenton's veracity was questionable; while Terry Venables, discomforted by the exposure of his contradictory evidence, stormed out of an interview.

Terry Venables's intransigence was encouraged by Graham Kelly. The FA's chief executive had come to detest Alan Sugar. In repeated telephone calls, the businessman cursed, 'Venables is putting the knife into me.'

In Sugar's mind, Venables and Kelly, inhabiting the same building, were perpetually plotting. 'He's upstairs with his tactics board,' insisted Kelly, 'not popping into my office discussing loans five years ago.' Sugar was unpersuaded. His appeal against the £600,000 fine, twelve points deduction and exclusion from the FA Cup won a revised punishment: only six points were deducted but the ban from the FA Cup remained and the fine was increased to £1.5 million. Vowing a second appeal and an application to the High Court, which eventually restored all Tottenham's points and its participation in the FA Cup, Sugar attacked the FA's 'outrageous fine . . . especially bearing in mind that all the information provided to the FA was on a voluntary basis'. The inaccuracy of that protest – the information was volunteered two-and-a-half years after the discovery of the 'Barnes file' and after Eddie Ashby had disclosed its contents to Granada TV – did not endear Sugar to his critics, especially as England's fortunes under Venables improved.

'Venables the Saviour' was short-lived. As England's performances during 1995 encouraged criticism, Venables's defences against his other pursuers crumbled. In early 1996, the Inland Revenue's investigation of his income since 1984 had produced the records of account number 59651156, his deposits at the NatWest Bank in Jersey. The statements of 1992 recorded that his deposit had increased from £71,000 to £670,473. Paul Kendrew asked Venables to explain the source of £950,000 in his several bank accounts, to produce the records of his account at the Orion Trust in Guernsey, to provide a copy of his contracts with Barcelona, and to explain how he had funded his purchases of the Royal Oak pub, 6 Oxford Gate, a flat in Kensington and a house in Brompton Park Crescent. Resolutely, Venables refused any explanations.

In exasperation, the Inland Revenue demanded an immediate payment of £54,000 for unpaid taxes.

Venables's plight could not be concealed. Although he successfully negotiated a settlement with the liquidator of Edennote, his company, at 50 pence in the £1, costing £580,000, others could not be so easily assuaged. Martin Roberts at the DTI was infuriated by the decision of George Staple, the director of the Serious Fraud Office, not to prosecute Venables on eleven charges. Roberts threatened Staple that he would refer the SFO's refusal to 10 Downing Street. In consolation, the DTI sought Venables's disqualification as a company director on the eve of the opening of Alan Sugar's libel action against his enemy. Venables found the pressure of coaching the England team and the fight for his reputation, even with Eddie Ashby's full-time assistance, too exhausting. In January 1996, he told Graham Kelly that he wanted either an immediate extension to his contract or he would resign after the Euro '96 competition.

Graham Kelly was appalled; exposure of Venables's deceit was irrelevant to him and he was proudly loyal to Venables. 'I tried to persuade him to carry on,' recalled Kelly, 'but he insisted on resigning because the FA was not supporting him. Like most managers, Venables is very stubborn and he would not be shifted. He had made up his mind.' With notable consideration, Kelly made a distinction between a child abuser and Venables's 'business mismanagement'. In Kelly's judgement, Venables was not disqualified to be England's football coach just because, 'he is not the most careful businessman in the world. He is of sufficient character to be England's national coach.'

Kelly accurately reflected the sentiment of the fans on the terraces; they were amused by Terry's dishonesty, and paraded their unconcern about being ripped off. Among those sympathizers was Tony Banks, the Labour MP and future minister of sport: 'I'm not required to judge Terry. I have no material evidence. There is no evidence. I don't want to be put in a position where I should criticize. I just would not want him to look after my pension. It's subjective. I admire him but I am under no illusions.' That conditional generosity was not limited to Terry Venables but extended to his self-proclaimed disciple, George Graham.

The fate of George Graham encouraged those who resented any regulation. In July 1995, Graham was banned by the FA for one year for his acceptance of money from Rune Hauge. To the further dismay of the FA's critics, the complete report describing Graham's corruption compiled by Robert Reid and Rick Parry had not been published. Discreet lobbying had protected Graham and Arsenal from further embarrassment. That discretion was compromised in November 1995. Reflecting footballers' general insensitivity, George Graham accepted £250,000 from the *Sun* for the serialization of his autobiography, promoting an aggressive whitewash of his conduct. Even Graham Kelly was outraged by George Graham's brashness and ordered the publication of the full report. The truth, however, did not hinder Graham's resurrection. At the end of his one year ban in 1996, he was appointed manager of Leeds. Few questioned the propriety of a corrupt manager returning to Premier League football. As a senior member of football's freemasonry, Graham was protected. On 26 October 1996, he accompanied his new team to play at Highbury. Graham's lack of shame was matched by the polite welcome from Arsenal's supporters, enhanced when the visitors were defeated by three goals. Graham stayed away from the Arsenal directors' box. Not because of any embarrassment, but out of anger.

The corrupt payments which Graham had accepted, it was agreed by the football fraternity, were exceptional. The problem was not widespread. His confession of dishonesty had become obliterated, a forgotten interlude in a forty year career. Graham's rapid resurrection – he also appeared as a frequent pundit on Sky Sports – was testimony to football's gospel. Even the Serious Fraud Office had abandoned an investigation. Few cared that Steve Burtenshaw, Arsenal's former scout who had admitted receiving £35,000 from Rune Hauge in 1992, had become QPR's chief scout after his dismissal by Arsenal in February 1995. 'There was no proof against him when he was employed by us,' said a director of QPR who, ironically, resolutely attacks dishonesty in football.

The mitigation extended to Rune Hauge; the lifetime ban imposed by FIFA was reduced on appeal to two years. Until he could officially resume business in March 1997, he operated unhindered using Frank Mathiesen, a Danish registered agent, and brokered the sales of Gunnar Halle, a Norwegian defender, to George Graham at Leeds, Ole Gunnar Solskjaer to Manchester United and Allan Nielsen to Tottenham. Ignoring Hauge, the clubs' managers, including Alex Ferguson, decided, would be counter-productive since he controlled the best Scandinavian players. Hauge's admission of paying bribes to other, unnamed British managers was assumed to be true. Finding more incriminating evidence, however, was proving to be difficult.

By 1996, after questioning over thirty witnesses in two years (the total would be sixty-six), Robert Reid QC, the lawyer and chairman, acknowledged a serious flaw in their technique. Those involved in the world of football were not accustomed to normal values of honest testimony. Lying was their lingua franca. Precise questioning, as was the custom in the High Court, was self-defeating. His stern cross-examination was preventing any cosy relationships developing with potential informants. 'We're not giving the suspects enough rope to hang themselves,' he realized. 'Too many avenues are being blocked off.'

The impetus to find the truth and impose any punishment was waning, and the organization of the inquiry by the Premier League was at best lacklustre. Making the arrangements for all three members of the panel to agree a place and date to interview a witness was problematic. Weeks would pass without a single interview. The panel's will-power was lapsing. The sight of endless lever arch files filled with 'inconsistencies, things we couldn't fathom and facts we couldn't understand' depressed Reid. 'This is spiralling out of control,' he conceded. 'We're hampered by the lack of powers of compulsion.'

At the heart of Reid's bewilderment was the identical but implausible stories of Frank McLintock, the agent, and Teddy Sheringham, the footballer. McLintock had described his drive north from London, his concealment in his loft of the £58,000 in cash which he had received from Tottenham, and his meeting that evening with Sheringham for a drink. Initially, Sheringham told Reid that he had never travelled in McLintock's car. 'I just went home,' said Sheringham in February 1994. Later Sheringham agreed that the two had driven alone in McLintock's car to a pub. Both denied meeting Ronnie Fenton, the assistant manager of Nottingham Forest, employed during the inquiry as a scout for Leeds and England.

Sheringham was the image of honesty. 'Did you get into the front or back of the car when you went with McLintock for a drink?' he had been asked in a throwaway question. 'Into the back,' replied the footballer. On rereading the transcript, Parry and Reid were puzzled. There were only two men in the car, so why would Sheringham sit in the back, leaving the front passenger seat empty? 'The story doesn't stack up,' grumbled Parry. He and Reid compared the statements, back and forth. Reid telephoned Brian Clough. Unsurprisingly, the manager sounded drunk. During their rambling conversation, Reid was struck by a throwaway remark. Unprompted, Clough mentioned a meeting between McLintock, Sheringham and Fenton at the Posthouse Hotel in Luton on the night of Sheringham's transfer. Until Clough's comment that meeting had never been mentioned. Reading the statements again Reid realized that all three witnesses had lied. Sheringham's car ride on the back seat suddenly made sense: the box containing £58,000 had been placed on the front passenger seat to give to Fenton. That evening, in Sheringham's sight, McLintock had handed Fenton the £58,000. Sheringham was recalled for questioning. 'I lied,' admitted the footballer, 'because I didn't want to get anyone into trouble.' The conspiracy had unravelled; the lies were blatant and foolish. The investigators' skill was to correctly interpret the deception.

To conceal the true fate of the £58,000 payment from Tottenham, Frank McLintock and his partner, Graham Smith, had provided a phoney invoice for building work which was dated before the cash was even received. Yet the builder denied receiving any money. The conspirators' foolishness was breathtaking. Parry expressed shock that the witnesses had 'lied again and again'.

Terry Venables was also repeatedly inconsistent. On one occasion, Venables denied knowing about the £58,000 payment until two days after the event; in another version he heard about the payment only four months later; and in his autobiography he offered a third explanation. Eddie Ashby's evidence was similarly inconsistent. In his desire to support Venables, Ashby could barely remember his previous version. 'If Terry changes his story now,' worried Ashby secretly, 'he'll drop me in it.' Parry and Reid agreed that both were lying; the evidence proved that on Venables's orders Ashby had asked for the cash from Tottenham's finance director, which he knew was not McLintock's fee but a vital ingredient of the transfer. One major flaw was the absence of any incontrovertible evidence that money had been paid to Clough.

The increasing popularity and wealth of the Premier League led to diminishing interest in the inquiry's conclusions. The twenty Premier League chairmen had a vested interest in dismissing the 'bungs' as unrepeatable history. Graham Kelly was optimistic that football was cleansing itself. That opinion was shared by Keith Wiseman on his election on 11 July 1996 as the FA's chairman, replacing Bert Millichip. Sleaze, pronounced Wiseman, was 'an odd residue of a difficult past'. In the future, he asserted, reflecting the FA's tolerance of conflicts of interest, there would never be another 'bungs' inquiry. One unexpected consequence of Wiseman's prediction was to discourage the critics and encourage the guilty to defy their accusers, disrupting the final stages of the inquiry in 1997.

Over the previous four years, all three panellists had assumed that they would agree to a unanimous report. In the final weeks, Parry, Reid and Coppell could agree that 'several witnesses have attempted deliberately to mislead the Inquiry in their evidence' which confirmed a 'cult of dishonesty'. But at the last moment there was a disagreement between them about the 'bung' for Sheringham's transfer. After Reid and Parry had written the report, concluding that McLintock had given the £58,000 to Fenton in the car park, they awaited Steve Coppell's agreement. To their surprise, Coppell decided to 'back off', asserting that the evidence was inconclusive. Reid was incensed; he admitted that much of the evidence was unpublishable and there was widespread criticism of George Graham's sentence, but that did not explain Coppell's stubbornness. With Parry and Reid, Coppell had been through drafts of the report, drawing out the evidence and the chronology. 'We all know which way it's pointing,' agreed Parry.

To secure Coppell's agreement, Reid drove to south London for a two-hour conversation in 'a tatty office in a single-storey building'. Together, Reid and Coppell reviewed the evidence. 'There's a consistency of lies,' said Reid, surprised by the change in Coppell's demeanour. 'We haven't got the evidence,' the football manager replied, adamantly refusing to sign the report. Reid, a distinguished QC, was puzzled; the evidence was clear, both to the lawyer and to Rick Parry, an experienced accountant and football executive. Both were shocked that Coppell should have difficulty with what key witnesses had admitted. Inevitably the cynics would suggest that Coppell's rebuff was 'a closing of ranks in the football fraternity'. Others were more blunt: 'He's been got at by football.'

The report – a frustrating conclusion to unfinished business – was passed to Kelly at the FA. 'A damp squib,' he said scathingly, uninterested why Coppell had not signed. 'After a lot of leaks and false starts about their conclusions, they passed the buck back to the FA to take disciplinary action without committing themselves. It meant yet more delay after so many years. Just dumped it on our desk after a simple fact-finding operation.' That damnation reflected the FA's antagonism towards regulating football.

The critics' headline after the delayed publication of the report in January 1998 would be 'whitewash'. Brian Clough, charged by the FA with misconduct, had retired due to 'deteriorating health'. Ronnie Fenton had moved to Malta. Rune Hauge's ban had expired. In the meantime agents had been legalized by the FA. 'Football is monster, monster clean,' smirked the agent Eric Hall in his distorted version of the report. And Terry Venables celebrated: 'I've been cleared . . . I knew I was innocent . . . but there was a concerted effort to destroy me, to jail me if possible.' Privately, his self-vindication was supported by Rick Parry. 'I don't think Terry is a villain,' he told a friend. 'He just surrounded himself with undesirables like Ashby. He's not fundamentally bent, just misguided. Terry lied because he was in a corner, to blur the truth. In the Sheringham transfer, Terry acted for Tottenham's benefit, not for his personal profit.' The four year inquiry had produced a lot of smoke, some token punishment and a commitment within the FA never to undertake a similar destabilizing investigation. Traditionalists, reformers and critics could no longer rely on the FA and Graham Kelly.

Graham Kelly was not regarded as a reformer but as 'a pawn', appointed by Bert Millichip to allow the chairman to enjoy the limelight without any challengers. The atmosphere did not change after Keith Wiseman's election to replace Millichip as chairman. Wiseman's ambition was to bring the World Cup to England in 2006 and to be elected to FIFA, a comfortable posting for life. Both those objectives precluded any desire by the FA to supervise the commercial activities of the Premier League's clubs. Kelly and Wiseman were proud of their idea to desist from interference in 'private' enterprises. Over the previous twenty years, Kelly complained, 'I've called for more financial monitoring and failed.' He recognized that his bureaucratic organization found difficulty in controlling a showbiz operation owned by rich individuals and partisan shareholders. Inactivity, he decided, was the only option, trusting tradition rather than intervention. He conceded: 'Bungs are a problem but there's no willingness by football to self-regulate its financial affairs.'

Similarly, Keith Wiseman preferred inertia to avoid antagonizing his critics. He repeated the reasons for the Premier League clubs' rejection of regulation: 'We don't want Big Brother looking over us.' According to Wiseman, football clubs were autonomous, free businesses without limits on expenditure. Lies, dishonesty and conflicts of interest were tolerated because some managers of clubs derided regulation. 'We don't want teams of lawyers and accountants poring over our records. Nor do we want the cost of that additional bureaucracy.' The clubs, he argued, were already subject to parliament's laws and many regulations. If the clubs were being ripped off, or exposed to Inland Revenue investigation, that was an issue for the clubs, not the FA. That was an opinion endorsed by Ken Bates. The senior status in the FA achieved by Ken Bates reflected the integrity of English football. 'I didn't bother to read the Reid report,' Bates proudly admitted. 'What for?' Ken Bates typified the attitude and character of the majority of English club chairmen.

4

THE CHAIRMAN: KEN BATES

The champagne and smoked salmon meal that Ken Bates shared with Rupert Murdoch in 1992 ranks among Bates's proudest moments. After a history of minimizing his taxes and encountering insolvent companies Bates was seated in the Australian's penthouse flat in St James's overlooking Green Park. Momentarily, Bates could forget his own grubby commercial history and enjoy the extravaganza of ranking as a player in the tycoon's constellation. 'I'll give you the Premier League for £50 million,' Bates offered, describing a deal which he would subsequently squeal to Murdoch was 'a marriage made in heaven'. In Bates's version of his life, brokering that marriage transformed English football, and he deserved the credit.

Ken Bates's extra delight was to have undermined David Dein, the vice-chairman of Arsenal, for the second time. In 1988, Dein had been party to a secret understanding with ITV worth £44 million to forge the then Big Five clubs into a Super League. Dein's collaborator Greg Dyke, the football fan and chairman of ITV's sports committee, had promised £1 million to each of the Big Five clubs – Manchester United, Arsenal, Tottenham, Everton and Liverpool – if ITV were granted the exclusive rights. ITV won the competition. In self-congratulation, Dein recalled that in 1965, a bygone age, BBC TV had paid £5,000 for the rights to highlights on *Match of the Day*, distributed as £50 to each club. In 1983, the television rights earned £5.2 million, but in 1985 the fees fell to £1.3 million. The casualties of the new contract would be the Second Division clubs who benefited from the FA's proposed agreement with the BBC. 'You tore to shreds a good deal for all of football,' Graham Kelly told David Dein in a tone of bewildered anger. The Lancastrian, although a modernizer, was irritated by the interlopers' partisanship. 'They're brash, rich and prepared,' Kelly grumbled about Dein and his supporters. His only sanction was to support Dein's removal on 18 October 1988 from the Football League's management committee in punishment for a conflict of interest. Bates relished Dein's embarrassment when he was criticized, albeit ludicrously, as an insider trader by no less than Robert Maxwell. 'All I wanted,' pleaded Dein in self-defence, 'was to get the best deal for football.'

In 1991, First Division clubs were earning £1.8 million for allowing televised broadcasts of their matches. More adventurous chairmen of the star clubs had vowed to terminate 'free' football on television and seek an agreement favouring themselves and excluding the other clubs. 'We're knocking on an open door,' reported David Dein, after presenting Graham Kelly with his plan for a Premier League. Kelly invited the BBC, ITV and the new Sky channel to bid for the television rights of the league of twenty-two clubs (soon reduced to twenty) to start in 1992.

Once again Dein forged an alliance with Martin Edwards of Manchester United, Philip Carter of Everton, Irving Scholar of Tottenham and especially Peter Robinson of Liverpool to support ITV. Ken Bates was not consulted. Bluster, threats and Greg Dyke of ITV Dein hoped would persuade Rick Parry, the Premier League's first chief executive, to side with ITV against Ken Bates and Sky. In a posture of bravado, Dyke told Parry: 'We'll be calling the shots. We've got twelve votes in our pocket.' That threat proved to be misconceived and counter-productive. Dyke, an uncouth populist, lacked the intellect and guile of Rupert Murdoch and Sam Chisholm, Sky's chief executive. Dyke had also lost Tottenham's vote; Alan Sugar, the new chairman, was contracted to supply Sky's satellite dish.

Sam Chisholm calculated that the key to success was to eschew the confrontational tactics of Dyke and Dein. 'Sam played Rick Parry well,' acknowledged a rival. Parry was invited to Sky's ramshackle headquarters in Isleworth; he was seduced by Rupert Murdoch on the telephone; and he departed with 'impressive pledges' followed by a written bid. By contrast, Dyke offered Parry only more threats.

In that confrontation, Dyke ignored Parry's opinion that a single broadcaster could not maximize football's potential profits. Parry favoured Sky working in association with a terrestrial station – either ITV or BBC. Dyke, he believed, was 'intransigent' by insisting on 'exclusivity' and rejecting co-operation with Sky. 'Dyke's trying to frighten the chairmen into an agreement,' judged Parry, encouraging Chisholm to finalize the 'dream ticket'.

Fearing stagnation from earlier losses of £14 million every week, Sky needed to secure live Premier League football to survive. Chisholm's target was Will Wyatt, the

deputy managing director of BBC TV. Four years earlier
the BBC had, embarrassingly, lost the rights of televising
Football League matches to ITV. Chisholm offered the
opportunity for revenge with the highlights of the new
Premier League matches. 'If you get football back on to
BBC,' joked Chisholm, 'you'll be made Lord Wyatt.'
Although he represented the world's biggest broadcasting
corporation, Wyatt lacked any real commercial experience. Thinking only of the short-term benefit, he
accepted Rick Parry's guidance that the BBC should join
Sky's bid. 'That gave credibility to the Sky offer,' rued a
competitor later. 'Wyatt's agreement was vital.' (In 2000,
Wyatt received a CBE for 'services to television'.) The
competing bids – Sky versus ITV – were to be discussed
by the Premier League chairmen on 18 May 1992.

'I want an assurance from you,' Dyke challenged Parry
on the eve of the decision, 'that you'll recommend ITV or
I'll go to individual clubs.' Parry was aghast. Encouraged
by Dein, Dyke was constantly undermining 'the spirit' of
the Premier League by pitting the clubs against each
other. 'I'm negotiating for all the clubs,' replied Parry
stoically. 'Individual clubs have no say.' Dyke, Parry
believed, was damaging the process. The daily telephone
calls which Parry received from David Dein, urging
ITV's cause, were further aggravation. Dein appeared to
be oblivious to the imminent revolution in broadcasting.
One relief was the other daily call from Ken Bates urging
resistance against Dein. 'There's going to be no ITV
stitch-up,' warned Bates, an emerging player in the dispute. As stipulated, Sky delivered a sealed bid the night
before the twenty chairmen met.

On the morning of 18 May 1992, adopting bizarre tactics, Greg Dyke's representative stood in the lobby of the
Royal Lancaster Hotel handing out envelopes to the

arriving chairmen containing ITV's bid of £262 million. Parry was incensed. Encouraged by Alan Sugar – who had already telephoned Chisholm urging Sky to 'blow 'em out of the water' – Parry also telephoned Chisholm and suggested, 'Bid again against ITV.' With gratitude, Sky outbid ITV and, thanks to Sugar's casting vote, a slender majority of chairmen accepted Sky's offer of £305 million for a five year contract. 'You were appointed to sell the Premier League to ITV,' Dein sniped at Parry. 'Each club has one vote,' replied Parry, sensitive that Dein had become an impassioned critic, but grateful for one vocal supporter. 'Shut up,' Bates snarled at Dein during the discussion among the members of the new Premier League. 'You've finally lost!'

David Dein's contemplation of revenge was brief. In the jungle of the new Premier League, it was dangerous to probe into the background of competitors, especially of Bates, a fearless pirate who habitually overwhelmed anyone daring to suggest an investigation of his financial activities. Selfish and vulgar, the chairman of Chelsea had cultivated a hint of aggression to conceal the secrets of his past and protect his current ventures. That manner had, in 1982, secured his ownership of Chelsea and subsequently saved the club from the consequences of insolvency. Bates's commercial history before his purchase of Chelsea had not been examined by the FA. The Association renounced any judgement about the probity of club owners, even if, like Bates, they were elected as members of the FA's executive committee. The world of football avoided judgements of its leaders, especially those who secured promotion to the Premier League.

Bates's journey to fame was strewn with mystery, strife and brushes with bankrupt companies. In self-justification for his brash aggression, Bates had pleaded that his

impoverished childhood had bred insecurity. Born on 4
December 1931, Bates's account of his life suggested that
at eighteen months his mother died and he was abandoned by his father to be cared for in a west London
council flat by step-grandparents. In his late teens, he
was reconciled with his father and, after abandoning an
accountancy course, worked with his father in a quarry
business near Manchester. At twenty-two, stocky and
outspoken, he married Theresa, the daughter of a wealthy
Irish country squire. Her family provided the money for
his first Bentley, bought the year after his marriage. The
quarry prospered and he began supplying ready-mix concrete to the growing building trade. Astutely, Bates
became master of an unsentimental business, undercut-
ting the established producers of concrete by locating his
plants in the nursery towns close to Manchester rather
than forty miles away, sharply reducing his transport
costs. Bates lived near Blackburn, and his natural pro-
gression was to become a builder. His activity attracted
Torquil Norman, an Old Etonian employed at Philip
Hill, a City investment bank. Norman had been told
about Bates by an acquaintance: 'There's this bright chap
in the north called Bates you should meet.' Norman was
impressed by Bates's humour, his Bentley and his concrete business which, boasted Bates, had produced
£700,000 in profits. Norman introduced Bates to Philip
Hill's directors who agreed to invest through Mineral
Separation Ltd in Batehill, a new company established to
invest in land leasing in Scotland and manufacturers of
carpets, uniforms, toys and marine equipment. 'We were
the first venture capital company,' recalled Norman.
'"Putting skates on business" was our motto.'

The City connection encouraged Bates's ambitions. On
28 January 1965, he launched Howarth, a construction and

property development company based in Burnley, on the Manchester stock exchange. In the same year, intent on fame, he used his new wealth to become chairman of Oldham Athletic FC. Football, he told his new audience, was a passion and only a club-foot had prevented his own professional career as a footballer. Howarth's share price rose and Bates acquired a succession of property companies.

By 1967 Howarth was struggling. Bates's expansion had proved to be unsustainable. In a statement to shareholders in March, he admitted, 'The recent past has been an unpleasant one and the present situation is difficult', but he was optimistic that, 'we have put the worst of our troubles behind us.' At the shareholders' meeting, Bates promised, 'I am not getting out. I am fully involved in the group.' There was also a shadow over his management of Oldham Athletic. A newspaper reported in 1966 that Bates had summoned the police to investigate the club's accounts and, in the following year, a director resigned complaining, 'Bates believes in a committee of two, with one absent.' His relationship with Torquil Norman was more amicable. Batehill had proved to be more profitable than construction and, through the company's financial relationship with Britten Norman, the stricken manufacturer of the small Islander aircraft, Bates had been introduced to the British Virgin Islands, a colony of 8,000 people.

During a business visit to the Virgin Islands in 1966, Bates met Norman Fowler, an American who had negotiated an unusual agreement with the British administrator of the colony. Development of the islands' economy, explained Fowler, had been hampered by suspicious natives and the absence of flat land around Road Town, the capital of Tortola, a mountainous island with a population of 2,000. With the approval of the British government, Fowler planned to exploit the explosion of tourism across the region by reclaiming 2.5 acres of water between the capital and an islet at Wickham's Cay. The new link would release 60 acres of land for the construction of houses, hotels and a marina. Fowler's operation had, however, collapsed. Every day's successful dredging was reversed during the night as the sea crept back over the reclaimed land. The fault, Bates realized, could be rectified by hiring a competent Dutch engineering company. A stark comparison appealed to Bates. Land in Road Town cost $3 to $4 per square foot, while in St Thomas, in the nearby US Virgin Islands, land values had risen to over $40 per square foot. The reclaimed land in Tortola, Bates believed, covered with a luxury holiday complex, would earn profits of possibly $50 million. Aged thirty-five, Bates saw an opportunity to earn money in a tax haven and avoid Britain's 90 per cent rate of income tax. Telephoning Torquil Norman from the Treasure Isle Hotel, Bates bubbled excitedly about 'earning enough in three years to retire for ever'.

Fowler agreed to transfer the rights owned by his company, the Tortola Development and Trust Co., to Bates. Once the deal was completed, Bates began negotiations with Martin Staveley, the local British administrator representing the Foreign and Colonial Office in London.

During his discussions, Bates's ambitions grew. Spotting Anegada, a flat, isolated coral island only accessible for the local population of 200 by boat, he proposed to Staveley that he imitate the property developments in the American Virgin Islands and, after constructing an infrastructure of roads, electricity and an airport, he would sell plots of land on the 15 square miles to Americans and Britons to build houses on a new tax haven.

Bates's power of persuasion was astonishing. In September 1966, contrary to the Foreign Office's advice, Staveley signed an agreement, a veritable coup for Bates. He had secured the right to reclaim Wickham's Cay and enjoy a ten year tax holiday for all the profits he would subsequently earn. In parallel, Staveley granted Bates a 199-year lease over all the island of Anegada, excluding only the 1,500 acres where the few inhabitants lived. On the British government's behalf, Staveley had also agreed that throughout the 199-year lease of Anegada, Bates's company and the island's new inhabitants would pay no taxes. Bates and Torquil Norman anticipated earning a further $50 million of profits. Three days after concluding the agreement Staveley's term of office ended and he left the island. News of the agreement only reached the Foreign Office four months later, on 20 January 1967. A baffled Treasury official in Whitehall would question why Staveley had signed away the Virgin Islands' single biggest source of future earnings. Inexplicably, Staveley would plead to his colleagues to have acted 'under pressure'.

To finance the development, on 25 July 1967, Bates and Torquil Norman floated Wickham's Cay Ltd, a company registered in the Virgin Islands. Torquil Norman secured a loan from Barclays Bank in New York, encouraging investors from London, including Michael Tollemache, an Old Etonian City broker. Others in London were less enamoured by Bates. In July 1968, after Philip Hill merged with Samuel, another merchant bank, the directors were unwilling to continue working with Bates, blaming his appalling manners. 'They felt that Ken wasn't one of us,' recalled Torquil Norman, who bought Batehill with Bates and relaunched the company by remortgaging their homes. The City bankers' disdain for

Bates was unsurprising since the aspiring tycoon openly confessed, according to the *Financial Times*, how he had earned his money by 'breaking the rules'. His strategy, he admitted, had not always been successful: 'I over-traded, made a penny do the work of three quid and headed straight for disaster – or that's what they said. Let's face it, there are a lot of people who want to see you fail because you don't go by the book. That may have been all right years ago, but nowadays we're a nation of spivs living off our wits.' Convinced of earning his fortune in the Virgin Islands, Bates cursed the City and flew towards the sun.

In July 1968, while the reclamation of the Cay was underway, Bates arrived in the Virgin Islands with his wife and five children. They lived in primitive conditions in Long Look, on Anegada, first in a caravan and later a house. Sitting in the sunshine overlooking the blue Caribbean sea, Bates nurtured his dreams. Executing an exit from Burnley was astute and his inevitable wealth at the end of the construction in the Virgin Islands would confirm his abilities. His departure from England had been fortunate. After selling his new home in Cheshire and resigning from Howarth, the company had revealed debts of £1.8 million and, on 24 July 1969, appointed a receiver. Bates was as unloved by the abandoned creditors as much as he was feared by his children. Robert, his son, complained of his father's explosive temper and denigration of his family by his habit of divide and rule. Neither complaint appeared to be of much concern to Bates. Convinced of his destiny, he began writing his memoirs, describing himself on a veranda in the Caribbean wearing shorts and drinking champagne, reproaching the world for failing to recognize the existence of an outstanding tycoon. In his artless prose, described by one reader as

'Ken at his egotistical best', Bates styled himself as the 'Master of the Game', the Cockney raised in a rough London council estate pulling the strings to outwit lawyers, accountants and other Establishment professionals despite his lack of education. The thin, uncompleted, typed manuscript, glorifying 'Ken Scoring', was vainglorious testimony to his strengths and weaknesses. Unintellectual, ruthless and rude, he begged to join the ranks of the global tycoons but lacked the self-awareness to recognize the consequences of his unsophisticated ignorance. Accomplished tycoons concealed their emotions, especially their lust for revenge; Bates's anger was raw and flaunted. Publicly denigrating others produced many enemies but became a self-inflicted wound.

After one year, the reclamation work at Wickham's Cay was nearly completed, while on Anegada, the infrastructure for roads, an air strip, a power station, a hotel and the first houses was evident. 'I went out and I made it work,' boasted Bates, but there were no celebrations. Bates's behaviour had incensed the local population. Not only was he vulgar, especially to local women politicians, but he had insensitively renamed Anegada the 'Crown Colony Caribbean'. Locals in Road Town blamed the inadequate drainage and sea walls along the new waterfront in Wickham's Cay built by Bates for flooding the town after a storm. They threatened violence against Bates's 'cavalier attitude' and worse, to punish the investor, the local government began enacting a law to limit the rights of aliens to own land and refused to enact the promised tax concessions. Those sanctions coincided with an economic recession in America, jeopardizing the entire project. The businessman's reaction to the crisis was incendiary, prompting 'The Battle of Bates'. In the

developer's opinion, however, he was the victim of agita-
tors in New York and antagonistic local civil servants.
'The outsiders wanted to nick the thing for nothing,' he
insisted. 'I had no problem with the local people.'

Others were equally certain about the cause of the
argument. In November 1970, the Foreign Office in
London had become concerned about Bates's continued
presence in the area. His personality, an official concluded, was 'totally unfit for these islands and I don't
think that things will get any better until he either
changes his attitudes or he gets out altogether'. The
'unrest' Bates was provoking, officials feared, would cause
'a political crisis and a probable breakdown in law and
order'. Their nightmare was a repetition of the coup in
Anguilla, a neighbouring British island, which had been
suppressed after a humiliating 'invasion' by British
troops. If Bates did not leave Tortola, the officials feared,
there would be a coup and Britain would be compelled to
abandon the islands.

Removing Bates was the problem. His agreement with
Staveley was legally watertight and in the opinion of
Lavity Stoutt, the islands' chief minister, Bates was a
'tough egg' who would 'tenaciously hold on to his legal
rights'. Haplessly, Stoutt and British officials hoped that
Bates would 'give way' without compensation. 'We think
that it is most important that we avoid any commitment
whatsoever to paying compensation to Mr Bates,' an official recorded. Bates shattered that illusion.

'I want $10 million,' Bates told the British administra-
tor after halting all work, firing his British staff, and
threatening to destroy the islands' opportunity to attract
future American investors. 'I do not intend to run a social
security scheme on the island,' he announced. His
employees complained of having been 'misled by Bates'.

Returning to England in October 1970, Bates invited Anthony Fairclough, the head of the West Indian Department at the Foreign Office, for lunch. Influencing the British government at the meeting was crucial to Bates's financial fortunes, but his bullying of Fairclough undermined his opportunity. 'I want £5 million or I'll get mean,' Bates threatened Fairclough. 'If there's no quick solution, the BVI's reputation will stink.' Bates, however, refused to present his accounts to justify his demand. His subsequent letters to 'get bought out' were criticized as 'offensive, abusive and unhelpful'. Bates's explanation is unambiguous: 'I've got contempt for civil servants.' Fairclough concluded that Bates was 'running a very big risk' and accordingly advised, 'no special favour is due to Mr Bates'. The civil servants' attitude changed in December. After vacillating between threatening compulsory purchase and offering compensation, the officials grudgingly decided to offer Bates a maximum of £2.5 million ($6 million). Their offer was rejected by Bates as 'a blatant piece of theft'.

At the end of March 1971, Bates was under pressure to accept the deal. Dislike of Bates had spread to Barclays Bank who had loaned him $1.5 million and, fearing delays in repayment of his loan, demanded total and immediate refunding. Bates was incapable of withstanding the bankers' pressure. 'Norman wanted to give up,' explained Bates. 'Life was too short to argue.' To the relief of the Foreign Office, in March 1971 the developer was sufficiently concerned to telephone in a panic to seek a settlement.

Bates had become the victim of his ignorance. Self-satisfied and boastful, he was insensitive to the government's own dilemma. Foreign Office officials had secretly acknowledged his entitlement to at least $6.8 million and

probably more. Securing 'an early settlement', the civil
servants agreed, was a 'political imperative'. More refined
tycoons would have perceived Whitehall's weaknesses,
but Bates remained oblivious. On 21 April 1971, he
accepted $5.8 million in compensation, less than he had
been offered one month earlier. 'It's grossly unfair,' he
moaned. At the request of Barclays, the money was
deposited by the British government at their bank in New
York. The bankers had confided their fear to the Foreign
Office that after receiving any compensation from the
British government, Bates would 'skip with the money
and leave his creditors in the lurch'. There was no evidence that Bates would behave in such a manner, but his
relationship with the bankers had clearly provoked unre-
strained spleen. In the final settlement, Bates's personal
profit from the British government was about $1.5 mil-
lion, the equivalent today of $10 million. The British
taxpayers' money was transferred by Bates to an offshore
tax haven. None of the shareholders or banks had lost any
money and Bates had paid all the creditors, but he had
failed to earn his anticipated fortune. In consolation, he
could use the compensation as seed money for a new
venture.

To reduce his tax bills Bates established a residence at
Hersilia in Monte Carlo. On the Côte d'Azur he met
Stanley Tollman, a South African acquaintance he had
recently met at the Dorchester Hotel in London. Tollman
was an aggressive and like-minded hotelier, who assumed
Bates's address as his own. Tollman was a distinctive
character; even in July he wore a dark brown mink coat.
Tollman and his brother had, it was said, 'been ducking
and diving for years', but the brothers were Bates's
chosen partners for his next enterprise in Ireland, where
he had settled with his family in 1971. Shankill House,

his home near Dublin, was an imposing mansion, suitable for an aspiring banker.

Life in the Virgin Islands had introduced Bates to the advantages of offshore banking. He had registered the Bank of Anegada, establishing himself as a banker and, to increase his investments in property and businesses, he applied for a licence to own a bank in Ireland. His timing was propitious. The country's banking regulations were still remarkably lax. Obtaining a licence from the Central Bank required only the production of a testament to the applicant's good reputation and proof of some assets. The finance for the proposed bank was provided by the International Trust Group, a company established in the Isle of Man shortly after Bates returned from the Virgin Islands. Among those recruited in Dublin by Bates were Giles Montgomery, a solicitor, and Tom Phelan, a well-connected accountant, apparently flattered by their new status as bankers. Together, in June 1971, they bought Kildare Bank, an off-the-shelf company. Two months later, the bank was renamed the Irish Trust Bank, with small premises at 5 Dawson Street. The next requirement was to find depositors.

To attract money Bates hired Brian Loughney, a persuasive salesman. Loughney's targets were the small savers in Ireland and the Irish communities in the United States lured by advertisements in New York's *Irish Echo*. To those emotionally attached to the Emerald Isle the Irish Trust Bank offered a safe haven for their savings, paying significantly higher rates of interest, tax-free. The same salesmanship enticed borrowers to the bank's branch office in Manchester, including George Best and Bobby Charlton.

Over the first year, the bank attracted 1,400 savers in Eire, England and America, who deposited about £3.5

million. Compared with methods used by Dublin's more
established banks their money was used in an unorthodox
manner. Bates's bank advanced a small number of large
loans to property companies. Among the recipients was a
loan of £1.4 million to the International Trust Group, a
company registered in the Isle of Man, which owned 20
per cent of the bank itself and produced two-thirds of the
bank's income; a further loan was advanced to purchase
land and property in Queensland, Australia, where Bates
would later live; and £250,000 was loaned to Moore
Holdings, a property company in Dublin owned by
Robert Noonan, one of Dublin's famous go-go specula-
tors, who would later own Chelsea FC.

Under Bates's management, the bank was also notable
for other striking features. The depositors were paid high
rates of interest but the bank lent money, especially to the
International Trust Group, at commercially low rates of
interest. Balancing the books to produce a profit was difficult. A second distinctive feature was the obscurity of
many ultimate borrowers. Peculiarly, while some loans
were channelled through the International Trust Group
in the Isle of Man, the legal borrower was another offshore nominee company whose directors were
anonymous. Unusually, the loan documents excluded
ITG from responsibility for the loans. In that manner,
the bank also made a loan to Hebrides Investments, an
anonymous company in Gibraltar, another tax haven,
which in turn lent money to a nominee company in
Cairns, Australia, to buy land in Queensland. Frequently
the loans were granted without proper collateral or a comprehensible legal framework.

One year after its creation, Adrian Byrne, responsible
for supervision at the Irish Central Bank, became concerned about Bates and his bank. In his aggressive

manner, Bates had bid on behalf of the International Trust Group in the Isle of Man for an Irish property company. Irritated by Bates, the company investigated his background and discovered stains on the hostile bidder's reputation. Firstly, the British government's fury with Bates concerning Anegada; secondly, the discovery that the 'Bank of Anegada' amounted to just a file in Bates's briefcase; and thirdly, that Bates was reported to have not disclosed his past directorship of Howarth, the insolvent property company. On 12 January 1972, Bernard Breen, the secretary of the Central Bank, wrote to James Keogh, a friend at the Bank of England, asking for any information about Bates. Keogh replied that while he could find nothing to Bates's 'discredit', none of his former bankers in England 'would be gladdened if he returned to them'. Keogh concluded that if Bates applied in London for a banking licence, 'I would have no option but to reject his claim.'

That was deemed sufficient for the Central Bank to apply to the Dublin High Court to revoke Bates's banking licence. The bank told the court that it 'did not regard Mr Bates as acceptable as a director of this bank' because he had omitted to mention in his application for a banking licence his directorship of Howarth. To Bates's good fortune, the bank's application was legally flawed and his counter-challenge was successful. Nevertheless, on 17 April 1972, Bates resigned as a director. Among the bank's new shareholders were Bates's five children – Fiona, Robert, Richard, Susan and Catherine – all of whom were minors, and Overseas Metals Ltd, an anonymous company registered in Gibraltar. Bates was replaced as a director by Freddie Pye, a former wrestler, a scrap metal merchant and the chairman of Stockport FC, who had spent a holiday with Bates in the Caribbean. Freddie

Pye's company, Pye Metals, secured a loan of £200,000
from the Irish Trust Bank through ITG in the Isle of
Man at a commercially low rate of interest.

Despite his resignation as a director, Bates continued
to work from Dawson Street and offered advice about the
bank's lending in his search for new opportunities.
Bankruptcies became the source of the gambler's fortune.
He was introduced to this by John Papi, a Kuwaiti
employed as an assistant to Martin Spencer, an insolvency expert at Stoy Hayward, the accountants. Papi's
skill was to find businessmen willing to take over companies in liquidation at no cost in return for repaying some
of the debts owed to the companies' creditors. In Bates,
Papi found a man determined to prove himself right.

The two met in 1974 at the Sherlock Holmes Hotel in
Baker Street, London. Both were attending a meeting of
creditors of the Court Hotels (London) Ltd. The administrator was Papi, and among the directors of the
insolvent company was Stanley Tollman. Bates was present as an interested observer.

Soon after their meeting, Papi offered Trafalgar
Travel, an insolvent subsidiary of Court Hotels, to Bates.
'You can make a bomb on this,' said Papi, suggesting
that he pay a small smount to the creditors and inherit a
good business. The Irish Trust Bank advanced a loan to
Stanley Tollman, Bates's partner. Trafalgar Travel's
profits in the first year were £2 million. Excited by
Papi's offerings, Bates also took over a publishing company on the brink of liquidation. Kemps Directories,
based off the Portobello Road in London, was bought
for £1 and earned Bates about £1 million; and with
Papi's help he took over Hales Owen Press, a printing
company, which was also profitably transformed. Papi's
best offer was the Montcalm Hotel near Marble Arch.

The cost was £1, plus repayment of £72,500 of debts to the creditors. Bates's Irish bank financed the purchase of the hotel from Barclays Bank, although Stanley Tollman and not Bates appeared to be the principal involved. Tollman was in the midst of creating a hotel empire which would eventually be declared bankrupt in a scheme which profited Tollman and his brother at the expense of many banks. Eighteen months after the original purchase in the early 1970s, the hotel was sold for £2.5 million. Throughout that period Bates often lived on the premises. He appeared to be averse to owning homes in England and preferred renting. People he encountered at the time recall that his pockets bulged with wodges of banknotes.

By any measure Bates was a fringe player, profiting from the crumbs of the phoney boom unleashed by the Conservative government. To join the bandwagon, he sought a substantial stake in Moore Holdings, an Irish property company managed by Robert Noonan. 'I want to appoint directors,' said Bates, convinced that the company was a rich picking. Noonan liked Bates but perceived all his self-destructive weaknesses. 'Buy more shares or quit,' Noonan challenged his banker. 'It's a fantastic deal.' Bates, certain that he understood property better than anyone, swallowed the bait and paid £300,000. Noonan took the money, bid farewell and smiled, 'He's bought dead stock.' Shortly after, Moore Holdings crashed. Like many other property dealers in Britain, Bates's dreams were shattering.

In 1975, the Irish Trust Bank was in difficulties. The bank had advanced long-term loans to property companies at fixed rates but was borrowing short-term to cover the debts. Interest rates on the short-term loans were rising sharply, propelling the bank towards insolvency.

To conceal its plight, the bank's accounts presented the unpaid interest payments from its borrowers as assets. That ploy was detected.

Since 1972, the Central Bank in Dublin had warily supervised the bank's accounts. A new law had closed the loopholes which had originally allowed Bates to obtain a licence. An inspection by Adrian Byrne's staff in late 1975 raised the alarm that too many loans were connected to anonymous offshore entities, that the loans' security was not properly perfected, that the loans were not being repaid and that there was insufficient income to repay the depositors. In particular, loans to Agamemnon and Temeraire, two companies with nominee shareholdings and unknown directors, were of special interest to the Central Bank's investigators. Both were buying derelict land in Dublin as a speculative 'site assembly'. Neither were paying any interest to the bank, and none of the bank's employees appeared to be able to name the owner of the sites. To verify his conclusions, Byrne asked Charles Russell of Coopers and Lybrand to investigate the bank's loan book. Russell confirmed that the bank was heading towards insolvency. 'You're taking big risks with other people's money,' Russell told Mel Kennedy, the bank's general manager, 'and that's against the rules of safe banking.'

Adrian Byrne, on behalf of the Central Bank, applied to the court to revoke the Irish Trust Bank's licence. Furiously, Bates counter-attacked. Although he was not a shareholder or director, he presented the evidence that the bank's loans were sound. He appeared outraged that anyone should question his talent or probity. Bates's plea was successful; and to Byrne's irritation, Bates appeared to leave the court with a swagger. Byrne was outraged that Ireland's most venerable institution had been embarrassed. On 19 February 1976, Byrne again applied to the High Court to close down the bank and appoint Paddy Shortall as the liquidator.

The court considered the application on 23 March 1976. During the hearing Bates and two other men, described in newspapers as 'heavies', entered the bank's premises in Dawson Street, and climbed a back staircase to the boardroom. Pushing past a female assistant, Bates seized a sack of documents. 'You can't do that,' an accountant shouted. 'See you in court,' replied Bates, leaving the building like Santa Claus, to be driven off by his wife. His appearance in court was sooner than he expected; thirty minutes after he had driven away, the judge issued a warrant for Bates's arrest. Later that afternoon Bates voluntarily sauntered into the courtroom. 'I believe you're looking for me,' he smiled. He explained that he had taken personal papers unconnected with the Irish bank and had not been a director since 1972. He had, he said, leased the premises to the bank and worked in an adjoining office. The judge ordered Bates to return the papers and granted the application to close the bank.

During their investigation of the bank's loans, Shortall and Russell discovered that the finances were worse than expected. Their most important witness was Bates, but he was occasionally unhelpful, storming out of the accountants' office when challenged to explain the flawed loans, whose consequences in 1977 were more serious than the banker had anticipated. Across Ireland, the tearful plight of the devastated savers had become an issue during the country's election campaign. Both major Irish political parties, anxious to deflect the bad publicity in the United States, promised to repay the depositors in full. 'Why don't you compensate the depositors?' shouted Shortall to Bates after the businessman denied once again all knowledge or responsibility for the fate of the money. 'Honour your guarantees at least,' roared Shortall. In Shortall's version Bates pulled out his cheque book and wrote a cheque for £280,000. Bates says it was paid through his lawyers but agrees, 'I was normally obstructive to Shortall.' That was an exceptional victory for Shortall. Over the following twenty-five years, Shortall would pursue the trail of the bank's loans across the world. Never once could he prove that a single loan had been made to a company associated with Bates, yet he reported to his superiors notable coincidences. In London, he met Bates at the Montcalm Hotel and the offices of Trafalgar Travel in Buckingham Palace Road, which had been bought by Stanley Tollman with loans from the bank; and in a remote hotel in Cairns, Australia, he was surprised to meet Tom Proctor, Bates's assistant, who offered to drive the liquidator to the land in Queensland which had been bought through a succession of nominee companies linked to Gibraltar and the Isle of Man. All of those investments, Bates told Shortall, were unconnected to himself.

The debacle did not embarrass Bates. On the contrary, he strutted with the pride of a victorious warrior. He had defeated the British government and he had outwitted the Irish government. His remorseless ability to dominate officials and employees proved his mettle. Liquidation also imprinted no stigma, only opportunities, for the businessman.

Two coach companies he controlled, Kirby Coaches and Transworld, were heading towards insolvency. Transworld's liquidation, on the petition of Trafalgar Leisure International, a company registered in the Isle of Man, caused some concern. Transworld's finances had been secured by his personal guarantee to Lloyds Bank.

Bates asked John Papi and Stoy Hayward to help avoid the worst effects. The insolvency expert produced an astute and legal lifebelt. In a technical paper chase, Bates became a preferred creditor of his own company by converting his debt to the bank into a debenture. He borrowed money to repay Lloyds and once Transworld was in liquidation, he was assured by Papi, acting as the liquidator, that the debenture holder, namely Bates, would have first call on the assets. 'I've taught you how to become a preferred creditor,' Papi told Bates. 'To reduce your costs.'

In John Papi's informed judgement Bates emerged from the 1970s with about £5 million. At fifty, compared with many businessmen in London, Bates's limited wealth testified to his limited skills. He possessed sufficient money to live moderately well, spending only on a regular cruise and the occasional charter of a yacht. His survival owed a debt to the astute and legal management of his taxes through an offshore company in Hong Kong and a bank account in Guernsey, and to Derek Evans, a partner of a small firm of accountants, Hargreaves Brown Benson in Lincolnshire. But most of all, in John Papi's self-interested opinion, to the insolvency expert.

In 1979, Papi flew to Nice. A maroon Rolls Royce was parked on the quay beside a yacht chartered by Bates. Papi was offering Osborne Marketing Communications, a company which was rich in assets but technically insolvent. 'You can make £4 to £5 million,' said Papi. Bates returned to England to meet the staff. The encounter proved disastrous. 'Right, let's meet tonight,' he told the truculent staff. Drawing a line down the room he barked, 'Right, those who want to stay, stand on that side. All who want to leave go to the other side and collect your P45s.' As usual, the nomad mistakenly thought that abrasiveness was the same as confidence. 'You've been so rude that they've rejected you,' reported Papi. Unconcerned, Bates temporarily fled from Europe. He grew his hair and flew to Queensland to cultivate sugar cane in the outback. On his return, he worked anonymously at Trafalgar Travel's offices near Buckingham Palace until a fateful visit by John Papi.

In November 1981, Papi took a taxi to Bates's office to offer the biggest prize. 'Chelsea Football Club,' the insolvency expert said, 'is looking for an investor.' Papi had heard the news from Martin Spencer, his former employer who had become Chelsea's chief executive. 'For £1,' said Papi, 'you can have the club and all its debts.' Bates, the frustrated tycoon yearning for applause, visibly gasped. Disbarred from invitations to any lucrative commercial party, he still ranked as a sprat, unknown among the City players who were earning real fortunes. Chelsea Football Club offered the final opportunity to wreak revenge against his imagined enemies.

For the first fifty years after its creation in 1905, the Chelsea Football and Athletic Club had languished, despite employing a handful of stars. The transformation had been achieved during the 1960s by Tommy Docherty. In successive seasons, Chelsea was promoted to the First Division, won the FA Cup and attracted new fans from the inhabitants of the King's Road, the stars of London's Swinging Sixties. During the 1970s the glamour faded. By 1982, the club had been relegated to the Second Division, was bankrupt and appeared to be doomed.

There was some irony in Papi's offer of a poisoned chalice. One year earlier, Martin Spencer had unsuccessfully offered Chelsea to Bates. 'They wouldn't entertain me,' replied Bates, aware that the club's owners were unimpressed by his pedigree. 'I'm not interested,' he said self-defensively. Twelve months later, the new circumstances dissipated his timidity. Barclays Bank were compelling Chelsea's owners to sell. John Papi's offer to Bates was an opportunity to recover from a humiliation in 1969: his resignation from Oldham FC. On that occasion, Harry Massey, the club's vice-chairman, said, 'Bates was too ambitious too quickly. His pace was too fast.' Nothing had changed in Bates's style over the years.

Acting on Papi's suggestion, Bates paid £1 for the football club and its debts of £600,000. His partner was Stanley Tollman, who became a fellow director. Curiously, in registering his ownership of at least two companies, Bates submitted a wrong date of birth – 8 April 1929 instead of 4 December 1931. The expert in insolvency had reason to anticipate acrimony during his management of the football club, although years later he explained his purpose at Stamford Bridge in romantic terms as one of 'a dreamer who is determined to make his dreams come true'.

Not having sufficient money, Bates did not buy a second company which owned the stadium and surrounding land. 'The club had debts of £2 million and was losing £12,000 a week,' explained Bates twenty years later. 'I couldn't face the exposure of greater debts.' Instead, Bates paid for an option to buy the stadium and land within seven years. To his critics, however, it appeared that Bates had been unable to understand properly the real consequences of the deal. Robert Noonan and David Mears, the vendors, had sold the club but had retained the freehold of the stadium and, soon after signing the deal with Bates, they sold the freehold of the ground to Marler, a property development company. Marler gave the football club notice to leave the stadium when the lease expired in 1989.

The next years for Chelsea FC were rancorous and perilous. The team, playing in a shabby stadium, languished in the Second Division while Bates fought bitterly against his own kind – property developers – to obtain control of the ground and prevent its redevelopment for housing. The feeling among the public towards football was hostile. Hooliganism and violence had erupted among vicious fans and the finances of many clubs were dire. Irving Scholar paid just £500,000 for Tottenham and Robert Maxwell paid £120,000 for Oxford United. Investors in a sport which spawned calamities were hardly idealists, but indulgent egocentrics. They enjoyed the fame but ignored their responsibilities. Bates appeared to be no different. On the contrary, Bates perfectly mirrored so many characteristics of Britain's football executives and, in turn, of modern Britain itself. His experience of rescuing some small businesses and teetering into insolvency with others was scant preparation to devise a business plan to improve Chelsea's financial predicament. Similarly, his reaction to the extreme hooliganism at Stamford Bridge was to apply to the council to erect an electrified fence in front of one stand. His application was rejected by the local authority. Unapologetic, Bates disregarded the continuing public protests. His fight against the ground's sale for development continued to win the sympathy of Chelsea's most truculent fans.

Bates was saved by two insolvencies. Among the casualties of the 1991 property recession was Marler, the owner of the stadium's freehold. Then Cabra Estates, the purchaser of the freehold, also fell victim to the plummeting property values and spiralled towards bankruptcy. In 1992, the freehold was assumed by the Royal Bank of Scotland, who in turn granted Bates a twenty year lease and an option to buy the stadium. Bates's stubbornness had won that particular battle, embellished by promotion to the Premier League. By any measure, securing Chelsea's revival and glory was a remarkable success. Basking in the gratitude and adulation of Chelsea fans, Bates went for glory.

Certain of the freehold Bates applied for permission to redevelop the stadium as a location not only for football but also a hotel and restaurants. 'Chelsea Village' would amalgamate all his talents: property, construction, travel, hotels and good living. But at that moment, a new recession in the British economy also hit Bates; he faced disaster. Over the previous decade, Bates had failed to improve Chelsea's finances. In common with so many football club owners, Bates was criticized for spending money without sufficient care. The last accounts for Chelsea Football and Athletic Club in March 1992 reported a pre-tax operating loss of £157,693 and an accumulated deficit of £1.5 million. In the report, Bates stated, 'The directors consider that the result for the year is satisfactory but the position at the end of the year remains unsatisfactory.' That caution proved to be understated.

Maybanks, the club's printers, were facing dire financial problems and issued a demand for the payment of £50,000 owed to them by the club. Chelsea was unable to pay many creditors, including the repayment of a £1.75 million unsecured loan to the Royal Bank of Scotland which was also pressing for repayment. The club owed a further £418,000 against tangible assets of £620,000 and a football team who were legally worthless if the club ceased to trade. Technically, Chelsea was playing football while insolvent, an infringement of the FA's rules, but Bates could safely rely on the FA failing to enforce its own rules.

The natural source of advice was John Papi, his best hope of keeping the club. They met for lunch at the Sheraton Park Hotel. By then Papi was personally on the verge of bankruptcy and under suspicion by the Insolvency Practitioners' Association for 'gross professional misconduct'.

Papi's solution to save Chelsea was a variation of the 'debenture' method which he had previously applied to save Bates's investment in the bankrupt coach company. The key to Papi's scheme was to obtain the support of the Royal Bank of Scotland, which risked losing its unsecured loan to the club. Papi negotiated to guarantee the loan's repayment if the bank agreed that Bates should become a preferred creditor over Chelsea's suppliers. In effect, in this scheme, which was approved by the courts, everyone in theory risked losing money except Bates and the bank.

Papi's plan was aided by an unnoticed mistake. The club's contracts with its football players, approved by the FA, were wrongly issued in the name of the Chelsea Football Club rather than the Chelsea Football and Athletic Club. 'You've fallen on your feet,' smiled Papi. 'It's a fortunate mistake. But we have to move fast to save the club.'

Papi set to work. Two new companies were created: Chelsea Village and CFAC. Under Papi's plan, the assets of Chelsea Football and Athletic Club would eventually be transferred to CFAC Ltd on 14 August 1992, saving the club but threatening all the creditors with the exception of the Royal Bank of Scotland.

Under the plan, for which both Bates and Papi claim individual credit, Chelsea Village should guarantee to the Royal Bank of Scotland the original loan of £1.75 million to Chelsea Football and Athletic Club. Bates, on behalf of

Chelsea Village, would secure a new loan of £1.75 million from the Royal Bank of Scotland to Chelsea Village. That new money was advanced to the Chelsea Football and Athletic Club and was secured on the club's assets. The new advance was classed as a debenture and would, in the event of insolvency, make Chelsea Village a preferred creditor. Next, the Chelsea Football and Athletic Club would be renamed CFAC Ltd, protecting the name 'Chelsea Football Club'. Next, the £1.75 million in cash would be repaid by CFAC to the Royal Bank of Scotland, protecting the bank's interest in the original loan. The final stage would be to transfer all of CFAC's assets to Chelsea Village. Everything was therefore set for CFAC to be placed into receivership, bequeathing the club to Bates free of the threat of insolvency. After taking legal advice, subsequently upheld in court, Bates approved the plan. On 17 August 1992, Bates and Tollman formally resigned as directors of CFAC.

Without notification to the club's creditors, Papi, on CFAC's behalf, transferred Chelsea's players, worth £7 million, from CFAC to Chelsea Village. That transfer would later be criticized by Christopher Morris of Touche Ross, the accountants, as 'unlawful'. The stadium was also transferred to Chelsea Village. Two-thirds of Chelsea Village's shareholders were anonymous offshore trusts, among them, it was repeatedly speculated, Stanley Tollman. In public, Bates spoke for 100 million of the club's 102 million shares. Among the casualties of the arrangement was the FA rule forbidding the anonymous ownership of over 10 per cent of a club's shares, but again Bates could rely on the FA's failure to enforce the rules.

To implement the plan, Bates flew with Papi to Guernsey. Sitting in the office of Patrick Marrin, an accountant, the two visitors watched the unfolding of a paper trail between banks and lawyers, prompted each time by Bates signing a succession of forms. By the completion of that circle, Chelsea Village became the CFAC's preferred creditor and the Royal Bank of Scotland possessed a secure debt in Chelsea Village rather than an unsecured debt with CFAC. On his return to London, Bates had secured possession of Chelsea free from the threat of insolvency, which he and the Royal Bank of Scotland stood to gain at the expense of the other creditors. To complete the process, the revenue of Chelsea's season tickets that year was not deposited in the old company's (CFAC) account. In June, Papi transferred CFAC's remaining assets of £620,000 to Chelsea Village, leaving debts of £418,000 owed by CFAC. The new company's shares were owned by anonymous trusts registered in Marrin's office, most notably, a 60 per cent stake owned by Swan Management, reputedly a vehicle of Stanley Tollman. Seven weeks later, unaware of those transactions, Maybanks, the printers, issued a formal winding up order of CFAC.

In May 1993, Chelsea Village, acting as the debenture holder of CFAC's assets, appointed John Papi as the receiver of CFAC. Formally, John Papi announced that CFAC 'had no option but to cease trading' and the company was placed into receivership. CFAC, disclosed Papi, owed Chelsea Village just over £1 million. On 30 June 1993, at a meeting of CFAC's creditors at the Sheraton Park Tower in Knightsbridge, Papi said, 'the company has a £2.4 million "black hole". There are not enough assets to cover the amounts owed.' CFAC was wound up. The club's creditors were outraged that Papi's liquidation had favoured Bates and appeared to discriminate against themselves. Papi did not recall Bates showing undue concern for their plight.

In late 1993, the creditors, bewildered by Bates's dealings, appealed to the FA to investigate Chelsea's unorthodox finances. The FA retained Christopher Morris of Touche Ross to examine the transactions. To his surprise, Morris received specific help from the Inland Revenue and Customs and Excise but, during the first months of 1994, he grew frustrated by the lack of cooperation and the absence of any documents. The official receiver was also perplexed. On 16 May 1994, the receiver also retained Christopher Morris to undertake a formal investigation. For the third time, an insolvency linked with Bates was under official scrutiny. Immediately, Morris dispatched Paul Mather to the Chelsea stadium to search for documents. 'They're all in that container,' shouted Bates, cheerfully pointing at the metal box. 'Help yourself.' Bates felt no fear. Six weeks later, in an application to the High Court, he won an order to halt Touche Ross's investigation. The court judged that John Papi's scheme had been legitimate but secured from Bates a guarantee that all the creditors would be paid. Christopher Morris hailed that assurance and the subsequent payments as his victory.

After defeating the Inland Revenue and Touche Ross, Bates faced one last hurdle. Mark Day, the FA's finance director, 'had a feeling that things were not quite as they should be' and probed Bates's takeover of Chelsea. Bates's response, disputing Day's authority, was brutal. Handicapped by minimal powers, Day was outwitted, not least because Bates, as a member of the FA's executive committee, had the right of access to his own files. Bates Day discovered had no hesitation in exploiting that to his own advantage. Day received no support from Graham Kelly or his other colleagues; his superiors pleaded impotence towards the controversial owner of a football club.

Bates was victorious and again won the gratitude of the fans. John Papi, the anti-hero of the operation, was less fortunate. Outraged by the insolvency expert's behaviour, Christopher Morris complained to the DTI and the Insolvency Practitioners' Association about Papi's 'gross professional misconduct'. In 1994, Papi's licence was withdrawn and four years later he was jailed for cheating the Inland Revenue. Papi had hoped that his payment for saving Chelsea from extinction would be 'Mandalay', Bates's house with 40 acres near Beaconsfield. Bates disputed their agreement and refused to meet again. 'You are unreliable and a fantasist,' Bates told Papi, whom he blamed for failing to maintain an efficient operation.

Now in his sixties, Bates had achieved a dream: fame. Unencumbered by other directors, shareholders and claimants, he could cast his eyes over the assembled hordes at Stamford Bridge on match days and sense the thrill of the emperors at the Colosseum in Rome. The roar of the crowd, the emotion and the sense of control fed his egoism. 'I'm doing what all the bloody moaners would like to do – I'm the chairman. A supporter's dream is to own a football club. Chelsea is the ultimate.' Unlike so many, his bid for stardom could be satisfied. 'The Romans,' he liked to say, 'didn't build a great empire by organizing meetings. They did it by killing anyone that got in their way.'

Bates's brash behaviour, until then familiar to a few, became his trademark; journalists were invited to his office to observe his bombastic telephone calls. His aggression was judged by many to be caused by insecurity, the fear that he might lose the club. Bates's private life reflected that turmoil; his marriage to Theresa, with five children, had collapsed after she discovered his affair with Pam, a model. He moved to Chelsea Wharf and began a relationship with a journalist. His personal life reflected his desperate haste. Conscious of his age and yearning to be crowned by public acclaim before he died, he launched what he called 'a dash for growth', hampered only by his limited wealth. His timing was fortunate; football had entered a glorious decade. The contracts with the television corporations were transforming football into a billion-pound business. Bates, like many other club chairmen, managers, players and agents, had good reason to be excited. By 1997 his investment had pushed his team to rank among the Big Five, a stunning achievement. Bates's exuberance and success, however, alarmed football's traditional fans, especially among the supporters of New Labour.

5

THE PASSING PURIST: ALASTAIR CAMPBELL

Alastair Campbell, the new prime minister's official spokesman, appeared agitated. The mood in the Cabinet room on 23 July 1997, nearly three months after New Labour's election victory, was unharmonious. Football was the topic, Campbell's passion. In opposition, New Labour had, partly under his guidance, proposed radical new policies. Influenced by the accusation of corruption against Bruce Grobbelaar, the goalkeeper, the Labour party was committed to imposing an independent regulator on football. The policy was supported by Tony Banks, the unexpected appointee as the sports minister who, like Campbell, also appeared to be irritated at that meeting. Across the table, Tony Blair was noticeably bewildered.

Banks, a vocal south Londoner, was complaining about a telephone call from a civil servant in Downing Street. In an imperious tone the official had rejected Banks's suggestion that David Mellor, the former Conservative minister, should be appointed as the chairman of the new Football Task Force. Banks, a reformed far left politician, disliked these Whitehall messengers. Initially, he believed that Alastair Campbell had opposed Mellor's appointment but he had been mistaken; although Campbell was ambivalent about whether the humiliated Tory was an ideal choice to implement his own idea of the Football Task Force. 'Don't people really hate David Mellor?' Blair asked James Purnell, the young special adviser, a protégé of John Birt at the BBC, and another football fan. 'He's the sort of person people like to hate,' agreed Purnell, who favoured the populist Tory rather than a tribal Labour appointee. Decisively, Purnell was supported by Angus Lapsely, the only civil servant in the room. 'Then Mellor's OK for me,' declared Blair. Campbell shrugged in agreement. At least the discredited Tory would be grateful for his reacceptance within the political establishment. Alastair Campbell would allow Mellor to believe that the appointment was his idea. The apparent favour would induce Mellor's gratitude.

Pertinently, Mellor shared the anger of all those in the Cabinet room that football, like politics, was mired in sleaze. Headline stories about match-fixing, agent's bungs, profiteering and dishonest managers were, he believed, just the tip of the iceberg. Mellor also agreed with his Labour opponents that their beloved game faced a greater danger. Money was replacing sentiment as the reason to own a football club. The Task Force was football's last chance of salvation.

The rules to protect and keep football clubs as a focus of local communities had been eroded. To safeguard football from financial predators, the FA had restricted clubs until 1981 from paying shareholders more than a 5 per cent dividend of the nominal value of the shares. That rule was deliberately undermined by clubs altering their legal ownership. Rule 34 of the FA's regulations forbidding directors to profit personally from the sale of club assets had been abandoned. Clubs could be sold to the highest bidder. Astute chairmen had, after secretly accumulating shares bought a generation earlier by loyal fans and retained by ignorant widows, floated their clubs for enormous profits. The Edwards family had spent between £31,000 and £41,000 to purchase 54 per cent of Manchester United's shares, and approximately £500,000 for a further 20 per cent. After the flotation in 1991, the club was valued at £429 million. Martin Edwards earned £33 million on the shares he sold and he still retained a 15 per cent stake. Sir John Hall, the chairman of Newcastle United, invested about £2 million for a 48 per cent stake, which was valued on flotation at £102 million. Peter Johnson, a Merseyside businessman, paid £20 million for a 66 per cent stake in Everton, which was worth £70 million. Doug Ellis bought 47 per cent of Aston Villa for £425,000 which, on flotation, was worth £42 million. The growing outcry by football's purists towards the windfalls – 'Football is a working man's game,' they protested – was aggravated by the revelation in 1996 that Sky's annual profits from 6 million subscribers had reached £374 million.

Convinced that they would receive further hundreds of millions of pounds when the next contract was negotiated in 1997, the club chairmen spoke of an opportunity for permanent change. Sentiment about the past was dismissed as an irritant. That brashness was provocative. The critics, especially articulate, educated, left-wing fans speaking on behalf of football's traditional roots in the community, complained that the new money-oriented owners were ignoring the emotional investment by poor fans in their local clubs. The slaughter of spectators at Hillsborough and Bradford had inflamed their anger against the Football Association and the clubs' chairmen. Eight reports on safety, the critics complained, had been ignored by the game's complacent owners. In the traditionalists' opinion, no one at the FA or in Westminster appeared to be concerned by football's mediocre leadership and flawed governance. Their fears were echoed by Lord Taylor in his landmark report in 1990 following the ninety-six deaths at Hillsborough: 'The picture revealed is of a general malaise or blight over the game due to a number of factors. Principally these are: old grounds, poor facilities, hooliganism, excessive drinking and poor leadership.' Lord Taylor blamed the same chairmen for eagerly maximizing their profits. 'It is legitimate to wonder,' he speculated, 'whether the directors are genuinely interested in the welfare of their grass roots supporters. Boardroom struggles for power, wheeler-dealing in the buying and selling of shares and indeed whole clubs sometimes suggest that those involved are more interested in the personal financial benefits or social status of being a director than of directing the club in the interests of its supporter customers.'

Taylor's criticisms had stimulated major reforms. The financial investment in new stadiums was applauded, but the projected prices of tickets were condemned as evidence of the chairmen's selfish promotion of football as show business. The debate between the chairmen and supporters was no longer confined to hooliganism but encompassed the soul of football.

David Mellor supported Alastair Campbell's ambition to redress the balance between the money-men and the fans, and impose an independent regulator on the game's managers. Only Campbell, a supporter of Burnley, and Purnell, an Arsenal fan, understood an exquisite irony. Both Tony Banks and Mellor were passionate Chelsea supporters and personal friends of Ken Bates, a chairman accused of several of the sins to be investigated. Neither was embarrassed by their friend, who opposed any regulation to cure the sport's diseases.

To ensure that the Task Force's birth was properly promoted Campbell planned to announce its creation in a briefing to a chosen *Mirror* journalist. He would also mention that Alex Ferguson, the manager of Manchester United and a godfather of football, had agreed to join the crusade to reform the sport. 'He can make things happen,' Alastair Campbell acknowledged about a hero noted for his ferocious temper, ambition and enmities. Alex Ferguson's prompt refusal to participate was not the only disappointment. The Task Force's budget was just £100,000, derisively insufficient to research and produce authoritative plans to compel the clubs to combat racism, improve access for the disabled, negotiate lower ticket prices and impose greater supporter involvement. Those complications were hidden from the public when Tony Banks and David Mellor posed on the pitch of The Valley (Charlton Athletic's home in south London) to publicize the new Task Force and their determination to clean up the game. Charlton was symbolic of football's crisis. During the 1980s the club had been declared bankrupt and was compelled to abandon its ground. Under the guidance of Richard Murray, its sober chairman, the club had been rebuilt with a supporters' representative on the board and, with new finance, had rebuilt its stadium to celebrate promotion to the Premier League.

That morning, David Mellor was openly emotional about the declining morality of the sport. In the 1960s, he fondly recalled, the players travelled to matches with the fans on Corporation buses. Now, they swept gracelessly into the grounds driving the latest Ferrari. The symbolism of uncontrolled fortunes contaminated the game. 'I feel frustrated that there's no desire to clean up football,' he emphasized in his unequivocal manner. 'The FA and the Premier League are in a position to do something and have the responsibility. But they're just too pleased with themselves. Unjustifiably pleased.'

The raw statistics confirmed to the architects of the Task Force a business unable to control its costs or its behaviour. Sky had agreed in 1997 to pay the Premier League £743 million for a four year agreement, a spectacular amount which would inevitably transform English football. In the previous year, wages had increased by 30 per cent – the average annual wage of a Premier League player was £550,000 – and the tabloid newspapers were reporting the familiar aggression, drunkenness and extraordinary excesses of stars only recently emerged from adolescence. To the loyalists, the Task Force was the last chance to save football from self-destruction.

'Everything depends on Number 10,' Banks told Mellor; adding rhetorically, 'But have they got the courage? Taking on football is a big deal.' In the years before the general election, Alastair Campbell and Labour politicians had discussed a Task Force to reverse the deliberate alienation of sport's traditional supporters by clubs maximizing their profits on tickets and merchandise. Both the FA and Premier League executives were criticized for ignoring democracy and compelling the alienated fans 'to pay through the nose'. Controlling the greed of managers, agents and players would be a crusade. 'Has Downing Street got the stomach to make it a priority?' wondered Banks. 'I'm not sure.'

Mellor cast aside those doubts after Alastair Campbell telephoned from his summer holiday. 'The fans want ownership of the game. . . . We're right behind the fans' complaints about how the game is run,' said Campbell, emphasizing his personal interest in the Task Force's success. Nothing, it seemed, was too radical for Campbell; personally and politically he saw the potential to slay dragons. New Labour would win the support of hundreds of thousands of football fans. The publicity would be invaluable. His object was not to resuscitate old sentiments but to challenge the game's ownership, most significantly, by an independent regulator. Football would be brought under control.

Alastair Campbell's arrival at the first meeting of the Task Force in Mellor's home in St Katharine's Dock by the River Thames on 2 September 1997 reinforced that conviction, although the first fissure had appeared. Racism and access for the disabled were easy topics to examine, but Adam Brown, a left-wing academic critical of the commercialization of football, mentioned the fans' desire for the return of terraces. 'That isn't part of the government's thinking,' said Campbell, sensitive to the political obstacles. There was no time for Mellor to close the gap. 'I've got to go,' Campbell announced. 'I've got a funeral to organize.' Princess Diana had just died.

Campbell left behind a group united in changing the status quo but divided about the cure. Could the 'core sporting character' of football club companies be protected, asked Mellor, or was football 'a speculative entertainment business run for financial gain'? David Dein, Ken Bates and the other Premier League chairmen were determined to reinforce the power of the richest clubs. Adam Brown and his supporters wanted the opposite.

Some in Mellor's camp were doubtful. His outspoken opinions on Radio 5 and in his newspaper column aroused some loathing. 'A problematic grandee,' concluded Adam Brown. After that evening, some inside

Downing Street were also puzzled. Mellor was entertaining those people he assumed to be the powerbrokers for breakfast at the Ritz. To his new friends, he appeared desperate to be liked and was possibly even hoping for a peerage. In Mellor's own opinion, he was seeking to negotiate unanimity among the rival interests. He was hampered by his reluctant reliance on Tom Pendry, a disgruntled Labour MP.

Tom Pendry was a 63-year-old former trade union official and had been an MP since 1970. His passion was sport, first as a champion boxer and then as a football supporter. His friends called him 'vain but lovable' and applauded his appointment in 1992 as Labour's shadow sports minister. 'You deserve it,' said John Smith, the party leader. Two years later, Tony Blair reconfirmed Pendry's appointment. Pendry believed that Labour's new leader owed him some gratitude. In 1982 Pendry had arranged Blair's candidacy in an important by-election in Beaconsfield. But their relationship became tarnished after Blair's election as party leader. Blair's first speech on sport had been written by Alastair Campbell without consulting Pendry, and the older politician had lambasted the newcomer from Fleet Street. Thereafter, Campbell was cool towards Pendry as he fashioned New Labour's policy towards football. The legacy of that argument threatened the Task Force with fatal consequences.

Tony Blair and Alastair Campbell agreed that their constituents were angry about the state of the sport. Fans had been encouraged to buy shares in their clubs at high prices from the chairmen, who had obtained the same shares for a pittance. After the flotations most of the share prices had fallen, hurting the fans, while the chairmen remained rich. The cake had grown but, due to the greed of the Premier League clubs, a declining number of clubs were enjoying the benefits. In their animated conversations with Gordon Brown, another football fan, Blair and Alastair Campbell criticized the 'obscene' wealth at the top and the penury at bottom. 'We've got to stop the fans getting ripped off,' was Alastair Campbell's message. 'They're getting a raw deal and the game is suffering.'

That sentiment had motivated Alastair Campbell to write an article appearing under Blair's name in the *Mail on Sunday* on 15 January 1995. The peg was the record transfer of Andy Cole, reported to be for £7 million, from Newcastle United to Manchester United, although the transfer price was registered as £6 million. The article's headline was 'How our soccer idols are betraying Britain'. Written from the heart, it was Campbell's purest expression of fear: 'I feel unease about what is happening in British sport . . . [not least] the get-rich-quick, something-for-nothing philosophy.' The article was a declaration of war against those who 'neglect sport at the grass roots, . . . because they are . . . obsessed with the commercial gains'. Targeted at 'some of the people at the top of our national game who think nothing of loyalty to club and community', the article was New Labour's warning that football was destined for 'sporting and social decline'.

'I was at first shocked, then puzzled,' wrote Campbell/Blair about Andy Cole's transfer. 'Shocked that he was going. Puzzled that, good though he is, lottery type money could be spent on a single player . . . But as a reflection of our society's priorities, Andy's transfer fee was as devastating as any hat-trick he scored.' Campbell/Blair complained about 'the sport's growing obsession with money-making . . . Loyalty doesn't seem to be enough anymore; rather it is exploited to make us pay more.' The article mentioned that after the transfer of Stanley Matthews from Blackpool to Stoke in the 'golden era' of 1961 for £2,500, the attendance had increased by 25,000. 'Could Andy Cole put 25,000 on a crowd?' Campbell/Blair asked rhetorically. Football has, they continued, 'a unique place in our culture and one that we must treasure. And yet I worry that the game . . . may lose touch with its roots . . . Fans are taken for granted, TV deals are ignoring the smaller clubs which desperately need support . . . and I worry that some of the allegations of illegal backhanders may be true.' In their morality sermon, Campbell/Blair condemned players who lacked shame, swore too easily, cheated, fouled and abused referees and who only thought about winning for 'the money it will bring'. The article was the foundation of the critics' manifesto for reform.

One week later, Alastair Campbell arranged for Tony Blair to be interviewed about the same theme: football was in danger of succumbing to commercial imperatives and was becoming distanced from the people. 'I do share the concern that the kind of money now involved in transfers could alienate those who follow it . . . I sometimes worry that the game is too much driven by money and not enough by the sporting spirit.' Critically, Blair supported 'safe standing' on terraces, an important demand by football's traditionalists. However, he added, while a government provided a framework for success, 'it is not the job of government to interfere in the daily running of football'. The solution was for football to listen to the fans' representatives.

Graham Kelly at the FA was unimpressed, especially by Blair's mischievously implausible assertion that, aged eight, he had visited Roker Park to watch Jackie Milburn, Newcastle United's legend, play in a match. Milburn had stopped playing for Newcastle when Blair was four years old. Kelly, like other football executives, was similarly underwhelmed by Blair's second newspaper article bemoaning the state of football, published on the day he would attend Stanley Matthews's eightieth birthday party. A succession of newspaper photographs reinforced his scepticism. Gordon Brown was photographed with Geoffrey Robinson, the local MP and millionaire, at Coventry City; Tony Blair was filmed playing 'keepy-uppy' with Kevin Keegan; and Alastair Campbell was recorded in the royal box at Wembley stadium with Tony Blair and their children close by. The image conjured by Campbell was of New Labour embracing football as part of family and national life. Kelly hated politicians using football for self-promotion.

One year later, in 1996, a committee including council-lors and representatives of professional football was assembled in the House of Lords to formulate the Labour party's manifesto commitments on football. Among its members were Tom Pendry, Jack Cunningham, the ambi-tious north-eastern MP, and Richard Faulkner, the vice-chairman of the Football Trust, an organization dis-tributing money provided by the football pools companies to improve the sport. 'There's a revolution in our game,' said Richard Faulkner, 'and that's an opportunity for change. The question is whether the change will be good or bad. If the share prices fall further, the fans will feel duped.' Most of those present would proudly claim fatherhood of the Football Task Force. They were united by their commitment to a Labour victory but divided by their personal ambitions and forceful personalities.

Tom Pendry, the shadow minister, drafted the mani-festo section promoting New Labour as the natural party for sport. 'We must strive to put Britain back on the sporting map,' promised Tony Blair, criticizing the Conservatives' '"laissez-faire" approach characterized by complacency and neglect'. Even football, complained Blair, was besmirched by Tory sleaze. New Labour's 'Charter for Football', Blair pledged, would allow the voice of ordinary supporters to be heard in the clubs. Market forces would not be allowed exclusive control of football's fate. 'Ideally,' Blair argued, 'football should regulate itself', but if the sport's owners and administrators ignored the warnings, a Labour government would impose an independent regulator.

Four days after Labour's election landslide on 1 May 1997, Tom Pendry was watching a football match at Millwall's ground, impatiently waiting for the telephone call from Downing Street. Like everyone, he assumed his automatic appointment as sports minister.

Inside the Cabinet room, Blair was consulting his trusted advisers. Alastair Campbell sat at his side. Sally Morgan, the prime minister's political secretary, disliked Pendry. The Old Labourite, she sensed, was a flirt and unpalatable for feminists because of his friendship with Aimi MacDonald, the actress. Alastair Campbell agreed, murmuring that the politician had 'an uncomfortable background', which some interpreted as criticism of his record as a businessman. No one spoke in Pendry's favour except Blair, and he preferred not to fight.

At Millwall's ground, Graham Kelly noticed Pendry was 'mortified' when the telephone did not ring. The telephone call from Blair on Monday morning was short. 'Tom, I'm sorry. I'm not going to give you the job.' 'Why?' asked Pendry. 'Because it's time to move on.' 'You can only move on if the right man is in the job,' Pendry shot back. Blair muttered something incomprehensible and the line was dead.

Tom Pendry was pole-axed. The news that Tony Banks had been appointed as sports minister paralysed the disappointed aspirant. Banks had been notorious as a representative of the loony left on the Greater London Council; he was a vociferous critic of capitalism and journalists; and he lacked the self-discipline required to manage a government department. Pendry blamed himself for allowing Banks to accompany Blair and Alastair Campbell to the Chelsea v. Newcastle match on the eve of the election. Tony Banks, an eyewitness related, was 'on such good behaviour. Charming. No swearing or drinking.' Alastair Campbell, Pendry believed, had delivered his revenge. The rejected politician's bitterness remained unabated for months. An unpredicted consequence was the destruction of Labour's commitment to neutralize the power of money in football, challenge corruption in the sport and, critically, to abide by its pledge to impose an independent regulator.

Bruce Grobbelaar's uncelebrated second acquittal in August 1997 brought football into the spotlight again and showed the need to find a solution to football's problems. The following month, Graham Kelly, under pressure from the new government, announced an inquiry 'into the manner in which football regulates its financial affairs' and to recommend how football could maintain its integrity and accountability.

Graham Kelly's choice as investigator was Sir John Smith, the 59-year-old former deputy commissioner of Scotland Yard. Smith assumed the FA was intent on discovering the truth about match-fixing, players betting on the outcome of their own matches and the finances of football. The reality, as the affable public servant soon discovered, was different. 'I think that I should look at the FA's ability to police the game,' Smith told David

Dein during an interview. 'That's not in your terms of reference,' replied Dein. To conceal the FA's impotence, Kelly preferred Sir John Smith to work within narrow terms of reference. 'You're unsure if I should go ahead,' Smith challenged Kelly. 'That's not true,' replied Kelly unconvincingly. 'The FA is a bad regulator,' Smith snapped. 'You don't want anyone to rock the boat.'

Sir John's misgivings extended to the Task Force, which he joined soon after his appointment. Fifteen organizations were represented. Mired in personal rivalries, its composition had proved to be unwieldy and ill conceived. David Mellor proposed to create a smaller working group to complete their reports swiftly. John Smith, sharing Mellor's concern to root out corruption, joined the working group just as a decision in Downing Street inadvertently threatened the Task Force's credibility.

Tony Blair felt guilty about disappointing Tom Pendry. To compensate the party stalwart, he agreed in October 1997, with the recommendation of James Purnell, his special adviser, that Pendry would be an ideal chairman of the Football Trust, administering £40 million provided by the football pools companies. Through the Trust he would also supervise the Task Force. The appointment would be announced in March 1998. Pendry's gratitude was eclipsed by the fury of Richard Faulkner, the Trust's vice-chairman, who had expected promotion to the chairmanship. 'A political fix,' seethed Faulkner, an agile lobbyist representing Littlewoods, the biggest pools company financing the Football Trust. 'Nothing to do with me,' replied Tony Banks. 'It's Number 10.'

Tom Pendry, in retaliation against Banks, whom he despised, and Mellor, whom he loathed, was reconsidering his allegiance to the fans, football's owners and the regulators. From his offices in Westminster and Euston, Pendry began sniping at the Task Force while Faulkner retaliated by agitating against the FA and the Football Trust. In the middle was Banks, not renowned for his diplomacy; he was principled on some issues but uncommitted to the enforcement of regulations. 'In the end,' he explained, 'football is entertainment. Theatre. Keep it in its context. Football doesn't amount to a great deal. All that matters in football is that your team is playing well – whether money is sticking to a manager's hands doesn't matter. In football, the element of the dodgy is always present. Football has honest crooks. Good people do compensate for the bad they get up to. I'm not stupid. All sorts of dodgy stuff goes on but more good has come out of it.'

Proudly, Banks paraded himself as a non-Blairite, unwilling to climb the greasy pole. 'They wanted profile and I gave them profile plus,' he said. 'I love sport, but it's a hobby, not life or death.' The following year, he would reject a seat in the VIP box at the Cup Final explaining, 'I do not want my enjoyment spoilt by sitting next to royalty.' The vanity and conflicts of New Labour's personalities were turning the government's policy towards football's finances and politics upside down.

The effect of Banks's nonchalance was similar to the indifference towards sport of Chris Smith, the minister of culture and sport. Smith did not believe that the nation owed a living to football but he was keen to cater to Downing Street's notion that New Labour was the party of fun, caring about the people's everyday concerns. Listening carefully to James Purnell, the special adviser speaking from Downing Street, Smith understood the political importance of football, despite one unkind critic's quip, 'What Smith knows about sport can be written on the back of an opera ticket.' Smith also lamented his perceived misfortune to be served by inadequate civil servants. Intellectually challenged, they were unknowledgeable about sport and 'hostile' to the agenda of the Task Force. Led by Robin Young, a socialite criticized for his department's slipshod management of the Dome, the redevelopment of Covent Garden, the bids for the Lottery and the management of Britain's museums, the subordinate officials were equally uninspiring. Colin Jones, Neil McKenzie and later Philippa Drew, Chris Smith complained, gave poor advice. Since neither Smith nor Banks had any confidence in their officials, Smith remained unguided while Banks appeared to be undisciplined, reluctant to read official papers or diligently attend meetings.

As Mellor marshalled his Task Force committee to research and quickly write the uncontroversial reports stressing the need to remove racism and accommodate the disabled, the urgency to produce the third report about 'investing in the community' and the final report about regulating football became pressing. Both topics were contentious although even the Conservative veteran of Westminster's intrigues did not anticipate the eruption of bitter enmity among football's vested interests.

The commercialization of football had politically polarized its supporters. Adam Brown, the senior research fellow at Manchester Metropolitan University, was typical of the educated Labour supporters who expected the new government's promises for the fans to be implemented. Before 1997, Brown had become aggrieved by the FA's failure to fulfil its promises to supporters. Ticket prices had increased by 16 per cent in 1997, four times the rate of inflation, and in some clubs by 400 per cent over the previous five years. Brown was also agitated by the continuing ban on terraces. All-seater stadiums had become, in his opinion, a ruse by the Premier League to increase their profits to the detriment of the traditional supporters. The fans at matches were now dispersed, ruining the chance of watching with friends, excluding casual supporters and causing the new danger of fans standing in seating areas. (The latest German designs guaranteed safety on the terraces.) Tony Banks's abject refusal even to listen to the arguments for safe terraces – 'That's not on the agenda,' he snapped – irritated Brown, who had embraced the Task Force as a political mission. His commitment alarmed the representatives of the FA, the Premier League and the club owners. In their opinion, Brown and his kind were interfering in their private business. 'The Task Force is flawed,' concluded David Davies, the FA's director of publicity, but his opinion was not voiced in public. Since the new government had a landslide majority an appearance of enthusiastic cooperation was required.

David Davies had been delegated to deal with the politicians by Graham Kelly. Davies had become close to Tom Pendry, Anji Hunter, the prime minister's assistant, and Alastair Campbell while working as a journalist at Westminster for the BBC. He joined the FA in 1994 and was pleased to be 'the point man' between football and the political parties. Davies wanted to prove that politics and football could mix. The lubrication of those relationships was helped by providing tickets to the best national and international matches. On those occasions Davies undertook to explain the new government's attitude to the FA's members. Football, he reminded the clubs' chairmen, received a lot of money from the government. Public money was financing the construction of a new stadium at Wembley, the new stadiums for clubs, and one-third of the cost of the bid to host the World Cup in 2006 was financed by Whitehall. Presenting himself as the man leading the FA towards reform, Davies warned the chairmen that the government would intervene if football did not properly regulate itself. The next test of the FA's commitment to veracity and proper regulation was the publication on 13 January 1998 of Sir John Smith's report, 'Football, Its Values, Finances and Reputation'. In summary, the former police chief urged the FA to 'put its house in order' but, to the satisfaction of his targets, he failed to provide a convincing indictment of his paymasters.

Sir John Smith's attempt to 'highlight malpractice' had become handicapped by the lack of evidence. He had accepted the task without the power to demand documents or compel witnesses to testify, and the FA had refused to provide an assistant or adequate finance. He assumed that because football, unlike gambling and racing, presented itself as part of the community rather than a business, he would receive the cooperation of witnesses willing to be named in his published report. That cooperation had not materialized. 'The witnesses are guarded,' he admitted, and he had been denied access to files. The result was an admitted lack of 'hard information' proving corruption. Nevertheless, his general impression was that 'things were not right'. Those he suspected, and those who refused to cooperate, would fail any 'fit and proper person test'. Former bankrupts and ex-criminals had influence in the management of the game – or worse, were owners of clubs in the lower leagues – and the FA appeared to be unwilling to investigate their financial affairs. Sir John Smith's solution was radical. He proposed a 'compliance and monitoring unit' to 'oversee the game's integrity and reputation'; he advised the FA to appoint an 'Ombudsfan' to investigate complaints by the fans with powers to demand evidence and to impose sanctions; and, to satisfy the activists, he recommended the nomination of an independent regulator. Since those recommendations precisely matched the government's policy, Smith was optimistic that the FA would adopt his ideas.

In public, Sir John Smith's report was welcomed by the FA. David Davies spoke about his 'optimism that Smith will be implemented', noting Smith's demand for an independent regulator. He solemnly reasserted the FA's determination to root out corruption in the game. Within the FA's headquarters, however, the report drew mirth. 'I can't remember Smith's report,' said Graham Kelly two years later. 'His report followed my compliance report into the wastepaper basket.' Keith Wiseman, as chairman of the FA's executive committee, understood how to satisfy the major clubs' requirement 'not to rock the boat'. Consistent with his former veto on compliance on behalf of the Premier League, Wiseman also rejected Smith's recommendations. The message from football's managers was similarly unambiguous. Sir John Smith's conclusion that footballers bet against their own team and that some West Ham players were guilty prompted Harry Redknapp, West Ham's coach and a famous gambler, to rage, 'What a load of cobblers . . . A joke.'

David Mellor and others of the Football Task Force were indignant about the ridicule and were wary about the lack of comment from Downing Street. Alastair Campbell, some feared, had lost his interest in reforming football's management. Mellor could no longer conceal his irritation about football's uncontrolled greed. The clubs' directors, Mellor cursed, deliberately uttered confusing messages in public. Sentimentally, they spoke of old values to protect football's traditions but behaved as modern business tycoons promoting superstars. On either count they were reckless consumers of money. 'We need some heavyweight political backing for significant change in the game,' Mellor argued, adopting the activists' language. 'Football needs to be reminded of its civic duties as our national game. It doesn't exist in its own little vacuum; it has relied heavily on the public purse.' The response to his blast was unsatisfactory: the FA uttered insincere platitudes, but the Premier League, fearing interference, openly voiced disenchantment with Mellor and others attached to the Task Force.

Peter Leaver, the Premier League's chief executive, understood football from his association with Tottenham. The combative lawyer, representing twenty chairmen, had been restrained during the first months of 1998 despite being irked by David Mellor's apparent lack of preparation before meetings of the Task Force and his habit of mouthing 'populist rubbish'. Recognizing the political direction coming from Downing Street, Leaver modified his irritation in public. Agreed reports by the Task Force about preventing racism and promoting access for the disabled were unobjectionable and published by May 1998 without complaint. Leaver's acquiescence vanished as Mellor commissioned the next reports about the community's control over the sport and the appointment of an independent regulator. Encouraged aggressively by Mike Lee, a consultant employed by the League, Leaver opposed any proposal which could hinder the Premier League's interests and denied the organization was a 'rip-off'. Those who blamed Peter Leaver for 'disruptiveness' failed to understand the influence of Mike Lee.

There was an irony to Mike Lee's robust championing of the capitalists in the Premier League. In his twenties Lee had been left wing, agitating for Marxism. Later, he joined the Labour party and was employed by Westminster Strategy, a public relations consultancy which also employed Jo Moore, who subsequently became infamous as Stephen Byers's publicist, advising civil servants to 'bury bad news' on 11 September, after the attack on New York's World Trade Center. Lee offered political insight to the apolitical football executives who did not appreciate the 'new environment'. Hearing the opinions and prejudices of those in the FA, Premier League and Football League, Lee believed that the reformers were proposing 'unrealistic and unworkable ideas' to interfere with independent businesses. In Lee's recollection, he was 'creative and honest', trying to balance his personal preference for modernizing football against the resistance of the club chairmen. Others remember a different attitude. In the Premier League, Peter Leaver recalls Lee urging resistance to any notion of the community asserting control over football. Lee even opposed Adam Brown conducting any research; the results, Lee explained, would only support Brown's prejudices. Football's supporters and their representatives, Lee told Denis Campbell of the *Observer* with unconcealed antagonism, were 'professional malcontents' and the Premier League would defy its critics. Lee's recollection of the dispute is different. Regardless of conflicting memories, the battle lines were drawn between the Premier League clubs and the reformers.

'They're out to block everything,' Graham Bean, at that time the representative of the Football Supporters Association, told Adam Brown. 'Lee's just arrogant,' agreed Brown. Unexpectedly, Tom Pendry had switched

allegiances and announced that the Football Trust would
not provide secretarial facilities for the Task Force. Mellor
'regretted' that Pendry had allowed himself to be used.
Others cursed the man who had 'curried favour by handing out Cup Final tickets'. The counter-attack was
similarly robust. Labour supporters channelled their
spleen about Mellor to Downing Street, complaining of
'shifting allegiances'.

James Purnell, the adviser to Tony Blair about football, was puzzled. 'What does Mellor want?' Purnell
asked his friends. Originally, Mellor had been courting
everyone but recently, fearful of the fans' criticism that he
was in the pocket of the Premier League, Purnell sensed
that Mellor was no longer pro-government. He was
beginning to make the process 'difficult'.

Among Mellor's targets was Gordon Taylor, the chief
executive of the Professional Footballers Association, a
trade unionist representing, in Mellor's opinion, 3,500
men able to kick but not think. Taylor's lifestyle, funded
by a salary in excess of £400,000, was, Mellor complained,
'outrageous'. The story that Taylor had flown in a private
jet on holiday and had spent £2 million on behalf of the
Association for a Lowry painting – a painting which Lord
Harris, the Tory peer, 'laughingly rejected at £800,000' –
aroused Mellor's spleen: 'Taylor thinks he's God because
he's got so much money sloshing about.'

The pretext for Mellor's row in May 1998 with
Taylor was the Task Force's third report about football
and the community. For Alastair Campbell and the
Labour government, re-engaging football with the community had been paramount. The chasm between the
highly paid football players and their poor fans needed to
be repaired to re-establish football clubs as the working
man's sport, a cornerstone of their communities. Mellor

began agitating against the FA for pledging to 'take account of community feeling' but doing nothing; and against the footballers for not devoting sufficient time to meeting their impoverished hero-worshippers, despite solemn promises. The players, Mellor wrote in the London *Evening Standard* on 12 June 1998, were idle, irresponsible and overpaid. Although contractually obliged to carry out three hours of community work each week, they were shirking their obligations. In reply, Gordon Taylor quoted statistics to prove the contrary. Those statistics were damned by Mellor as 'decidedly dodgy evidence' concealing the stark truth that there were just '0.20 visits per player per year'. Taylor had misrepresented the number of players involved in community work, alleged Mellor. Taylor responded by demanding Mellor's resignation as chairman of the Task Force. 'He's pompous,' sniped Mellor.

The public spat exploded the semblance of unity in the Task Force. Mellor became the focus for football's disdain of interference. Taylor and others wrote to Tony Blair demanding the politician's dismissal, arguing that he had used the position as 'an extension of his populist rabble-rousing media career'. His removal, Taylor added, would be 'warmly endorsed at all levels of a game which has become heartily sick of his vacuous posturing'. Mellor's many enemies joined the chorus. At stake was the ultimate prize: the appointment of an independent regulator. Leading the attack against the reformers was Mike Lee, goading Peter Leaver to be combative, and receiving support from Tom Pendry. Resentful towards Tony Banks and angered by the minister's friendship with Mellor, Pendry announced that the Football Trust would no longer support the Task Force. The protagonists were inflamed.

Early on the morning of 21 July 1998, Leaver struck. Just before a Task Force meeting in Euston, Leaver searched out Mellor in the chairman's office and asked him to resign. 'Your journalism,' Lever complained, 'proves your bias.' Angered, Mellor's response was robust: 'I was never appointed to be independent, but because of my experience and sympathy with football's grass roots.' The conflict between the men shocked Richard Faulkner: 'Leaver's general attitude seems to me to be destructive.' Adam Brown agreed: 'He's plain rude.' Leaver returned the criticism: 'The best advice I received from Lee was to stand up against Faulkner. He's the ultimate nose-in-the-trough man, milking his position and pushing a populist line to get a peerage.' Eventually, Leaver would regret becoming so publicly exposed, but that was only after his own abrupt dismissal by the Premier League.

'Let's call Peter Leaver's bluff,' suggested Adam Brown on 22 July 1998. 'It's cards on the table time . . . We cannot proceed with endless wrecking tactics.' Professor Roland Smith, the chairman of Manchester United, agreed: 'Leaver is trying to sink the whole ship.' The battle was taken to Downing Street. Recalling the earlier enthusiasm, the government needed to be persuaded, urged Adam Brown, that there was 'significant political capital to be made out of tackling greed and social exclusion'. Tony Banks brokered a peace. That Tuesday evening, the minister persuaded Leaver to withdraw his objections to the Task Force and to help redraft the third report, 'Investing in the Community', published on 23 July 1998. 'It all went very well,' sighed Mellor, content that all sides appeared to agree to the appointment of an independent regulator. To the reformers it appeared that a milestone had been passed in resolving the ultimate issue: how much money the Premier League would donate to the football community.

In late October 1998, Andy Burnham, the devoted administrator of the Football Task Force, was summoned to the Football Trust's headquarters in Euston to explain the final draft of 'Investing in the Community'. Graham Kelly, Peter Leaver, Nic Coward and David Sheepshanks were waiting for the 28-year-old New Labour activist and Everton supporter. Their mood was ugly. In the manner of a Star Chamber, they had agreed their tactics to ambush and destroy the young football enthusiast. Two hours later, eyewitnesses noticed Burnham emerge, crushed and tearful. The yob culture prevalent on the terraces had been carried into the committee room. 'It was a bad-tempered time and a sour atmosphere,' complained Burnham to an eyewitness. His modest challenge to the FA to expunge selfishness from the football establishment had been torn into shreds. He vowed revenge.

The argument was about money. Burnham's commitment was to 'change the world' of football. His draft, echoing a firmly socialistic sentiment, suggested a strategy to 'put the game in order' by controlling football's commercialization. 'English football,' Burnham had written, 'depends on the redistribution of income. It has been a feature of the game since it began.' Over the previous six years, the Football Trust had given £88.5 million to thirty-one major English clubs in the Premier League. In the same period, the Premier League had earned £1.1 billion (£1.05 billion from television) and, Burnham complained, invested none of that huge revenue back into the grass roots to support the poorer clubs or schoolboys deprived of facilities. The Premier League, he had recommended, should accept a 10 per cent levy on its income for the benefit of all the 43,000 clubs affiliated to the FA.

Reaching that recommendation had been fraught. Mike Lee, representing the Premier League, had aggressively questioned the levy. Lee fumed about everything, not least Burnham's piety: 'English football depends on the redistribution of income.' Lee damned those thoughts as 'socialistic', an irony considering his Marxist pedigree. Negotiating with Lee, Burnham discovered, was akin to trading with a second-hand car salesman. Agreements which were assumed to be 'finalized' were suddenly subject to renegotiation. The two men were barely speaking. In Mike Lee's opinion, 'the arguments were part of the process. I was being constructive if difficult, but I'm not combative.' James Purnell in Downing Street had sought to mediate an agreement but had failed. David Mellor had never underestimated the 'forces of football's establishment'. Stubborn self-interest would resist any change. 'Like you,' Mellor wrote to Adam Brown, the academic, 'I was dismayed by their reaction to the report and, as we approach the critical issue of regulation, football politics will intrude more and more.' The Premier League's lobbyists were seeking to undermine the government's policy.

Peter Leaver, David Sheepshanks and Graham Kelly protested to Chris Smith that the Task Force's new remit was unauthorized. Their damnation appeared to be conclusive. In a telephone call to Burnham by Colin Jones, a civil servant at the Department for Culture, Media and Sport (DCMS), Burnham was told, 'Your negative proposals are disgraceful.' The Task Force's draft, Jones warned, would not be submitted to the appropriate Downing Street committee. Only a bland report would be submitted. Rapidly, Jones was outmanoeuvred by Tony Banks, keeping the faith against the Premier League. To the distress of the Premier League's executives,

Burnham's report was cleared for publication with a recommendation that the 10 per cent levy, to be imposed on the League's income from television, should be distributed to football's grass roots. Reluctantly, the Premier League accepted the principle of a levy, without agreeing 10 per cent, but in return for a price.

In August 1998, the Office of Fair Trading (OFT) had launched an action in the High Court, accusing the Premier League of acting as a cartel against the public interest. Unexpectedly, nearly all of football's antagonistic groups united with the government to oppose the OFT. All feared that the destruction of the Premier League would prevent collective bargaining, would undermine the FA's authority, and would weaken the sport. David Mellor, after a 'pitched battle within the Task Force to get common ground', offered to testify in the Premier League's favour. In return, he expected the Premier League to agree to the 10 per cent levy on its income. A minority of the activist reformers criticized the unholy alliance for endorsing the Premier League and Sky as 'good for football' and, three weeks after the OFT launched its case, they believed their opposition was proven.

On 7 September 1998, Sky TV announced a £624 million takeover bid for Manchester United. Those committed to resisting the commercialization of football were incensed by Rupert Murdoch's threat. His bid threatened to subordinate the Premier League to Sky's interests, widening the gap with the rest of football. If successful, Sky would be sitting on both sides of the negotiating table, eroding fair competition and the FA's governance of the sport. The projected finances confirmed their suspicions; Murdoch expected to earn just £25 million a year on the investment. That uncommercial profit portrayed the bid as a strategic ploy to turn the Premier League into a subsidiary of his television station. Football's traditionalists feared that Tony Blair, who before the election had flown to Australia with Alastair Campbell to obtain Murdoch's endorsement, would abandon the Task Force's principles.

On 21 September 1998, to challenge the government Adam Brown suggested that the Task Force should issue a statement officially opposing the takeover. The divisions among the members became wider. 'You're trying to hijack the Task Force,' charged Mike Lee in a telephone call. 'Leaver's also been ranting on the phone,' Brown reported to Andy Burnham. The Premier League again lobbied Colin Jones at the DCMS. 'There'll be no statements,' Jones warned Brown.

In west London, on 11 January 1999, at the Wormwood Scrubs playing fields the festering disagreements manifested themselves. Ministers, politicians, football groups and members of the Task Force gathered as a publicity stunt to launch the 'Investing in the Community' report. The most notable absentee was Gordon Taylor of the Professional Footballers Association. Taylor knew that football players disliked community work and would support his snub to David Mellor, an implacable enemy. Graham Kelly was secretly pleased by Taylor's publicized defiance. 'I would have been antagonistic towards any view supported by Mellor,' said Kelly. Personalities threatened to overwhelm all the well-intentioned policies, while the existing regulators turned a blind eye to the sport's notorious suspects.

6

EL TEL: PART II

In November 1998, a fraud squad attached to Hampshire police announced a four-month investigation into Terry Venables's purchase of five Australian players during his management and ownership of Portsmouth Football Club between 1996 and 1997. The police had been summoned by Martin Gregory and Peter Hinkinson, the club's abandoned shareholders. The complainants were uncertain whether Venables had bought the five players to improve the club's performance or for another reason. Subsequently, Venables was completely exonerated.

Venables had arrived at Fratton Park in August 1996 after hastily resigning as England's coach to fight a libel case launched by Alan Sugar. Eddie Ashby, under investigation by the police for managing Tottenham while disqualified as a bankrupt, still continued as Venables's intimate adviser. 'At Portsmouth,' Ashby recalled, 'I was Terry's sweeper. All the people were coming to me and telling me his deals. Because Terry was away, I ran it from the inside.' From his office, Ashby watched his employer being driven away in a black Rolls Royce, registration number 1 VEN, by Soki, a glamorous Serbian woman. The appointment at Portsmouth was a honeymoon for Venables and Ashby.

Terry Venables had considered several offers after resigning as England's coach. Martin Gregory, the owner of Portsmouth, had been particularly energetic in his pursuit of Venables. The club was immersed in debt and in despair Gregory, whose inherited fortune originated from Blue Star garages, ranked among the many convinced about Venables's ability to perform miracles. To secure him, Gregory had even conceded that Venables could also continue to coach Australia's national team on the other side of the world, an appointment he had taken after resigning as England manager. He ignored the cynics' warnings that Venables would only remain until a better offer arrived.

Three thousand Portsmouth fans greeted El Tel as a messiah to rekindle Fratton Park's glory days and restore the spirit of a club heading towards oblivion. 'I could be here one year or ten years, who knows?' Venables announced in the stadium on 11 August 1996. 'It's a statement of intent. I'm fully committed to Portsmouth.' Venables was masterful in the art of conveying his sincerity and in promoting the propaganda of his unrivalled abilities. Standing alongside the Lord Mayor of Portsmouth, Venables promised the crowd to build a new stand, a new ground and a bright future. Any doubters were reassured by Venables's purchase in February 1997 of 51 per cent of the club for £1. 'Fucking amazing,' swooned Venables to Ashby about Gregory's acceptance of a pittance for the shares. 'As far as I'm concerned,' said Martin Gregory welcoming Venables's appointment as chairman, 'it's the best news I've had in a long time. We stand on the threshold of exciting times and with Terry at the helm I'm convinced that we can finally fulfil Pompey's potential.'

Despite the club's perilous finances, Venables began a spree of transfers which did not always appear to benefit Portsmouth. Relying on three trusted friends, Ted Buxton, his favourite scout, and the agents Eric 'Monster' Hall and Tommy Lawrence, Venables approved the purchase of John Aloisi, an Australian striker, from Italy and Matthias Svensson, a striker playing for IF Elfsborg of Sweden.

Ted Buxton had 'spotted' Svensson, an 'ideal player', in November 1996. Elfsborg's transfer price was £75,000. With Venables's approval Tommy Lawrence was asked to finalize Svensson's transfer. 'Lots of whoopsies in this,' Lawrence told Ashby. The financial transaction was unusual; under Lawrence's direction, the transfer fee was not to be paid directly by Portsmouth to Elfsborg but to Stephen Carter, a lawyer in Dulwich employed by Lawrence. There was another peculiarity. Kjell Hallen, Elfsborg's vice-chairman, was told by Lawrence that he should invoice Stephen Carter for £200,000, and once the money was received Hallen should return £125,000 back to Carter. The solicitor subsequently concluded that the £125,000 would be Lawrence's profit. 'I think this was an attempt to derive as much from the transaction as possible,' agreed Carter.

In correspondence with the Swedish club, Paul Weld, Portsmouth's secretary, confirmed on 18 November 1996 that he would transfer £200,000 for the player. Three days later, Carter received the details of Elfsborg's bank account. Over the following days, however, the directors of the Swedish club became nervous; the complications were causing overwhelming anxiety. By 2 December, Kjell Hallen decided to halt the charade. 'It's too much [sic] people involved in this transfer,' Hallen told Weld in a fax. Hallen wanted a direct transfer of £75,000 from

Portsmouth and no opaqueness. The enrichment of
Lawrence by the Swedes was terminated. Nevertheless,
Venables ordered Ashby, 'Pay Lawrence £20,000 for his
services'. Buxton was also paid a fee by Portsmouth.
Ashby was vexed. During his two years at Tottenham,
Ashby had been introduced to football's devious prac-
tices. He had seen the unusual commissions lubricating
the transfers of Gascoigne and Sheringham. At
Portsmouth, in Venables's absence, Ashby was no longer
an active observer but at the centre of Venables's bid to
become rich. Ashby had just negotiated a £200,000 loan to
Portsmouth from a local supporter and disliked the diver-
sion of so much money to Lawrence and probably others.
Ashby's stance caused a strain in his relationship with
Venables. In his memoirs, Eric Hall would claim that
Ashby had demanded a bribe to facilitate the deal and was
upset not to receive any money. Unsurprisingly, Ashby
uttered a similar allegation against others. Suspicion and
self-enrichment at football's expense surrounded
Venables.

Apparently unconcerned about the club's finances,
Venables bought four more Australian players – Robbie
Enes, Hamilton Thorp, Craig Foster, Paul Harries –
although they would be frequently absent, at his own
request, to play for Australia. Venables's critics, however,
were silenced by his sale in 1997 of Lee Bradbury, a
striker, to Manchester City for £3 million, a colossal sum
for a questionable talent. After the sale, Venables billed
Portsmouth £300,000 for his services agreed under his
contract, a healthy bonus to the £300,000 he earned from
promotional contracts with Admiral, a clothing manufacturer.

Venables was squeezing a dry carcass. Building work
for the new stadium was threatened by the failure to pay

the contractors; suppliers were complaining that their bills
were unpaid; the players worried that there was no money
for their wages; and fewer supporters were watching
matches. In April 1997, creditors' writs and court judgements began arriving at the ground. 'Our position isn't a
nice one,' sighed Paul Weld. Insuperable financial prob--
lems easily disillusioned Venables. A football club without
money was unable to satisfy his ambitions.

The embarrassments at Portsmouth were aggravated
on 23 October 1997. Eddie Ashby was convicted at
Knightsbridge Crown Court of breaching the bankruptcy
laws and, to his surprise, he was sentenced to four
months' imprisonment. During his first weeks at
Wormwood Scrubs and Stamford Hill prisons, he
believed that his wife would receive a regular income
from Venables, not least from a 15 per cent stake in a
major project.

In 1996, Ashby had arranged the purchase on
Venables's behalf of a twenty-bedroom hotel and 300
acres of land in Mas de Panorama near Alicante in Spain.
Arranged to avoid taxation, the plan was to convert the
property into a football academy. Ashby transferred
£550,000 to Venables Holdings, an English company.
Next, he asked Alan Chick, an offshore facilitator in
Guernsey who was also caring for the private trust of
Geoffrey Robinson, the discredited paymaster general in
the Labour government, to establish Oakcliffe Holdings.
On Venables's behalf, the new offshore company bought
the Mastapo complex for £750,000. Ashby was a partner
in that transaction until his conviction.

Standing on the court steps in Knightsbridge minutes
after Ashby was taken to a prison cell, the football coach
disowned his loyal assistant. 'I knew nothing about his
bankruptcy,' Venables declared. Few were convinced, but

Venables had his own problems. He had lost heavily in
the libel action arising from his autobiography. The case,
brought by Alan Sugar, had cost the publishers £101,000
in damages, plus costs of £1.5 million. During the hear-
ings Venables had been declared to be discredited by two
judges. Venables's own fate had become perilous.

On 2 December 1997, Portsmouth's new but uncompleted stadium was opened at Fratton Park but, after two
games, was closed for safety reasons. Three days later,
Venables awarded himself £150,000 as a performance
payment, sold his shares back to Gregory and resigned
from the near-insolvent club. For his original £1 investment Venables had earned in two years over £550,000,
but some players complained of remaining unpaid.
Among the aggrieved was Paul Walsh, an injured striker
expecting £500,000 from the club on an insurance claim.
To Walsh's anger, the club had allowed his compensation
to disappear into a 'black hole'. Months after Venables
had left the club with his own pay-off, Walsh was still
struggling to recover the money paid to the club by the
insurance company.

Early the following year, in January 1998, Venables
appeared in court to face nineteen charges of serious misconduct under the Company Directors' Disqualification
Act 1986. Specifically, in his purchase of Tottenham,
Venables was accused of including false information in
the 'offer document' and perpetrating 'an undisclosed
and sham loan'. The DTI investigation of Edennote,
Venables's private company, reported that the football
manager had produced untruthful financial accounts.
Edennote's 'long running insolvency', the inspectors
reported, was 'characterized by dealings and transactions
of obvious impropriety'. Ashby, his co-conspirator, was
accused of unlawfully signing cheques and negotiating

with banks on Venables's behalf. Venables was accused of being 'non-cooperative' with the official receiver and the Inland Revenue. He pleaded guilty to the nineteen offences. He was fined £500,000 and disqualified from acting as a company director until 2005.

Venables's admission of guilt surprised Graham Kelly. In the wake of successive scandals at Doncaster, Chester, Brighton and Portsmouth football clubs, the FA's chief executive promised in May 1998 to enforce 'the highest standard of administrative behaviour' in football clubs, but there was little evidence of purposeful interest.

The convictions of Ashby and Venables satisfied Alan Sugar. He and his staff had provided information and some affidavits to the DTI to prove the dishonesty. Football's realities, however, influenced Sugar's opinion. In his eagerness to enhance the value of Tottenham – worth about £74 million in 1998 – his attitude towards the game's morality became tempered.

Since Venables's departure, Tottenham had declined successively under two managers, Ossie Ardiles and Christian Gross. Sugar was visibly desperate to find a cure. As the directors pondered how to save their club, they searched for a candidate with a proven record. Only one name was deemed to be suitable: George Graham, the disgraced manager employed by Leeds. Graham, Sugar agreed, would be ideal, not least because he would want his revenge against Arsenal. In the discussion among Tottenham's directors, Graham's dishonesty and the 'bung' were barely mentioned. Soon after Venables's conviction, Graham was approached on Sugar's behalf and he agreed to a four year contract, to start on 1 October 1998.

By any reckoning, the appointment of George Graham by Alan Sugar was a defining moment in English football.

Not because of the outcry that the appointment provoked,
but by the complete absence of any controversy or condemnation. Graham Kelly's passivity was unexceptional.
Sugar's endorsement of a dishonest man did not surprise
Kelly. George Graham's one year ban, believed Kelly, was
'a quite substantial punishment which had passed slowly'.
Although Sugar had complained four years earlier about
Kelly's preference to avoid the consequences of a serious
probe of Venables's activities and concluded that the FA
was 'a toothless tiger, without any real controls over the
clubs and players', he appeared to have adapted himself to
life and survival in football's jungle. He was not surprised
when, that same year, Terry Venables re-emerged yet
again at another Premier League club. In February 1998,
Venables was invited to save Crystal Palace, a loved but
unglamorous south London club, from relegation.

In 1990 Crystal Palace had reached the FA Cup Final
but during the following years slid towards the bottom of
the top flight. Disenchanted by football, Ron Noades, the
club's enigmatic chairman, had welcomed the approach in
1997 by Mark Goldberg, the 34-year-old owner of a computer servicing company in Bromley which he valued at
about £100 million. Like so many self-made millionaires
whose fortunes had been earned by brashness –
Goldberg's trick was to wave wads of cash in front of his
salesmen – the effervescent tycoon had originally dreamt
of scoring goals for Crystal Palace. Instead he offered to
buy the club and create a team able to defeat Manchester
United. 'As a Palace fan,' said the man aspiring to copy
Ken Bates, 'I've suffered a lot of frustration over the
years.' Swayed by Noades's description of life as a club
owner – 'It's great. I went to lunches in Downing Street
with kings and ambassadors' – Goldberg dreamt of
clutching a glass of champagne in the directors' box and

gazing at the crowds roaring below the giant red letters embossed on the new 'Mark Goldberg Stand'.

In self-promotion Goldberg pledged unlimited money for the club's benefit, although his business record was not pristine. In the early 1990s two of his companies had been declared bankrupt and during his campaign to sell hospitality trips to the 1998 World Cup, he had wrongly claimed to enjoy the endorsement of Alex Ferguson. But his motives were unambiguous. 'In business,' Goldberg pouted, 'I've never wanted to be second, only number one.' Within five years he expected his investment in Crystal Palace would be worth £100 million. Ron Noades understood Goldberg's self-delusion. 'Everyone thinks he can run a football club,' Noades told Goldberg, 'but it's the most difficult business in the world.' In his dismissive manner, Goldberg spoke of the dividends he would earn from the profits. 'I have never earned a dividend from Crystal Palace,' Noades told him, 'except when I wound up the old club. There's no profits in football.' Like so many star-struck businessmen intent on jettisoning their anonymity at any price, Goldberg fantasized about fulfilling his dream.

Goldberg's bid to Ron Noades on 12 November 1997 was characteristic. Although Crystal Palace was at the bottom of the Premier League, he offered to pay £30.1 million for the club. 'Stupid,' concluded Noades. The bid was £12 million over Noades's own valuation and, not surprisingly, he accepted the offer in February 1998. The money was to be transferred in three stages over one year while Noades remained as the club's chairman.

In March 1998, Goldberg sought to renegotiate the agreement. Crystal Palace was on the brink of relegation and the high purchase price had deterred any City support. Goldberg sold a stake in his computer business for

£23.75 million and agreed that, until he paid the full
amount, Noades should retain the freehold of the club's
property, including the stadium. 'It's a stupid deal,'
Noades told Goldberg. 'You're paying too much.'

Goldberg was not listening. Yearning for fame, he had
turned to Terry Venables, the architect of Crystal
Palace's 'Golden Years' in the late 1970s, with an offer of
the managership to save the club from relegation. 'I have
studied Terry's history quite carefully,' explained
Goldberg, 'and I am convinced that I can work with him.'
This was just after Venables's disqualification from acting
as a director until 2005. Goldberg was undeterred,
despite Venables's initial reluctance.

Goldberg's offer to Venables proved to be irresistible.
After pocketing £135,000 simply for opening negotiations, he secured a five year contract worth £3.5 million,
a house worth £650,000, a tax-free cash payment of
£750,000 and share options valued at £2 million.
Goldberg's trust in Venables was complete: 'We're like
brothers almost. We respect each other. Totally. Terry
Venables is the master of all masters. He is the authority
on football.' Noades cautioned Goldberg: 'Venables's
problem is that he comes with an entourage and that will
be expensive.' Convinced he could tame Venables,
Goldberg paid Noades £80,000 to relinquish his chairmanship and depart.

Venables showed little sympathy for Goldberg's financial plight. He began buying thirteen new players, some
in peculiar circumstances. Among the first was David
Amsalem, a 27-year-old Israeli left back. Venables had
been offered the player by Barry Silkman, an amiable
agent based in north London, acting for Pinhas 'Pini'
Zahavi, a shrewd Israeli agent. 'Look at the videos,'
Venables told John Griffin, the club's trusted scout.

'He's no good in defence,' Griffin reported. 'Could I train him?' asked Venables. 'Yes,' replied Griffin, 'but he's too old to become a good defender.' Nevertheless, Venables bought Amsalem for £850,000, notionally from his club, Maccabi Nevealon, but in reality from a consortium. Ron Noades was baffled by the transfer. 'He's worth at most £250,000,' he told Goldberg. 'I gave you his recent medical to show his real value. Get out of it.' Goldberg was deaf: 'I know what you're talking about but I'll go ahead.' The purchase proved worse than Noades predicted. Amsalem was a disappointment and the fate of his transfer fee was puzzling. Maccabi Nevealon claimed not to have received the first instalment of £266,666 from Goldberg and finally complained that less than £100,000 was ever received from the club's owner. Amsalem would be resold to another Israeli club for £25,000.

At the end of the 1997–98 season, Crystal Palace was relegated from the Premier League. Goldberg's gamble on Venables had failed. Although £6 million were added to the losses, Venables's buying continued, ostensibly to prevent the club's slide towards the bottom of the First Division. His purchase of two Chinese players, Fan Zhiyi and Sun Jihai, for £1 million aroused particular speculation. Venables had relied upon the recommendation of Ted Buxton, his favourite scout, that the two Chinese were ideal for Crystal Palace. In reality, neither player proved to be suitable and the Chinese authorities complained about receiving only £600,000. The fate of the remaining £400,000 of the club's payment was never resolved. Both transfers would be investigated, but no action was taken. Venables also decided to rely on Lee Bradbury, the striker he had recently transferred from Portsmouth to Manchester

City for £3 million and who was swiftly rejected by the
club. In October 1998, Goldberg agreed to pay £1.5
million for the player. One year later, Bradbury was
resold for £300,000.

Graham Kelly did not consider investigating the
unusual transactions at Crystal Palace, even after the circumstances surrounding the transfer of Walter del Rio,
an Argentinian midfielder, to Crystal Palace had been
revealed. Walter del Rio had been offered to Crystal
Palace by Jon Smith, the ambitious joint owner with his
brother Phil of First Artist, a football agency. Jon Smith,
born in 1952 in Barnet, was a former pop promoter in
Los Angeles who had never played football but recognized the potential wealth of the football business.
'Everyone wants to put their nose in the trough,' he said,
unashamed about his motive, 'and the trough is enormous.' Premier League clubs, Smith knew, were paying
millions of pounds every year in agent fees. The chairmen of Britain's football clubs, he believed, would have
reason to fear the increasing power of agents.

The outset of Jon Smith's career as a football agent in
the late 1980s had coincided with the collapse of commu-
nism in eastern Europe. Whole teams of east European
players were offered for sale to west European clubs,
either for the east European club's survival or for private
profit. One obstacle to employing the players in Britain
was the European Union's law that players should be EU
nationals or entitled by birth to EU passports. For those
players who were ineligible, unscrupulous agents in south-
ern Europe used forged documents to invent Greek or
Italian grandparents or great-grandparents. With those
'great-grandparents', east European players applied for
Greek or Italian nationality and became eligible for
employment by EU clubs.

Jon Smith represented Bulgarian players who had already been transformed by other agents into Greek citizens and could be 'legitimately' sold to Scottish clubs. 'A fabulous trade,' Smith told his friends. 'Money ended up in banks which had nothing to do with the clubs. I don't think anyone acts by the strict letter of the Bible.' In his genial manner, Smith candidly asserted a truism for many in the football business: 'Morality was important in the past, but it's not so important now.' Regularly, he would be asked by chairmen or managers of famous clubs during negotiations, 'How does the deal stack up?' The question was code for an explanation how the chairman or manager would be paid his cut. Smith's reply was reassuring: 'You can introduce any third party you like into the deal, but any payment will be invoiced and presented to my auditors.' The chairmen nodded. Shortly after a transfer was concluded, an invoice for an 'interpreter' was presented by First Artist to the club and the payment forwarded to an offshore bank, nominated by the club's executive. Sums in excess of £150,000 were not unusual. In Smith's corporate world, so long as those payments were listed in his company's financial accounts and approved by his auditors, there was no wrongdoing. Convinced of the growing power which agents would exercise, Smith's principal purpose was to be included in 'the deal' and, like his competitors, Smith was prepared to assist any participant regardless of what outsiders would deem to be a conflict of interest. Commissions in football, Jon Smith believed, were no different than a company director enjoying a night at the Royal Opera House at a client's expense. That attitude encouraged carelessness.

The purchase of Walter del Rio from Boca Juniors was agreed with Terry Venables on the basis of a fax sent on 20

August 1998 from Buenos Aires to Steve Wicks, an employee of First Artist and a former professional footballer who had been captain of Chelsea and QPR. Written on the headed notepaper of Boca, the fax recorded that the player would be loaned to Crystal Palace for one year for a fee of $200,000 payable to Jon Smith and First Artist. Smith forwarded the fax to Mark Goldberg. Simultaneously, First Artist faxed Crystal Palace an invoice for $170,000 plus $29,750 VAT, describing the sum as a 'FIFA agency loan and finder's fee'. On 15 September 1998, a second invoice was presented for $317,250. Of this, $270,000 was described as a 'FIFA agency fee representing 50 per cent of the ownership of Walter José del Rio'. The invoice also contained the phrase, 'This fee is to be passed to the owner of the player's rights, Tony Barradas.' Crystal Palace were also to pay £118,317 to Marcello Houseman, the alleged Argentinian agent of the player. On the basis of those various incomprehensible invoices, First Artist received £91,000 commission. However, unknown to Mark Goldberg, Walter del Rio had been released by his club on a free transfer on 17 June 1998. There was no reason for Goldberg to pay Boca Juniors for the player. The fax purporting to come from Boca was a forgery sent from a fax machine in a shop in South America. Jon Smith's description of del Rio's status had been inaccurate. Smith insisted that he was also a victim of the forgery.

Jon Smith was embarrassed by the revelation of his company's misrepresentation but his relationship with Crystal Palace was barely affected. He was not asked to repay the commission, although Goldberg's £30 million investment was evaporating, propelled by Venables's decision to try to buy John Hartson from West Ham for £7.5 million, an unexpectedly high sum, at the very moment that the manager had been ordered to reduce the team from forty to twenty-five players. (Hartson in fact later went to Wimbledon.) Distraught that the inevitable casualty of sliding down the league table was Crystal Palace's expensive squad, Terry Venables resigned at the end of January 1999. His departure was cushioned by Goldberg paying six months' salary in compensation. Venables's appointment, admitted Goldberg, had been 'a mistake'. The fabled manager had failed to motivate the players, conceded Goldberg, who added, 'The club is actually in a sound financial position.' That was inaccurate. The club's deteriorating finances prompted Ron Noades to issue a writ for the non-repayment of a £1 million loan. Goldberg's total debts after less than one year's ownership were over £20 million. Two months later, in March 1999, the receivers were appointed. 'I was a sucker,' Goldberg conceded. His reign had lasted fourteen months. By the end of the year, Goldberg would be declared personally bankrupt and branded 'dishonest' and 'a liar' by a High Court judge. Like so many attracted to football, Goldberg's recklessness had been self-destructive.

Mark Goldberg's plight attracted little sympathy, although the relationships and deals during his brief ownership aroused unresolved questions about Venables's activities within the club while disqualified by the DTI, the true value of Venables's transfer deals, the representations of First Artist and the abrupt insolvency of a major club. Some answers might have been discovered by David Buchler, the administrator of the club's insolvency, but he resigned citing the unpleasant working conditions. An explanation might also have been unearthed by a DTI inquiry but, to the complete astonishment of Ron Noades, the DTI investigation examined whether Goldberg had been the victim of a fraudulent valuation of the company and its assets. In March 2001 an application under the Company Directors Disqualification Act 1986 was made by the DTI for Mark Goldberg to be disqualified from acting as a company director. David Lee, a financial investigator, conducted an inquiry for the new administrators. Lee identified many riddles and provided replies to rebut the financial demands of Noades and Venables. But amid all those circumstances, there was a curious lack of interest about Crystal Palace's fate on the part of the FA. An investigation was not even considered, despite the club's dubious route to insolvency. The fate of the club and its management – a certain investigation for an independent regulator – barely interested the FA. Not even the vulnerability of the club to agents persuaded the FA to reconsider its nonchalance. Believing that football's wealth would continue to soar, the FA's officials were under pressure to resist interfering, despite Graham Kelly's promise in May 1998 to enforce 'the highest standard of administrative behaviour' in football clubs. That piety was meaningless and, soon after uttering that assurance, Kelly himself became the victim of a coup within the FA.

7

FIASCOS AND DISILLUSIONMENT

Football's magnates were intolerant of Graham Kelly and Keith Wiseman, the FA's new chairman. Towards the end of 1998, both men were walking into a trap of their own making, condemned for ignoring the requirements of football's rich professionals.

Keith Wiseman, a 53-year-old solicitor and coroner, was a former county tennis champion and eager football supporter. His election as the FA chairman in 1996 was unexpected. Few had anticipated that he would secure victory by embarrassing Dave Richards, the Premier League's unimpressive candidate, and, not surprisingly, the machinations that secured Wiseman's election sowed permanent resentment among Richards's sponsors. Soon after Wiseman further angered the Premier League's chairmen; he requested an annual payment of £250,000 in compensation for his loss of earnings. His request was rejected, and his reduced demand for £75,000 was also refused.

Wiseman's agenda was to change the FA, in particular by transforming the FA from an amateur association into a commercial corporation. Among the FA's many weaknesses he identified the antagonism between Graham Kelly, scorned as a clerk, and the self-regarding Premier League professionals personified by David Dein. Wiseman sought to broker a truce between those personalities, and between the Premier League and the other clubs in a business cursed by muddle and short-sighted self-interest. His plans and opinions were rejected.

Wiseman's personal ambitions also aroused friction. He sought election to UEFA, the European football association, and his defeat evoked derision among members of the FA. Soon after he purchased 1,150 shares in Southampton FC valued at £1 each. After the club's flotation, the shares were worth £1.27 million. Traditional fans were shocked by Wiseman's so-called 'profiteering' and demanded answers from Graham Kelly. His response was self-condemnatory. Despite extensive coverage in newspapers and television, Kelly denied any knowledge of Wiseman's jackpot and refused to launch an investigation. 'It's nothing to do with the FA,' insisted Kelly insensitively. 'The FA's rules have not been breached.' To his critics, Wiseman's ambitions appeared to profit himself rather than football. Despite his denials, Wiseman's critics accused him of appearing as a would-be 'wheeler-dealer'. In the newspapers they even castigated him as a master of 'odious machinations', a 'mealy-mouthed conspirator' and a 'scheming, self-serving chairman'. And that was before Wiseman sought election as England's representative to FIFA. Wiseman had reasoned that English football, excluded from influence at FIFA for so long, would be enhanced by a place in FIFA's council, not least to promote England's bid to host the World Cup in 2006.

In 1998, the reports of the FA's prospects to win the competition to stage the World Cup were not encouraging.

Doubts had existed ever since the bid was launched in February 1997 at a party in Downing Street hosted by John Major, featuring Bobby Charlton, Tom Finney, Tommy Lawton and other football personalities.

The bid was the brainchild of Bert Millichip, an 83-year-old who had recently retired as chairman of the FA. In Millichip's version, he had agreed during a conversation in 1993 in Las Vegas with the representative of Germany's FA that England would receive Europe's block vote in support of a bid for the World Cup in 2006. Millichip's recollection was doubted by Rick Parry, after his conversations with European chairmen. 'England has got no chance,' Parry told Millichip before the government's formal announcement. 'Thanks very much,' replied Millichip, determined to ignore the warning. Parry was unsurprised by Millichip's hauteur. Over the years in the FA, Millichip had been seduced by an expensive lifestyle and if England hosted the World Cup he would be guaranteed unlimited freebies until he was ninety-two.

Graham Kelly had not considered doubting his mentor's hazy recollection of the alleged conversation in Las Vegas. In autumn 1996, Kelly had appointed Alec McGivan, a Labour activist who had managed the public relations for the successful Euro '96 competition played in England, to organize the new bid. 'The FA didn't know what it was taking on,' admitted McGivan. 'Euro '96 had been handed to England without competition. The bid for the World Cup would be contested by other countries.'

The first surprise was a reply to John Major's invitation to the Downing Street launch. In a fax from Gerhard Aigner, the director general of UEFA, Graham Kelly read that the European football association was supporting a

German bid, as agreed between Millichip and the German representative in Las Vegas. 'We were gobsmacked,' recalled McGivan; while Graham Kelly and David Davies were 'left a bit shocked'. The suggestion of a converse agreement had been unexpected. According to the German version Millichip had agreed in 1993 in Las Vegas that in return for Germany not opposing England's bid for Euro '96, England would support Germany's bid for the 2006 World Cup. Keith Wiseman, Millichip's successor, decided to ignore Aigner's message; the new chairman lusted for the glory. Pertinently, UEFA was unable to provide any written record to support their version, encouraging Wiseman and then Kelly to ignore what they euphemistically called 'the gentlemen's misunderstanding'. Over the following four years, both assumed, the disputed conversation would become unimportant. As proof of the FA's isolation from football's politics, neither man chose to telephone the six other European football associations represented at UEFA to verify their prejudice in favour of Germany. Instead, the FA's executives pursued their bid, relying upon government support.

The Labour party's election manifesto had embraced the bid but misgivings had surfaced after Alec McGivan and the FA's organizers had spent £50,000 to lobby for support during the 1998 World Cup in France. They had managed to entertain only two FIFA executives to lunch. That embarrassment was compounded by growing qualms about the reliability of the accounts provided by the FA's own executives. Towards the end of 1998, Tony Banks, the sports minister, was regularly encountering representatives of UEFA and European football associations who mentioned the Las Vegas 'gentlemen's agreement'. Repeatedly, McGivan, Kelly and Wiseman derided those assertions.

'There are no minutes showing any agreement,' they chanted. 'It's the corruption of football,' cursed Banks. 'One can't commit a country on the basis of a gentlemen's agreement. But I couldn't, of course, say to the FA, "You're liars."'

Keith Wiseman barely helped the cause. In his effort to restore the influence which England had lost since the retirement of Stanley Rous in 1974, he boasted that he would lead England to 'impose ourselves on the leading footballing nations of the world'. The occasion of his tactlessness was during the vote for a new president of FIFA in 1998. Wiseman ignored the agreement among UEFA delegates to vote for Lennart Johansson, and instead supported Sepp Blatter. Wiseman's justification for alienating the Europeans was Blatter's tempting promise to support England's bid for the World Cup and galvanize sympathy for England among other football federations.

The focus of England's bid was a new stadium at Wembley; construction had been formally agreed in 1996. Fearing that the combined bureaucracy of the FA and Sports Council would delay construction, Graham Kelly had proposed in autumn 1997 entrusting the project to Ken Bates, to 'put a bomb under the Sports Council' and 'bulldoze Wembley through'. Bates's nomination had provoked gasps of astonishment and amused applause but any criticism was silenced by Kelly's mention of Bates's successful transformation of Stamford Bridge into Chelsea Village. Neither Kelly nor the FA's councillors understood the flaws of Chelsea Village's financial model or were aware of Bates's financial history. Graham Kelly's endorsement of Bates as reliable was accepted by the councillors. That acquiescence symbolized many of the FA's defects but was seized by Bates as an endorsement of his trustworthiness. At that moment, Warburgs, the City bankers, were arranging a £75 million, ten year loan for Chelsea bearing an annual interest payment of £6.85 million. The loan was approved in December 1997 and the club's shares rose to 161 pence, valuing Chelsea at £250 million. Bates earned substantial profits by reducing his shareholding to 17.7 per cent while other offshore trusts owned by his associates reduced their stakes to 28 per cent. Bates's status in London had been enhanced.

Over the following months, Kelly and Bates, as the chairman of the English National Stadium Development Company Ltd (later the Wembley National Stadium Ltd), negotiated with Derek Casey, the portly chief executive of Sport England (the quango responsible for distributing National Lottery money) a grant to build and manage the new stadium. In July 1998, the government approved an allocation of £120 million from the Lottery to the FA, as the principal user of Wembley, with the obligation to raise the remaining finance privately. Public money would support the country's richest sport with the proviso that the stadium was shared by football, rugby and athletics. The Lottery grant was subject to fifty-two pages of conditions compiled by Casey. For Wembley to qualify as a truly national stadium, Casey stipulated the numbers of the public to be admitted, the seat prices and the conditions of all the FA's commercial agreements, including those with television companies. Bates's contempt for any restrictions was echoed by Graham Kelly. Casey's stipulations, protested Kelly, 'are an unnecessary interference in how we run our business'. The denunciation reflected the FA's foolhardy manner of managing and regulating the football business towards the end of 1998.

Keith Wiseman's strategy to win the bid for the World Cup included his plan to be elected as England's representative to FIFA. His success required the support of the Welsh Football Association. To vote for Wiseman the Welsh FA demanded a loan of £400,000 every year for eight years. Although this was expensive, Wiseman and Kelly secretly agreed to commit the English FA to pay £3.2 million. In the international football world, buying votes was common, but in England, Wiseman's ambitions displayed an unusual insensitivity to his own and Kelly's vulnerability.

The unauthorized arrangement with the Welsh FA was discovered after an invoice for £400,000 arrived at the FA's headquarters in November 1998. Critics of Kelly and Wiseman were quick to condemn the 'outrage' and their 'grave error of judgement'. English football's turbulence precluded any tolerance of the hapless FA executives. For differing reasons, David Dein, Labour politicians and others favoured confrontation. Dein's complaint was specific: Kelly and Wiseman had committed a terrible folly to vote for Sepp Blatter instead of Lennart Johansson as FIFA's chief executive. 'Johansson had worked hard to arrange England's readmission to European football,' said Dein. 'That was no reward for his help.' On 15 December 1998, the FA's executive committee unanimously passed a vote of no confidence in Kelly and Wiseman. Kelly resigned immediately but Wiseman refused to go. Pleading that he was the victim of a smear campaign, Wiseman hoped to reverse the decision at a meeting of the whole FA on 4 January 1999. His stubbornness reminded some of his misguided opinion, voiced in 1996, that Robert Reid's 'bungs' inquiry was 'an odd residue of a difficult past' which would not be repeated. Wiseman's hope of a reprieve was misplaced. After a two hour meeting, his dismissal was confirmed, despite the perception that some were motivated by ambition for his job. His humiliation was complete.

The reality of English football in early 1999 was unedifying: the national sport was uncertain whether the business was in the midst of a revolution or gripped by paralysis. Geoff Thompson, appointed as the FA's temporary chairman, was an invisible 54-year-old small-club bureaucrat who epitomized the macabre quip that English football was managed either by the inmates of death row or by worthy, well-preserved flannels. The FA's plight worsened on 6 February after Glenn Hoddle, the coach of the England team, was forced to resign for espousing the notion that the disabled were being punished for sins committed in a former life. The FA appeared to be rudderless and seemed unfocused in regulating the game and its opaque finances.

Chaos in the FA coincided with the climax of a bitter feud in the Premier League revolving around Peter Leaver and Sir John Quinton, the chairman. Without informing the Premier League's members, Leaver had concluded a consultancy contract with Sam Chisholm after his resignation from BSkyB. In return for advice about the future of the Premier League's contractual relationships with television, Chisholm would be paid between £50 million and £60 million. On reading Chisholm's contract, Peter Ridsdale, the chairman of Leeds, exploded. Leaver was ordered to terminate the agreement. Chisholm's compensation was £10 million – 'for doing nothing', as Ridsdale deplored. After completing the settlement, Leaver and Quinton were asked to resign on 11 March 1999 for acting without authority. 'I was pleased to get out,' said Leaver, 'because a few of the Premier League chairmen were hypocrites who were never straight in their dealings.' Few football chairmen had kind words for Leaver, who departed presenting himself as the disgusted eyewitness of alleged transgressions involving unpaid taxes, unauthorized loans and a file of unusual contracts between the Premier League and sponsors.

The swirl of huge income from Sky seemingly masked any rancour and turmoil; an image was sustained of an energetic enterprise, regardless of the chaos. In 1999, twenty-one Premier League and Football League clubs were listed on various stock exchanges. The first flotation, in 1983, had been Tottenham's to pay off debts of £5.5 million incurred in rebuilding their stadium. During the 1990s other major clubs followed, unleashing unexpected new investment. Sky bought a 9.9 per cent interest in Chelsea for £39.4 million, valuing the club at £404 million, and there were similar stakes in Leeds, Manchester City and Sunderland. Sky's 6 per cent stake in Manchester United at 230 pence per share valued the club at about £600 million. Sky's investments prompted rival bids to counter Murdoch's influence. ITV bought a 5 per cent stake in Arsenal for £47 million and a 10 per cent stake in Liverpool for £20 million. A third investor, NTL, a cable company, invested £26 million in Aston Villa, (although for less than the flotation price in May 1997 of £11 a share), undisclosed millions in Middlesbrough for a 5.5 per cent stake, £11.5 million in Leicester City, and about £14 million in Newcastle for a 9.9 per cent stake, plus a loan of £25 million for five years.

The escalating wealth fortified football's status among sceptical ministers. Tony Blair and Alastair Campbell had not revised their criticism of four years earlier, but the government's support of the bid for the World Cup necessitated New Labour reconciling itself with the representatives of the national sport. Like the Dome in Greenwich, the stadium at Wembley would be a towering

monument to New Labour's philosophy in the new mil-
lennium. There appeared to be good political reasons for
the government to embrace the Football Association with
enthusiasm.

On 15 March 1999, Wembley National Stadium Ltd
(WNSL), a subsidiary of the FA, bought the old stadium
and a 24-acre site from Wembley plc, a publicly quoted
property company, for £103 million. Unusually, the contract stipulated that 7 acres of additional land around the
stadium would be returned without compensation to the
vendors if the redevelopment of the stadium had not
started by the end of 2002. That commercial aberration
reflected the FA's inflated valuation of the land. The site
had been privately valued for the FA at £64.5 million.
Three years later, the same land would be valued at £30
million. Those who replaced the 'amateur' Graham Kelly
had paid the additional £35 million (or £73 million) for
'good will'.

Three months after the purchase, Wembley National
Stadium Ltd, under Ken Bates's chairmanship, was
running two separate tendering processes on substantially different terms for the same construction contract.
The process was subsequently criticized by a parliamentary committee for being 'contrary to best industry
practice' caused by 'possible conflicts of interest'. Even
the FA subsequently admitted, 'we did not have a completely transparent process'. There was also an absence
of harmony.

Ken Bates had become antagonistic towards the condition of the Lottery grant requiring the construction of an
athletics track around the football pitch. 'I'm not prepared
to sacrifice the interests of football who will finance the
stadium,' Bates told Derek Casey of Sport England. To
build a new stadium, complained Bates, with a permanent

athletics track placing football fans too far from the pitch was 'madness'. Wembley would suffer the same fate as the redundant Olympic stadiums in Barcelona and Sydney. Casey was sympathetic to those wanting a replica of the Stade de France in Paris, the location of the World Cup in 1998. Retractable seats allowed the French stadium to be easily converted to serve football and athletics. But the French government had contributed nearly £500 million towards the stadium's cost of £670 million and guaranteed an annual subsidy. Britain's Lottery had given the FA only £120 million and Wembley was to be thereafter self-financing.

Casey's niggling pressure enraged Bates. The FA's agreement with Sport England for a national stadium, he fumed, was 'a total recipe for disaster'. While football and rugby would guarantee twenty fixtures every year, athletics could guarantee none. Only three athletics events, including the Olympics, ever attracted more than 5,000 spectators and, realistically, there was only one foreseeable event, the World Athletics Championship, planned for London in 2005, which would use Wembley. Bates's assessment was confirmed by David Moorcroft, the chief executive of UK Athletics. Their compromise, to avoid an uneconomic white elephant, was a stadium which was built for football but could be converted for athletics. Casey surrendered and agreed with Bates; their plan required the endorsement of Chris Smith.

During April 1999, Rod Sheard, the architect of Sydney's Olympic stadium, had unveiled a revolutionary solution for accommodating the two sports. Within a perfect stadium for football, a massive concrete platform, sufficient to take the weight of 140,000 people, could be installed across the pitch for a world athletics competition. The only disadvantage was the installation and dismantling of the platform. The combined transformations would take about one year, cost £23 million and reduce the number of seats from 90,000 to 73,000.

Instinctively, Chris Smith disliked the platform. After a second presentation in mid-July 1999, he again complained, 'It's Heath-Robinson.' Troubled by the installation, he envisaged a platform raised on hydraulic rams. 'Wembley's not a West End theatre,' scoffed a Wembley executive. 'We're talking about acres of thick concrete 20 feet above the ground. Hydraulic rams would cost up to £100 million, and you don't know in years' time if they'd be still working, if you even ever need them. There's no value for money.' Smith was unconvinced. He wanted the Stade de France, even though his government was unwilling to match the French government's subsidy. 'I'm not satisfied,' he insisted, unpersuaded that a similar platform in Monte Carlo's stadium had proved successful. Smith wanted hydraulic rams. 'You've got a closed mind,' he complained to the architects. 'These are not difficulties.'

The real difficulty was the government's relationship with football. Smith was a member of a secret government Wembley monitoring group which included representatives of football but excluded the administrators of athletics. While Smith would publicly say, 'Wembley was never a government project. It was an FA project,' he sought, on the government's behalf, overall control to advance football's interest. To his misfortune, Robin Young and his other departmental officials were bereft of a strategy and appeared to be uncertain about the commercial and technical requirements for a stadium. While the minister grappled for answers, his advisers remained silent, disdainful of the pressing deadline to reveal the new stadium to the public.

The politician's interference had become intolerable for Ken Bates. Without any expertise, he cursed, Chris Smith believed he knew better than the professionals. 'Shall we cancel the public launch of the stadium?' Bob Stubbs, Wembley's frustrated chief executive, asked Smith. Floundering but fearful of annoying Downing Street's ambition to host the World Cup in 2006, Smith emphatically rejected the suggestion. 'Absolutely not,' the minister replied. The demand for a stadium similar to the Stade de France was abandoned and Smith's reservations appeared to have been unequivocally resolved. Pleasing the football lobby was imperative. 'I was caught up by the momentum,' Smith explained, 'of beating Germany to stage the World Cup. Everyone thought it was urgent.'

On 29 July 1999, beaming with satisfaction, Chris Smith hosted the launch party in Wembley, unveiling Ken Bates's singular version of a national stadium for football and athletics. Among Smith's audience in the dilapidated old stadium were the contented representatives of football's establishment. 'The new stadium,' enthused Smith, 'is stunning and a magnificent venue for athletics.' In the same week as England's bid to host the 2006 football World Cup intensified, Smith seized the opportunity to associate himself with Tony Blair's passion for the prize, which would climax in Wembley. The new stadium symbolized New Labour's embrace of the national game and Smith, normally uninterested in sport, understood the political advantage of gluing himself to Downing Street's 'football mania'.

Ken Bates was ebullient. Unanimously, everyone praised his ability to produce a realistic design, although the cost had doubled from £136 million to £240 million and risen again to a tentatively fixed-price contract of

£334 million. The additional cost was Bates's scheme to construct an all-year business centre rather than a mere facility for twenty fixtures every year. In his replica of Chelsea Village, Bates reasoned that Wembley's profits depended upon corporate hospitality. Since Derek Casey insisted on 75,000 tickets for the public, which would produce no profits, Bates added 15,000 corporate seats, including over 100 corporate boxes, to generate Wembley's income. His blueprint was swelled by a Hilton hotel, offices and a banqueting suite for 5,000. The business plan had been endorsed by the FA, Sport England, Deloitte Touche, the accountants, Investec, the merchant bank, and, most importantly, by Chris Smith at the public launch. That morning, few doubted football's victory, especially those complaining of defeat.

Unseen but standing close to Smith at the meeting was Simon Clegg, the chief executive of the British Olympic Association. Clegg was cursing and inclined to undermine the politician's optimism. Minutes after the launch Clegg ensnared Philippa Drew, the senior civil servant accompanying Smith, and vented his spleen. 'It's outrageous,' fumed Clegg. 'Wembley has been hijacked by football. It's meant to be a national stadium, fit for Olympic athletics. But it's too small for the Games. We've been ignored.'

At the very moment that Smith and all the leaders of Britain's sports organizations lionized Wembley's new stadium as the ideal venue if the Olympics were ever held in London, Clegg set about sabotaging that conviction. 'Britain will never get the Olympics,' he raged. 'That's ludicrous,' replied Drew, who had recently transferred to the DCMS from the Prisons' Department at the Home Office. On her return to Whitehall that afternoon, Drew, acting on Kate Hoey's instructions, blithely began to overturn the solemn prediction by Tony Banks, the sports minister: 'Wembley is a project that we simply cannot allow to go wrong.'

On that same day, in a gesture towards the government's commitment to football, Tony Banks had resigned to become Britain's ambassador to win the World Cup in 2006. 'After a few months as minister,' Banks explained, 'I knew I wanted to give it up. I didn't like it. Alec McGivan was distressed, so I agreed to ask Blair if I could be the special envoy for the World Cup.' The new stadium would be the showpiece for that championship.

Kate Hoey, Tony Banks's critic, was appointed the junior minister in his place. Twenty-four hours after the ceremony at Wembley, Hoey had completed reading through the departmental files, noting especially Clegg's protests since 1998 about the lack of consultation. Athletics, she believed, had been 'marginalized' because 'everyone had fallen under the spell of the World Cup'. The proposed stadium, she concluded, had become 'a stitch-up by football'. The major culprits, she opined, were Ken Bates, the officials within her own department and football's greed.

Kate Hoey possessed no technical qualifications or specialist advisers to challenge the reconstruction plan proposed by the Australian architects. Guided, as she admitted, by 'instinct', she condemned the concrete platform as 'a complete and utter nonsense. No other country had done it that way.' In her opinion, the platform undermined the 'legacy value' of a national stadium for athletics and was 'a waste of money'. By 21 September 1999, her antagonism towards Bates had solidified. Invited for discussions to her office, Bates refused and sent Bob Stubbs. In Bates's opinion, Kate Hoey had discredited herself by saying soon after her appointment that Wembley's twin towers would have to be incorporated in the new design – at a cost of an extra £40 million. To the businessman, the minister appeared to shoot from the lip without justifying her government's interference. 'I don't like incompetent women,' said Bates. 'I don't like bullies,' replied Kate Hoey.

'Why aren't we building a Stade de France?' Kate Hoey asked Bob Stubbs. 'Football wouldn't have it,' replied Stubbs with stark honesty. That confirmed Kate Hoey's anger. 'I want a national stadium with a legacy,' she said, ignoring the absence of government subsidies and the redundant stadiums in Barcelona and Sydney. Kate Hoey's next question was self-revelatory. 'What influence do I have over this?' 'We have £120 million from the Lottery,' replied Stubbs, 'and as long as we stick to the conditions, you have none.' 'You're saying you can do what you want?' 'Yes.' 'I'm not having that,' said Kate Hoey, resenting her impotence and offended that a businessman would decide the use of Lottery money.

Searching for allies, Kate Hoey alighted on Simon Clegg of the British Olympic Association. Three weeks later, on 13 October 1999, the two were closeted in her office. Both had similar ambitions: Clegg wanted an Olympic stadium and Kate Hoey wanted a Stade de France or a dedicated athletics stadium. Both dismissed the arguments that such stadiums were financially unsustainable. To succeed, they united to destabilize Ken Bates, who by then had antagonized both. 'Clegg's chasing a dream,' scoffed Bates. 'He hasn't got a pot to piss in.'

Ken Bates had been emboldened by a meeting of the FA council on 8 September 1999. The agenda listed 'Wembley' as an item for decision. The single word embraced the FA's largest investment, posing a serious risk of the FA's bankruptcy and the destruction of English football if the development was mismanaged. For months, Peter Middleton, the chairman of the Football League and a banker who had resigned as a director from Bates's Chelsea Village board, had urged caution. The reconstruction of Wembley, Middleton believed, would automatically transform the FA into a property company and the organization lacked the necessary expertise. Any project, he reasoned, that was to be financed by debt rather than equity was certain to be more expensive. That afternoon, Middleton again cautioned his fellow members. 'There will be an insufficient revenue stream,' he predicted. 'Wembley cannot be rebuilt on that basis.' The bland faces prevented him continuing to warn, 'Wembley is a monument for Ken and he can't succeed. We need more information.' His audience was not interested, their minds were elsewhere. Football, not finance, was their passion and they were all glancing at their watches. Thirty-five minutes had been allocated for the entire meeting. Each man was calculating the departure time to reach the airport to catch a plane for Warsaw. No one wanted to miss England's match against Poland. Everyone was impressed that Ken Bates had improved the seating, décor and food at the old Wembley stadium; there was no reason for further discussion. Bates's management was reconfirmed. But Bates's opponents in Whitehall were not so easily deflected.

Simon Clegg and Kate Hoey executed their coup on 19 October 1999. Everyone associated with Wembley's reconstruction was invited to a meeting in the basement of Sport England's headquarters near Euston station. Before the meeting, Clegg had persuaded Kate Hoey that once the proposed platform for athletics was inserted into the stadium, the view of many spectators would be obstructed. Enthusiastically, Kate Hoey adopted the 'sight line' obstacle to undermine Wembley's suitability. Blithely, she ignored the architect's computer models, which dismissed Clegg's criticism as bogus. At worst, the models showed, 2,000 spectators would not see one runner on an outside track for one second. 'The architects are bound to say that,' smiled the junior minister. Clegg persuaded Kate Hoey to seek an independent review of the architects' plans by the consultants, Ellerbe Becket. Subsequently, Chris Smith would deny 'there was collusion between Clegg and Hoey', although he agreed, 'Clegg found a more sympathetic ear with Kate Hoey than from Tony Banks.'

The spleen of Kate Hoey and Clegg was directed at Derek Casey, Sport England's chief executive. 'Casey has failed to produce a strategy,' complained Clegg. 'He has been ineffectual. He has given in to the interests of football and he has failed to safeguard the Olympic dimension.' In Kate Hoey's opinion, Casey had been 'browbeaten' by Bates, a 'domineering' businessman who had 'taken complete control and wasn't listening to anybody'. She did not disagree with the condemnation by the representatives of athletics of Casey as a leading 'villain', 'a control freak', an 'oily politician brilliant at survival', and an 'excessively cautious bureaucrat'. Casey would robustly reject those criticisms, saying that 'Clegg was happy' until suborned by Kate Hoey. Even David Moorcroft, representing UK Athletics, had supported the FA's proposals until July, when he unexpectedly switched to Kate Hoey's camp mouthing the expensive mantra, 'I want a legacy.' Kate Hoey's coup was to persuade everyone, including Casey, to commission Ellerbe Becket to investigate Bates's scheme. Four weeks later, Kate Hoey claimed her second victory.

On 17 November 1999, Chris Smith and Kate Hoey
were the guests of Ken Bates in the old Wembley stadium
to watch England play Scotland. A verbal exchange at
half-time plunged Wembley's redevelopment into a spiral
of disaster.

Relations between Bates and the politicians had
sharply deteriorated over the previous weeks. At their
meetings, Smith had been regularly embarrassed by Bates
in front of his senior officials. 'How will we expand the
stadium from 80,000 to 90,000 spectators?' asked Smith,
expecting a technical explanation. 'Just add another 10,000
seats,' snorted Bates flippantly. The businessman refused
to endear himself to Labour politicians. Hoey rejected
Bates's invitation for lunch to discuss her concerns.
'Power-broker meals,' said the junior minister, 'mean
hidden deals.' The antagonism had gradually persuaded
Smith that Bates's plan for athletics was, as Kate Hoey
argued, unsustainable. As the government was inclined to
consider bidding for the Olympics after securing the
football World Cup in 2006, Smith became nervous about
Wembley's suitability for athletics. He had become
obsessed by the 'duplicity' of Derek Casey of Sport
England. 'We were meant to have the Stade de France at
Wembley . . . Casey has failed us,' grumbled Smith.
'Wembley won't give us a legacy,' agreed Kate Hoey.

Bates's harsh warning to Smith at Wembley on 17
November gave the advantage to Hoey. 'Forget the "sight
line",' said Bates, 'and the platform and all your other
objections. Your real problem is the warm-up track.'
Under Olympic rules, a minor stadium was required to be
built close to the Olympic stadium for the athletes to use
prior to the race. The only suitable site adjacent to
Wembley was covered by industrial buildings. 'You'd
need to issue compulsory orders to clear the area,' said

Bates, knowing what thoughts had instantly been triggered in the politician's mind: costs of about £20 million, the loss of jobs and land lying unused, possibly indefinitely, until an Olympic bid was accepted. Smith's response was instant: 'We've got to get athletics out of Wembley.' Kate Hoey was delighted. 'Yes!' she said gleefully. By any measure, that exchange revealed the chaotic political management of the Wembley stadium. While the two politicians went into overdrive to calculate an effective exit from Wembley, neither pondered the discrepancy between paying £20 million for the extra land at Wembley and the £190 million necessary for a dedicated athletics track, possibly at Picketts Lock in north-east London, or the £4 billion price of the Olympics.

Chris Smith later explained his conversion against Wembley. 'I didn't realize the obvious before July 1999,' he said, 'that you can't have a perfect football and athletics stadium.' He blamed everyone for failing to explain that truism, not least Derek Casey who, he claimed, 'ignored the fundamental incompatibility between football and athletics'. Just how the reconstruction of Wembley, the home of British football and praised by a parliamentary select committee as a venue for a major athletics competition, could have been derailed by the hypothetical notion of holding the Olympic Games in London was never explained. Not least, because in March 1999 Simon Clegg had told a parliamentary select committee that a British bid for the Olympics was not dependent on Wembley's reconstruction. The only suitable site for the Olympics Clegg believed would be in east London. Nevertheless, Clegg had become outraged about how football's billions had bought prestige and political patronage, an opinion shared by Kate Hoey. The junior minister was uninterested that the International Olympic

Committee had denied Clegg's criticism that the new stadium would be too small; and she ignored the scientific evidence that the 'sight line' of only very few spectators would be obstructed. Kate Hoey wanted to believe Clegg. Subsequently, his role would be condemned by a parliamentary committee for having 'exercised an influence on the Wembley national stadium which has not been justified, an influence exercised ironically to the detriment of athletics'. But by then Clegg could claim victory.

On 1 December 1999, Chris Smith invited Derek Casey and Bob Stubbs to read the Ellerbe Becket report in the Houses of Parliament. Within just two weeks, the American consultants had been expected to examine 1,000 drawings and computer models. By their own admission, it had been an impossible task, but political necessity had smothered practicalities. Just thirty minutes after entering the room, Casey and Stubbs were told by an official that Smith was about to announce to the House of Commons that Ellerbe Becket had revealed 'five serious problems' for athletics at Wembley, especially the 'sight lines'. The minister appeared willing to torpedo the FA's project on the basis of a hastily commissioned consultant's report. 'I was shocked,' recalled Stubbs, 'that Smith used such a piece of work to justify a decision and say our plans were fundamentally flawed.' Others dubbed Smith's behaviour 'madness'. Most assumed that the minister, unable to grasp the mathematical calculations, had panicked. Smith rejected that impression: 'I believed that it was important to share my concerns with the House at the earliest moment. I've learned on the job. Is that a bad thing?' Smith would be criticized by a parliamentary committee for confusion and inaccuracies, and by others for behaving 'impulsively' and 'like a butterfly'.

On 22 December, Smith formally told the House of Commons that athletics would not be part of Wembley. Jubilant, Kate Hoey began campaigning for a dedicated athletics track at Picketts Lock in north-east London as the venue for the World Championships in 2005. Cast off, Wembley became a battleground between Westminster and football's personalities. Bates was a common target.

In the collision of interests, Chris Smith, Tony Banks, James Purnell, Andy Burnham and even Alastair Campbell recognized that Labour's policy for football had become 'a mess'. Within just two years, their dream of reforming football was crumbling. 'We've given full support for 2006, for Wembley and for an Olympic bid,' complained one of the special advisers, 'and all we've got in return is football discrediting us and the Task Force. It's all one way. Football is in charge. We've made a mistake.' Downing Street's special adviser sensed uncertainty, even disorientation: 'The FA's in a mess, the Premier League is greedy and we haven't achieved our manifesto commitments.' The plans to distribute money from the Premier League to the grass roots and to create an independent regulator were unfulfilled. The government's disillusion delighted football's administrators. Their business was on the verge of an important victory: to be free of any interference.

8

THE FA: MASTERS OF DELUSION

The vitriol was blatant and mutual. Football's aristocrats were contemptuous of their critics and, in return, were despised for demanding unconditional victory. The leaders of the Football Association and the Premier League were condemned by Lord Faulkner as 'venal' and 'egoist'. In reply they damned Faulkner, the vice-chairman of the Football Trust, as 'grubby' and 'unreliable'. In the middle were Labour ministers and their special advisers. Their battle was over the appointment of an independent regulator for football.

'Surely it's inconceivable that the government would allow itself to be blackmailed by the football authorities in this way?' Richard Faulkner challenged Chris Smith. The Labour peer was outraged by the Premier League's ultimatum to enfeeble the proposed regulator – 'Should the government proceed with this weak and biased Establishment lapdog, it would be against the wishes of football supporters.' Faulkner's critics had good reason to fear independent scrutiny.

In March 2000, the battle to regulate football was reaching a climax. The astonishingly abusive acrimony had intensified after the warring factions on the Task Force failed to agree on a unanimous recommendation. Disagreements had become personalized after Richard Scudamore proposed an Independent Scrutiny Panel. 'How will it work?' asked Adam Brown, the academic. 'I don't know,' replied Scudamore flippantly. 'This is arrogant and ridiculously weak,' countered Brown in dismay. 'Scudamore is outrageous,' declared Faulkner in September 1999. 'He's accelerating the polarization between the Premier League and the rest, damaging the national sport.'

Their sentiments towards Mike Lee, Scudamore's consultant, were similar. 'Mike Lee's a nasty piece of work,' cursed Adam Brown, suspecting that Lee had sought to ridicule the Task Force. An 'anonymous' insider had told the *Daily Telegraph* that a 64-page draft on 'commercial issues' 'is riddled with embarrassing typing mistakes, factual errors and historical inaccuracies, and has so infuriated the football authorities that they intend to rewrite it from top to bottom'. Lee firmly denied his culpability, although he openly blamed David Mellor's 'confrontational and opinionated chairmanship' of the Task Force for alienating the Professional Footballers Association, the Premier League and the FA. The Premier League chairmen, revealed Lee, were 'fed up with Mellor' and demanded that he should be 'removed'. Lee complained that Mellor's suggestion of a regulator with powers of investigation and expulsion, 'would be like having cuckoos in the nest'.

David Mellor had also become disillusioned. Uniting the professional football organizations with the fans, he lamented, would have been 'beyond the Archangel Gabriel'. Those involved in football, he sighed, quoting Dr Johnson, 'are fair-minded people. They never speak well of each other.' In particular, he was irritated by James Purnell. At recent meetings Downing Street's special adviser had rarely spoken and refused to persuade football's aristocrats to honour the process. 'You're willing to wound but not to strike,' Mellor told Purnell, suspicious of a cosy deal between Downing Street and the football authorities. 'You're letting football off the hook.'

The mood had changed since Mellor's appointment as chairman of the Task Force. Lee's bombardment of Downing Street had been effective. Many Labour politicians who had accepted the invitations from the FA and Premier League to hospitality at the major football matches, especially at Wembley, had fallen for the argument that football was a sport, not a monopoly business that should be controlled by a Football Regulation Bill. Alastair Campbell's will to challenge football's aristocrats had diminished. The brokers of the retreat were James Purnell and Andy Burnham, recently appointed as Chris Smith's special adviser.

Elements in this resistance to change were money and patronage. The money was to fund the new Football Foundation, inheriting the mantle of the Football Trust; and the patronage was the appointment of the chairman of the Foundation.

At the beginning of 1999, the Premier League had agreed to pay a levy on the income from Sky to support football in the community. The size of the levy had not been agreed and many, including Richard Scudamore, disliked the commitment. Informally, the Premier League threatened to withhold any money until the government excluded the notion of a regulator. A crisis meeting was convened on 16 December 1999 in Downing Street. James Purnell and Andy Burnham discussed the threat with Dave Richards and Mike Lee of the Premier League.

In the midst of their argument, at Alastair Campbell's request, Tony Blair passed through the room. The noise abated. The government, said the prime minister, would pay 5 per cent towards the Football Foundation if the Premier League agreed to the same. 'OK,' agreed Richards, committing the Premier League to contribute £80 million over three years. We've achieved the unthinkable, thought Burnham.

The next step, the appointment of the Foundation's chairman, was a sensitive issue. Richard Faulkner, the vice-chairman of the Football Trust for eleven years, expected the position. His unexpected rival was Tom Pendry. By mid-1999, Pendry had become disillusioned with Westminster and decided to retire at the next election. He hoped to receive a peerage and the chairmanship of the Foundation as a reward for his services. Both required the approval of Tony Blair. The recommendation to the prime minister would be influenced by James Purnell who, coincidentally, was searching for a parliamentary seat. Conveniently, Pendry introduced Purnell to the committee of his own constituency of Stalybridge and Hyde. Pendry endorsed Purnell's qualities. Soon after Purnell won the nomination, and Pendry was appointed the Foundation's chairman. His office was located in the FA's headquarters. Not surprisingly, he became antagonistic towards an independent regulator.

Pendry's appointment infuriated Richard Faulkner, angry about his exclusion from any official position in football's politics and by Pendry's opposition towards a regulator. 'I want,' said Faulkner, 'a wholly independent, powerful, permanent body able to scrutinize clubs directly and where necessary undertake investigations to ban offshore ownership like Chelsea's.' The football aristocrats criticized Faulkner for showing 'naked hostility'.

His ambition, it was whispered, was to be appointed the regulator.

The venom prevented the Task Force agreeing about a regulator. Pleas by Purnell and Burnham for a compromise failed. Two reports were written. One by the football authorities, a minority on the Task Force, promised an 'Independent Scrutiny Panel' without powers or sanctions; while the report of the majority, by Mellor, Faulkner and Brown, recommended an investigative regulator – an Independent Football Commission – who would be 'independent of any direct involvement in the game'.

James Purnell was outrightly hostile to a regulator. In his report to Tony Blair, he mentioned how football 'hated outsiders' questioning, influencing or instructing them about their business. New Labour, he advised, should not be minded to antagonize the national sport by imposing a semi-independent regulator suggestive of a Soviet, nanny state. Instead, he suggested that the government should support self-regulation to change football's culture. The message from Purnell to Chris Smith and Andy Burnham was blunt: 'it is a delusion that football will ever be regulated by the government or an independent official digging deep'. The publication of two reports, an inevitable embarrassment, was compounded by the revolt of Kate Hoey.

On the evening of 21 December 1999, the day before publication of the reports, Kate Hoey called at David Mellor's home. The reformers in the Task Force, Hoey believed, were Labour's true allies. Confronting the football establishment over the appointment of an independent regulator was the cornerstone of purging football of over-commercialization and corruption. She disparaged Chris Smith, her superior minister, as indecisive, without any understanding or qualifications to challenge the football authorities. 'He's all over the place, only interested in himself, loves worship, and is anxious to please Blair,' she complained. The presence of Andy Burnham, a passionate football supporter, within her department inflamed Kate Hoey's suspicions. Once, frustrated by Hoey's 'unhelpfulness', James Purnell had sought to change her mind by arranging a telephone call to her from Anji Hunter, the prime minister's personal assistant, to confirm: 'This is what the PM thinks.' The admonition had failed. That night, against her own government, Hoey encouraged Mellor's campaign for an independent regulator.

The following day, 22 December 1999, Kate Hoey did not attend the launch of the reports at the Atrium in the Millbank Tower, near Westminster. 'She just refused to come. Not her baby,' sniped Purnell about a woman criticized as a non-team-player. Hoey's absence confirmed that the government had shifted away from the fans. 'A sorry state of affairs,' sighed David Mellor, aggrieved that no one even bothered at the end to thank him for his work. In that surreal atmosphere, Purnell and Burnham promoted the FA's 'minority report' as 'progress' while dismissing the 'majority report' as 'recommendations by other members'. As journalists moved forward to interview Mellor and Brown about the split, Mike Lee intervened to give the 'official' version. Lee knew the battle was nearly won. Sidelining Mellor had been an important victory for the football aristocrats. But Lee's celebration was premature.

The counter-attack was launched on 1 March 2000. Adam Brown and ten others wrote to Tony Blair urging the government to appoint an independent regulator as recommended by the majority report. Blair's reply was to be delivered by Chris Smith, who in turn consulted

Richard Scudamore. Downing Street's desire to satisfy the football authorities would be met by Scudamore's proposals. The sport, said Scudamore, on 16 March, would only support an Independent Football Commission (IFC) appointed by the Premier League and Football Association. But, according to some, he pledged not to veto any candidate for chairmanship associated with the Task Force. Smith agreed that was ideal. 'The supporters won't like this,' protested Adam Brown. 'I'm not interested in the supporters,' replied Chris Smith.

Chris Smith's public announcement in April 2000 endorsed Scudamore's blueprint for a regulator. As window-dressing, Smith emphasized the IFC's purpose to improve football's 'transparency and accountability', to reduce the costs of tickets and to control merchandising. Deftly, the politician glossed over the proposed regulator's impotence – his lack of authority to undertake investigations or impose sanctions. The majority faction in the Task Force prepared to retaliate in the final battle: the nomination of the IFC's chairman. Their last attempt to impose controls on the football business depended upon that appointment.

Richard Faulkner offered himself as a candidate. To his admirers, he was a man who 'tried to do the right thing'. On 5 April 2000, Adam Crozier, the new chief executive of the FA, and Richard Scudamore promised Faulkner that neither would veto his selection or even seek to influence the appointment. That appeared to confirm Scudamore's pledge to ministers three weeks earlier. With that 'welcome' assurance, Faulkner bubbled to Kate Hoey that his selection was guaranteed due to 'my excellent relationship with Adam Crozier'.

Faulkner had good reason to believe in Crozier. Unlike Graham Kelly, Crozier presented himself as a powerbroker with commercial experience, despite leaving the Telegraph Group's advertising department amid rancour. At the FA, he was applauded by David Dein, his mentor, and by Peter Ridsdale, as a professional who would introduce the reforms ignored by the previous regime, including a 'financial police' office of four accountants to review clubs' accounts every five years as a 'health check'. Crozier was hailed as a modernizer, yet Faulkner's optimism about the chief executive was misplaced.

During April, Crozier and Scudamore reconsidered their undertaking. The chairmen of the Premier League would not tolerate any challenge to their autocracy. Faulkner, some antagonistic members had warned, would cause trouble. 'He's not decent,' complained Rick Parry. 'He's a grubby individual, too conflicted, wearing three hats: lobbying for the Football Trust, the Labour government and for his PR firm.' The sight of Faulkner entertaining Labour party grandees in the royal box at Wembley had irritated those who complained, 'Faulkner got his peerage on the back of football.' To help disable any regulator Scudamore decided to ignore what others claimed to be his pledge to the ministers on 16 March and veto any candidate who had been connected with the Task Force. 'There are limits,' Scudamore told Kate Hoey on 20 June 2000. He later denied ever offering the pledge. The exception, added Scudamore, was Sir John Smith, who had not been identified with the Task Force and 'would meet our independence test'. The Premier League, Scudamore concluded, would leave the final decision to the DCMS.

Adam Brown was outraged. Football's veto of Faulkner, Brown warned Purnell, would be 'over my dead body'. By rejecting legislation, Brown told Purnell, the government had allowed the football establishment to 'play an

unscrupulous game and take the upper hand'. All the hard
work on the Task Force, he concluded, had been 'wasted'.
Purnell was unsympathetic. Simply appointing a regulator,
he still believed, would be interpreted as a major achievement in Number 10, although the regulator's status had
changed. His task would not be to remove corruption in
football but to strengthen Scudamore against the chairmen
of the Premier League. Remoulded by that philosophy
Purnell was insensitive to the fact that the prime minister's
selection of Jack Cunningham as the chairman of the proposed IFC would inflame the reformers.

Tony Blair's motives for helping Jack Cunningham, an
ex-minister, dubbed 'Junket Jack', were characteristic; and
Cunningham was unsurprised by the nomination. 'When
I lost my job,' chimed Cunningham, 'Tony promised me
something.' Just prior to losing his cabinet post amid criticism of his competence and luxurious lifestyle,
Cunningham had taken on a mortgage for a new home in
Northumberland. Although he earned £90,000 per annum
for his consultancies in addition to his MP's salary of
£48,371, the hedonist sought more money. Cunningham
had rejected the prime minister's first offer and soon after
James Purnell telephoned to test the water with a second
offer. 'Would you be interested to chair the IFC?' asked
the special adviser. 'Yes, if the terms are right,' replied
Cunningham. Before Blair formally telephoned
Cunningham, it was agreed that the pugnacious fixer
would be paid £25,000 per annum plus £25,000 expenses
and he could naturally also expect free tickets and hospitality at all the matches. The appointment of Jack
Cunningham was supported by the football establishment.
'I would not have been uncomfortable with Cunningham,'
said Rick Parry who, despite his own commitment to
investigating corruption, condemned regulators as 'a bit of

nonsense' and accepted Cunningham as 'safe, straightforward and rather good'. That opinion was endorsed by Richard Scudamore.

Jack Cunningham did not anticipate any resentment when, on 11 September 2000, he met the members of the Task Force for the first meeting in a conference room at the Department for Culture, Media and Sport in Trafalgar Square. Arriving with Sean Coster as his official secretary, Cunningham addressed the small group as subordinates. 'I'll be based at the FA's new headquarters in Soho Square,' he pronounced, 'under the terms of reference agreed to by the FA. I'll be paid by the FA.' Cunningham was insensitive to the frisson of irritation among his audience, unaware that his opening statement undermined their long campaign for an independent regulator. Blithely, he continued to expound that since the FA's total budget was £150,000, there would be no salaries or expenses for the other members. Only he would be paid. 'I'll handle all the press enquiries,' concluded Cunningham. 'Everything will be done through me.' The politician demanded the spotlight.

His audience became hostile. Each sensed that Cunningham identified them as 'mere rubber stamps for decisions taken by Cunningham, Scudamore and Coster'. Adam Brown raised the first doubts: 'What about your relationship with Newcastle?' 'I haven't got one,' snapped Cunningham, an odd denial since his entry in the House of Commons register of interests listed 'gifts, benefits and hospitality' from Newcastle United. Football fans in the north-east bore a serious grievance. Cunningham had recently supported a scheme by Newcastle's directors to deprive 4,000 supporters of their old seats, despite their purchase of bonds to rebuild the ground. Some investors had lost money. The fans' anger had been inflamed by a secretly recorded denunciation of Newcastle's supporters by two directors of the club in a Spanish brothel. Cunningham was unconcerned by the appearance of his partisanship.

'I've got some concerns about your objectivity,' said Sir John Smith, the former police chief who had expected the post, 'if you're located and paid by the FA.' 'I'll be independent,' Cunningham replied curtly. So far as Cunningham was concerned, his appointment was final. Oblivious to the resentment, he departed. 'We've got to get rid of Cunningham,' suggested Faulkner later that day. 'He's so arrogant,' agreed Sir John Smith, voicing the unanimous conclusion. Their plot was to embarrass the government. Lord Faulkner, the lobbyist and ringleader, was still grieving that Tom Pendry had been anointed the chairman of the Football Foundation at a ceremony in Downing Street on 25 July attended by Tony Blair and Kevin Keegan. This latest twist reinforced his conviction that the Premier League was 'blackmailing' the government and making a 'mockery of two-and-a-half-years' work' having 'sold out thousands of football fans'. Kate Hoey, the minister of sport, was a natural ally.

Efficiently, Faulkner organized coverage in the Sunday newspapers of the row with Cunningham. Kate Hoey, Faulkner told his contacts, was 'resisting but needs a lot of help. Chris Smith must be persuaded not to sell out to the Premier League . . . It is vital that John Smith declines to serve and that becomes publicly known asap.' He was pleased with the results: 'Denis [Campbell] and Patrick [Barclay] have done us proud today,' he reported to Kate Hoey.

The letter Faulkner drafted for supporter groups to send to Blair was defiant. The government, he wrote, was participating in 'seedy horse trading with the football establishment . . . It seems that the secretary of state is so concerned about not offending the Premier League that he is prepared to entirely exclude the wishes of football supporters and capitulate to the Premier League's demands.' Faulkner accused Tony Blair and Chris Smith of 'siding with the establishment whom the Task Force was set up to reform'. The proposed IFC, he protested to the prime minister, is a 'weak and biased establishment lapdog'.

Purnell and Burnham were furious. The revolt against Cunningham meant that they had failed to deliver Downing Street's agreement with Scudamore and Crozier. Principle had interfered with philistinism. The embarrassing publicity was added to by Faulkner's 'unhelpful' questions in the House of Lords about Cunningham. The special advisers suspected Kate Hoey had briefed her Labour colleague. News had filtered out that Hoey had targeted Faulkner and Scudamore while they were eating in the Barry Room in the House of Lords and that she had picked an argument with Scudamore. The following day, Faulkner sought to broker a compromise.

Over lunch with Adam Crozier on 10 August 2000, Faulkner proposed that if Sir John Smith rather than Cunningham were chairman the Task Force could work with the FA's version of self-regulation. But, warned Faulkner, if the FA and the government persisted with Cunningham, the Task Force would publicly denounce the plan. Crozier was suspicious while Richard Scudamore was scathing. Faulkner, he seethed, had proved himself totally unreliable and was 'not considered to be one of us'. Faulkner's compromise was rejected.

Sir John Smith, a fundamentally decent public servant, was agitated. Richard Faulkner, he decided, was

right. The government should impose statutory regulation on football. In a letter on 19 September 2000 to Sean
Coster at the DCMS, Sir John Smith declared his refusal
to participate in the IFC on the FA's terms or with
Cunningham as chairman: 'We are gravely concerned at
the way that [football's] reputation for integrity and fair
play has diminished over time . . . The football authorities have been found seriously wanting . . . We all have
had our confidence so shaken by the tenor of the initial
meeting.' To forestall a crisis, Chris Smith agreed to meet
John Smith and four others on 3 October 2000.

While the politician and his advisers groped uncertainly to escape their predicament, the resistance of the
Premier League clubs to any outside regulation had stiff-
ened. 'John Smith irritates me beyond belief,' said Parry,
echoing a common complaint. 'His report was superficial,
the product of David Davies saying, "We must be seen to
act." And Smith didn't even bother to come to see me
although I'd spent years on the bungs inquiry. He said he
couldn't get a train to Liverpool because of bad weather.'
A new battle line was drawn.

Chris Smith hated confrontation, but his orders from
Downing Street, relayed through Burnham, were
unequivocal: 'Cunningham is immovable. He's furious.
He refuses to resign. And he demands that his chairmanship be announced.' Obediently, Chris Smith repeated to
his visitors that Cunningham had been chosen as 'a result
of a "cross-departmental" decision. The choice cannot
be questioned and it is therefore irrevocable.' Sir John
Smith's written reply was equally unyielding: 'That being
the case, we feel unable to play any further part. We do
this with deep regret.'

The minister asked Burnham for guidance. Burnham
in turn consulted Purnell. Both agreed that Cunningham

had lost the media battle and 'should be dumped'. Their method was painless. Philippa Drew, the civil servant, was ordered to announce on 26 October 2000 that the appointment of a regulator required adherence to the Nolan principles of formally advertising and interviewing the candidates. Cunningham's appointment was smartly airbrushed from history. The two special advisers sought revenge. 'This isn't a crisis,' Purnell and Burnham agreed, 'but it's a pain and we're not going to reward John Smith for his putsch.' Sir John Smith's comment – 'the Premier League needs to be less selfish and consider the wider interest of football' – categorized him as the enemy. The advisers' message to Crozier and Scudamore was reassuring for the football cabal: 'Sir John Smith is unreliable, difficult and has effectively blackmailed us.' Neither cared to consider that the former deputy commissioner of Scotland Yard was an incorruptible public servant and was standing his ground in a tough environment. He was disqualified out of fear that he might become effective. Sir John Smith was not told about the veto; instead, he was encouraged to apply to become the IFC's chairman. In a telephone call by Scudamore to Sir John, who was visiting Kansas City in America, the football executive allayed the former police chief's suspicions. 'Are you thinking of applying?' asked Scudamore. 'Yes,' replied Smith. 'Good,' soothed Scudamore.

Kate Hoey had been similarly labelled as dangerous. Her public spats with Ken Bates and Richard Scudamore matched her antagonism towards Adam Crozier. She damned the FA executive as a glib, superficial Walter Mitty character. The Labour MP had little sympathy for a marketeer of football whose salary had just been increased by an additional £100,000 to £375,000. She believed he appeared more interested in power than the sport. Other than cup finals and international games, he was infrequently seen at unglamorous League matches across the country. Isolated from the grass roots, she alleged, he was too limited intellectually to understand the inevitability of football's crisis.

Adam Crozier similarly bore no respect for the politician. In particular, he was appalled by her support for the reintroduction of safe terraces in stadiums to allow the young and poor access to football. The Premier League clubs feared loss of income if the seats were removed and, in self-defence, invoked the police's criticism, which blamed terraces for all of football's troubles. Crozier did not want the debate to start and Purnell and Burnham were ready to oblige. On the eve of Kate Hoey releasing a report advocating the reintroduction of safe terraces, Burnham sent the Press Association a statement in Chris Smith's name criticizing the proposals for 'adding nothing new'. After discovering that Burnham had checked 'Smith's statement' with the Premier League before its release to the Press Association, Kate Hoey yelled, 'That's sabotage.' She never spoke to Burnham again. Their dispute delighted the football cabal; Kate Hoey's alienation from Downing Street was emboldening.

Finding a safe regulator was not as easy as Philippa Drew and Richard Scudamore had anticipated. Drew admitted failure after repeatedly 'trawling through the DCMS data base'. To help Drew Scudamore paid Spencer Stuart, the headhunters, £20,000 to produce ten names. Their recommendations included Howard Davies, the City regulator, Sandy Leitch, the chief executive of Zurich Financial Services, Terry Burns, the former permanent secretary at the Treasury, Peter Levene, the chairman of Deutsche Bank, Peter Sutherland, the chairman of British Petroleum, and Keith Oates, chairman of

1. The ambitious Chelsea chairman, Ken Bates

2. Rick Parry, the respected chief executive of Liverpool, is accustomed to the backstabbing among the Premier League's chairmen

3. Arsenal's ambitious vice-chairman David Dein (l) and manager George Graham (r) watch their team play in 1995. Six months later, the FA banned Graham for a year for his acceptance of money from Norwegian agent, Rune Hauge

4. Adam Crozier (r), chief executive of the FA lost the support of Peter Ridsdale (l), chairman of Leeds United, which prompted his resignation in November 2002

5. One of the Big Five, Manchester United's Peter Kenyon (l) with former chairman Martin Edwards who agreed to resign after allegations about his behaviour on 29 November 2002

6&7. 'The Doug Ellis Stand' – a satisfying sight for chairman Doug Ellis at Villa Park, home of Aston Villa FC

9. Richard Scudamore, the chief executive of the Premier League, opposed Labour's proposals to create an independent regulator – beyond the control of the Premier League – to investigate the football business

8. Agent Paul Stretford has said, 'I'm really worried about the lack of professionalism and I am frankly appalled at the behaviour of some of the so-called agents that certain players have signed with'

10. Graham Kelly, former chief executive of the FA, also resented external intervention and criticism. However, he did call for financial monitoring but this was ignored

11. Former Nottingham Forest manager Brian Clough holds a bronze bust of himself. After the FA investigated his purchase of Teddy Sheringham from Tottenham Hotspur in 1994, Clough was charged with misconduct. He retired due to 'deteriorating health'

12. Eddie Ashby was found guilty and imprisoned for helping Terry Venables manage Spurs and a night club in breach of the bankruptcy laws

13. Norwegian agent Rune Hauge admitted to paying money to British managers. His lifetime ban imposed by FIFA in 1995 was reduced on appeal to two years but he carried on operating unhindered

14. Throughout his colourful twenty-five-year career, agent Dennis Roach (centre) has become accustomed to both criticism by irate football managers and scrutiny by the FA, while Sugar and Venables' 'football marriage made in heaven' ended in an acrimonious battle

15. Jerome Anderson, posing with Dennis Bergkamp and Ian Wright, is a passionate Arsenal fan and ranks among the club's most popular agents

16&17. The extravagant ambitions of the Smith brothers (Jon left, Phil right), founders of First Artist agency have aroused controversy

18. Tony Blair plays 'keepy-uppy' with Kevin Keegan, publicizing New Labour's dedication to cleaning up British football

19. Culture Secretary Chris Smith and Sports Minister Kate Hoey. Hoey clashed with football's leading figures over plans for the new Wembley stadium. She was sacked in June 2001

20. Former Conservative MP David Mellor (l) and Labour Sports Minister Tony Banks (r) during a photo opportunity launching the Government's Football Task Force

21. Peter Leaver QC (l), chief executive of the FA Premier League, and Robert Reid QC unveil the Report of the Commission of Enquiry into Transfer Dealings in 1997

22. Graham Bean, a former detective constable, is the solitary symbol of the FA's self-regulation

23. Harry Redknapp, former manager of West Ham, signs copies of his autobiography in which he advocates that those in football 'should make the bucks while you can . . . if there is a chance to earn a few quid, take it because it doesn't last forever'. He told the author, 'Money is not my God'

24. Terry Venables has been investigated and confessed to dishonest behaviour. Nevertheless, in July 2002, he arrived as the new manager at Leeds United, and was hailed as the club's saviour

25. Sir Alex Ferguson welcomes Rio Ferdinand to Manchester United in July 2002 after a record-breaking £30 million transfer fee

Byzantium International. Rejecting their work with deft understatement as 'unhelpful', Drew consulted Chris Smith. He suggested Michael Parkinson, the TV presenter. Drew approached Parkinson and sent an application form. The notion of Michael Parkinson as football's policeman reflected the confusion within the department; they had not anticipated Parkinson's commitment to football journalism.

Bereft of further ideas, Philippa Drew raised the possibility of reconsidering Sir John Smith. That idea, Richard Scudamore declared, was intolerable. 'The football authorities,' Scudamore told her, 'would abandon the IFC proposal if Sir John were to be chosen as first chairman.' In Scudamore's opinion, Sir John Smith's support for the 'majority' Task Force report and his role in Jack Cunningham's demise disqualified his application because of a 'conflict of interest'. The politicians were startled by Scudamore's apparent misunderstanding of the term, 'conflict of interest': the real 'conflicts' were the reasons for appointing a regulator. Government reaction was contradictory. Chris Smith pondered how his department would bow to Scudamore's veto, while Kate Hoey asked Geoff Thompson, the FA's chairman, for his reaction to Scudamore's 'amazing statement' to 'oppose John Smith and the entire proposal'.

There was no reply from Thompson. The neat solution, the football executives decided, was to follow the procedures and formally interview Sir John Smith for the post. 'Are we wasting our time being here?' asked Smith during the interview. He looked directly at Scudamore who had remained silent throughout. 'Oh no,' replied Drew. 'We are all independent.' That evening, Scudamore telephoned Smith at home. 'Please realize that there's nothing personal in this,' said Scudamore in a

voice which the former deputy commissioner recognized
from his career chasing criminals. Unpleasant, thought
Sir John; he felt unusually debased. Scudamore was defiant. Defeating Sir John Smith, Lord Faulkner and their
accomplices, it appeared, removed an unsightly wart from
the Premier League's bid to present a smooth image.

Six years earlier, Tony Blair and Alastair Campbell
had raged about Andy Cole's transfer for £7 million. The
latest transfer fees made Andy Cole's price tag look like a
pittance, and football's warlords were inflicting further
embarrassments on the government.

The estimated cost of Wembley's reconstruction had
risen again; on this occasion from £475 million in early
2000 to £660 million. The cost of the actual stadium was,
according to Ken Bates, fixed at £316 million, the extra
millions were for the site and to develop the surrounding
infrastructure. Bates, as the representative of the FA, had
immersed the project in controversy.

At the beginning of the year, two English contractors had complained about the 'adversarial' tendering
process, mentioning the 'change of culture' by Wembley
National Stadium Ltd (WNSL) under Bates's chairmanship. There was no reaction from Chris Smith's
office. Preoccupied by the bid for the 2006 World Cup,
Smith and his officials had also overlooked another concern: the company had named Multiplex of Australia as
the preferred contractor, the same company responsible
for completing the stadium at Chelsea. No one in
Whitehall queried the failure of the WNSL directors to
offer the contract to public tender despite the use of
public money. A subsequent investigation would report
a 'perception . . . that the process had not been entirely
fair'. Consistent with the familiar customs of the football business, others mentioned 'possible conflicts of

interest' and a 'risk . . . in the highest possible standards of transparency'.

Ken Bates was untroubled by those perceptions, scorning a consultant's review that the directors of the project 'may have been misled' about important negotiations with the contractors. Bates's brazenness undermined his credibility. Some senior board members of the FA believed that Ken Bates's experience as a property developer was proving inadequate to manage the Wembley project. Although the business plan, prepared by Investec and Chase Manhattan, two merchant banks, endorsed Bates's confidence about his 'first-class design with a first-class builder', his presentation to 300 City experts at Chelsea's stadium had been unconvincing and his problems were growing. The dotcom bubble was bursting and the stock market had begun to slide. The project's bankers had made mistakes. Bates, with a talent for insulting those whose sympathy he required, could not staunch the growing pessimism.

The changing sentiment was influenced by the repeated refusal of Adam Crozier to deliver signed contracts committing the FA to using Wembley, its own project. Without those agreements Wembley was not guaranteed an income and the banks were unwilling to loan money on realistic terms. 'Crozier's excuse,' complained Bates, 'was that the agreements were delayed by the lawyers.' Some politicians were delighted by Bates's failures but the responsibility was Adam Crozier's and the FA's. Repeatedly, the directors of the project ignored warnings from Tropus, hired as project managers, about 'irregularities'. 'The Wembley fiasco wouldn't be happening,' Kate Hoey told the prime minister, 'if we hadn't bid for the World Cup.' The FA had become entangled in another problem of its own making.

Labour's manifesto in 1997 had committed the government to support the FA's bid to host the World Cup in 2006. Two years later, seventeen full-time staff and an international manager on secondment from the Foreign Office were helping Tony Banks, Alec McGivan and England's football stars to visit over twenty countries, some more than once. Bobby Charlton and Geoff Hurst were paid £300,000 and £200,000 each as retainers, plus fees and expenses for each foreign visit. In 1999, FIFA executives and members of their technical committee were welcomed to England in ostentatious style. Housed in five-star hotels, they were taken on shopping trips, visits to the theatre and entertained at Hampton Court before meeting Tony Blair and the Prince of Wales. The prime minister was always available for important photo-calls. The financial investment was substantial, provoking internecine bickering.

Kate Hoey was a principal opponent, who believed that Bert Millichip had undertaken not to bid for the World Cup and recoiled about public money being wasted on hype, receptions for foreign delegations, vast expenses spent by Tony 'the minister of tickets' Banks, and government planes and helicopters. Her anger spilt over into apparent sabotage. Ignoring Downing Street's authorization, she refused to sign letters to the Ministry of Defence requesting the aircraft. Livid that Alec McGivan appeared to have direct access to Downing Street, she sniped to the *Evening Standard* of London, 'McGivan is treated like God.' Everything Kate Hoey was told by Banks appeared to be reported in the *Daily Telegraph*. Chris Smith, she alleged, was 'bending the rules' in negotiations with hotels. 'I just resented the way we seemed to be lowering the standards while Chris Smith didn't want to challenge things that were wrong,'

Hoey complained. 'He always looked for the easy way out.' Her invective sparked retaliation. Chris Smith telephoned and demanded an apology to McGivan. James Purnell criticized Kate Hoey as 'unhelpful'. Banks criticized her as 'disloyal'. The personal antagonism was mutual. Kate Hoey's opposition to the bid was not unique. Many in England believed Germany's version, rather than Bert Millichip's, of his conversation in 1993 in Las Vegas.

Although in public Alec McGivan had no choice but to support Millichip's version that there was no deal at Las Vegas, in private he seemed less certain telling Jo Gibbons, his press officer, 'there could have been a deal but there's nothing on the record'. The pretence was self-defeating. 'It's an albatross which will not go away,' complained Tony Banks in private about the 'conversation'. Banks's limitations as a special envoy had also become apparent – the socialist resented the process of lobbying powerbrokers at FIFA. 'It's a gentlemen's club,' he scorned. 'So many people in football loathe each other but smile and kiss when they meet. They know how to behave in public and how to conceal their hatred.' Banks, accustomed to Westminster intrigue, was especially disdainful of Franz Beckenbauer, the smooth-talking German champion who applauded capitalism. Sophisticated foreign sportsmen appeared to be anathema to English socialists. Banks also resented the FA, which he discovered was staffed by unlovable and pompous officials excluded from the centres of power in the international game.

The disappearance of Graham Kelly, whose shy manner was a nuisance to the bid, had been blessed as an advantage by Tony Banks and Alec McGivan, but both similarly lacked the experience to broker international deals. McGivan, a Labour supporter but 'not a heavy hitter', was unfamiliar with the politics of international football. Bereft of personal relationships with foreign football associations, the director of the bid focused on individual FIFA representatives, oblivious to the influence exercised in those countries by government ministers and the leaders of the national football organizations. While praised by his detractors for organizing the nameplates and serviettes at the grand dinners, McGivan was criticized for lacking an overall strategy. Haplessly he and Banks watched South Africa secure Latin America's support while Germany negotiated Asia's votes. 'We haven't got enough cards in our hand,' lamented Banks, blaming the FA's 'lack of clout' on England's refusal to bribe like some other countries. 'We are unwilling to be corrupt,' he announced proudly. 'We are too accountable for rules and unwilling to put women and cash into delegates' rooms.' Yet the notion that English, unlike European, football was clean ignored the evidence that the transfers of some players in England had been accompanied by 'bungs' and that Graham Kelly had been recently dismissed for the secret inducement offered to the Welsh FA. Consistent with that self-delusion, the FA decided to compete with its rivals by contributing £1 million to a football training school in the Caribbean and to finance the employment of a coach and the staging of a youth tournament in Thailand. Those votes, it was hoped, would neutralize the alienation of UEFA's delegates by England's support for Sepp Blatter rather than Lennart Johansson during the voting for a new president of FIFA.

At the beginning of 2000, Banks, McGivan and the FA believed, despite the uncertainty of Wembley's reconstruction, that England's bid would be successful. Their conviction ceased on 16 June 2000 after outbreaks of hooliganism among English fans in Belgium. Six days later Banks and McGivan flew to New York to meet three FIFA members whose support was crucial. 'England cannot win,' they were told. During their return journey, the two men agreed to recommend that England's bid should be withdrawn. In his presentation to the FA on 27 June 2000, Banks revealed that besides losing votes because of hooliganism, seven out of the eight European nations with votes on FIFA would support Germany's bid. Banks's report was contradicted by Bobby Charlton who said that withdrawal would be associated with hooliganism and would permanently scar English football. That opinion was endorsed by Adam Crozier. 'We want to carry on,' David Davies told Banks. The FA still believed that England enjoyed more support than Germany. Banks was incredulous. The FA's leaders were truly pitiful and deluded; the managers of English football were their own worst enemies.

Hours later, Banks appealed personally to Blair in his private office at the House of Commons. 'We've got no chance,' he urged. 'Even if it's a manifesto commitment we've got to withdraw the bid.' It was agreed that Banks would again urge the FA to withdraw. Adam Crozier and the FA again refused. Loyally, Banks agreed to continue the battle on the FA's behalf.

All the weaknesses of English football coalesced in that decision and its implementation. The previous criticism of Graham Kelly as naive could similarly be directed at Adam Crozier. The insularity of England's football establishment was reconfirmed. The delusion that their failure to build one stadium at Wembley would not reflect upon their ability to organize a whole competition demonstrated their limitations. English football's crudity was displayed in the days before FIFA's decisive vote on 5 July 2000.

In a preliminary meeting the eight UEFA countries met in Luxembourg. After three years of 'living and breathing the bid', Banks argued his case gracelessly. Unless UEFA supported England, warned the politician, the World Cup would be awarded to South Africa. There was a stony silence, not least because before 1997 Banks had supported South Africa's bid. 'You haven't bothered to read England's submission,' continued Banks. 'You've got closed minds if you only bother with Germany's bid.' Insults might be successful in Labour party caucuses, but in Luxembourg Tony Banks had committed a tactical disaster. 'That's an insult to Germany,' Lennart Johansson said calmly.

The English bid was resoundingly defeated yet the lesson had still not been learnt. In Zürich the following day Banks's tactics were more unusual. He and McGivan briefed journalists that because England was promised more support than Germany, South Africa was certain to win after a split vote. In private conversations, the English lobbyists also whispered about South Africa's perils and how football matches in the dark continent were played on mud pitches. The shock for the whisperers, just before the announcement of the final decision, was the publication of FIFA's technical report. England's facilities were ranked third behind Germany and South Africa. Compared to England South Africa was judged to possess superior transport, telecommunications, security and stadiums. 'We were spitting blood about the total stitch-up,' Banks admitted. 'It's a scandal,' agreed McGivan.

Their naivety remained uncured; they retained their optimistic belief in Sepp Blatter's assurance to support

England. In the contest between Lennart Johansson and Blatter, the Swedish president of UEFA had collected the European, Gulf and some Asian votes; Blatter had secured the support of Africa and South America. England's largesse to win Thailand's support failed: Worawi Makudi, the Thai delegate, owned a Mercedes franchise in Bangkok and supported Germany. Sepp Blatter returned England's support for his presidential bid by arguing South Africa's case. England's humiliation was complete. The truth was buried in Downing Street. 'It was a big mistake,' James Purnell admitted, 'to think we could win. We did not understand the international politics of football.'

The credulousness of Purnell and Andy Burnham remained, both believed that the removal of the discredited old guard – Kelly, Wiseman and Leaver – had revolutionized English football. They thought that the replacement of the men wearing blazers by the money-men enjoying hand-to-hand combat ought to have guaranteed England's success. Only Kate Hoey was impenitent. The distress in Downing Street, she gloated, was 'huge'. Blair, Campbell and Purnell had been misled. Finally they understood the agenda of those involved in the FA. At last, she believed, all three would be cautious about further involvement with football. Wembley was the first casualty.

In November 2000, thirty banks rejected Ken Bates's business plan for the new stadium. Bates's notion that the hotel and conference facilities located in a remote industrial zone could be profitable was derided. Forlornly, Bates sought allies but discovered that he was spurned by Crozier and a chorus condemning his plans as 'grandiose'. The mood was turning hostile. His own club's net debts were doubling from £37.5 million to

£66.9 million, with an overall debt of £140 million. Turnover had fallen by £13 million to £93.6 million, and the company's trading losses, caused by the two unsuccessful hotels and five restaurants, were rising by £3.5 million to £11.1 million. Most damning of Bates's commercial weaknesses was his sale of only three of the stadium's fourteen corporate boxes, offered at £1 million per year. His dream of a profitable club was shattering. Chelsea's share price was falling from £1.20 towards 30 pence, valuing the company at £52 million. Everything was turning sour, including the football team's fortunes.

A damaging critic was Tropus, the project management consultant for Wembley stadium. In the consultant's subsequent submissions to a House of Commons committee they expressed surprise that Bob Stubbs, the chief executive of WNSL, had advanced money to Multiplex, the Australian contractors, on the basis of a letter submitted on 1 September 2000 by the contractor. According to Tropus's submission, Stubbs had ignored the legal consequences of the letter. In Tropus's opinion, without any suggestion of illegality or impropriety, Multiplex used the letter to exploit its position and increased the cost of its work from £316 million to above £400 million. Stubbs vehemently denied those criticisms. Nevertheless, the apparent mismanagement of the project influenced the banks' final refusal to provide any loans. Bates lost the confidence of the FA. In a bruising confrontation with Crozier and other club chairmen Bates was removed from his chairmanship of Wembley's development company on 8 December 2000. Retreating 'very hurt', his humiliation was welcomed by his adversaries. 'The FA,' said Chris Smith, 'made a mistake giving Wembley to Bates. There was no sense that they took a grip on what was happening.' Kate Hoey was more damning: 'Bates is a bully. He embarrasses people. It's a tragedy that years have been wasted, but I know what we did was right.' The politicians barked too quickly.

To the government's irritation, financial experts disproved their criticism. Sir Rodney Walker, a building engineer, appointed by the FA to save Wembley's reconstruction, endorsed Bates's business plan as 'largely sound if the luxury bells and whistles are removed'. Without the hotel, offices and banqueting facilities, Walker reported, the original plan was feasible. Two years later an independent quantity surveyor judged the design of the stadium to be 'value for money'. The hiatus had been caused by Bates's manner and his style of management. To government ministers, the confusion confirmed the FA's incompetence and Adam Crozier corroborated their fears in his own words.

In his after-dinner speech to Lancing College old boys at a London hotel in March 2001, Crozier attacked greedy agents, insolvent clubs and a culture of 'fear, suspicion and mistrust' inside the FA. His inheritance from Kelly, he said, was 'the biggest shambles I've ever seen'. To avoid the blame for mistakes, he disclosed, decisions within the FA had been indefinitely delayed. The state of the English clubs was equally bad. 'Fifty per cent of all the professional clubs in Britain,' he revealed, 'are technically insolvent. They are bust.' The examples Crozier chose to demonstrate the iniquities within English football were stark. An unnamed Liverpool player had paid a fine of £80,000 in advance to Gérard Houllier to be released from training; and there was suspected corruption in Aston Villa's purchase of Juan Pablo Angel, because only £2 million of the £9 million ($12.5 million) transfer fee was paid to his club, while the remainder was taken by agents.

Crozier's portrayal of English football was accurate, but to placate the uproar he later apologized.

There was good reason to question clubs' finances. The dream financed by Sky had soured. English football had attracted a lot of money but also huge debts in pursuit of glory. Financial results in 2000 and forecasts for 2001 proved the precariousness of the business. While Manchester United's shares at 400 pence each valued the company in March 2000 at £1 billion, its profits slid that year from £22.4 million to £16.7 million and the club's value would be halved. Chelsea was valued at £413 million in 2000 on a turnover of £76.7 million with losses of £3.5 million and debts of £37.5 million. In 2001, Chelsea lost £6.83 million on falling turnover and accumulated an overall debt of £140 million. The club's share price fell further towards 16 pence. Bates dismissed the criticism of his financial management as 'lurid' and 'nonsense' and affirmed his 'excellent' position, but his aggressive gloss could not impede the developing crisis.

Leeds, on a turnover of £57 million, had debts of £21 million rising to £37.5 million in 2001 and £78 million in 2002. (In September 2001, Leeds's losses were £7.6 million on a record turnover of £86 million.) The company was valued on the stock exchange at £35 million but its players were valued at £198 million. On flotation the club's share price was 19 pence but by mid-2002 the price had slid to 7 pence. Newcastle's debts in 2001 rose from £46.6 million to £65.8 million and its share price fell from £1.35 in April 1997 towards 21 pence. In 2000, Liverpool spent £40 million on wages and costs on a turnover of £46.6 million. In 2001, the club spent £48.8 million from a higher turnover of £82.3 million. Charlton's share price fell from 80 pence in 1997 towards 17 pence. Playing in Europe had become vital to the financial health of spendthrift clubs, but only the Big Five could be likely to qualify and there were no guarantees. In 1999, Manchester United earned £26 million from the European Champions League. In 2002, that income was uncertain. Bolstered by merchandising and full attendance at its huge stadium, Manchester United could nevertheless effortlessly survive but other clubs lacked those resources. To prevent the anticipated financial crisis required common sense and leadership.

New Labour's relationship with English football had become a liability, damaging many reputations including Chris Smith's. Fearing his dismissal after the imminent general election, Smith seemed willing to humiliate the FA. On 24 April 2001, Adam Crozier had written to the DCMS concerning the finance of Wembley stadium suggesting a 'partnership' with the government. In return for guaranteeing a £30 million loan from the banks, the FA asked the government to contribute a subsidy of £150 million. Crudely, Crozier offered to keep any agreement 'under wraps' until after the election. The begging letter, in the opinion of those disenchanted in Whitehall, confirmed the unreliability of a relationship with the FA. A public divorce, officials calculated, could prove advantageous. To embarrass the FA, Smith's department leaked Crozier's letter to a newspaper at the beginning of May 2001, for publication on 6 May. That marked the end of New Labour's love affair with football. Football, it was implicitly agreed, would no longer receive the government's embrace. For the football business, that was a good deal; self-regulation suited the mavericks.

Two days after the Labour government's re-election on 7 June 2001, Chris Smith and Kate Hoey were dismissed. 'Was it Wembley?' Hoey asked Blair on the telephone. 'Is that the reason?' 'No,' replied the prime minister. 'It's no reflection on the work you've done, Kate. I just have to make room for new people.' Kate Hoey cried. Blair lacked the courage to be honest.

On the same day, Andy Burnham and James Purnell were taking congratulatory calls from friends. Both special advisers had been elected to parliament. Their contribution towards Labour's football policy had been rewarded. Among those grateful for their retreat were football's magnates and those aspiring to wealth. Without a regulator, football's aristocracy could behave as if in the Wild West.

THE MANAGER: HARRY REDKNAPP

Even among hardened football fans the transfer of Rio Ferdinand from West Ham to Leeds on 25 November 2000 for £18 million provoked sensational gossip. Not only was £18 million a record for a British defender, but the roll-call of those involved raised questions about the process of the negotiations and disbursement of the money. The absence of an independent regulator permitted the colourful participants in the transaction to plead confidentiality and disappear. The gossip, however, persisted.

The focus was on Harry Redknapp, the raucous manager of West Ham. Born in London's East End on 2 March 1947, Redknapp was the son of a docker who, after his apprenticeship at West Ham's youth academy, became an acknowledged football player and successfully passed the ball to the legendary Geoff Hurst. The former barrow boy and aspiring second-hand car dealer was appointed a club coach. In 1994, he was appointed West Ham's manager, a living symbol, portraying all the traditions of English football.

Football and money were Harry Redknapp's preoccupation during his seven years' management of West Ham.

The pugnacious Cockney frequently boasted that other than Sandra, his blonde wife, football was his 'obsession'. No one doubted his love of football. In Harry Redknapp's life that passion nearly equalled his ambition for personal wealth. 'At the end of the day,' he pontificated with sincerity, 'no one gives a monkey's about you once your career's over so in my view you should make the bucks while you can.' In Redknapp's view a manager's insecurity justified greed. 'Do your best,' Redknapp recommended, 'don't rip anybody off on the way, but if there's a chance to earn a few quid, take it because it doesn't last for ever.'

Harry Redknapp was emphatic that he had never taken a 'bung' or that as an established gambler he deserved the sobriquet 'Readies Redknapp'. Before signing his contract with West Ham, he was told by the club's lawyers to carefully read the 'ferocious clauses' forbidding any secret payments. Their existence provoked Redknapp to declare with unexpected passion, 'I don't need to be greedy like George Graham. I don't need to jeopardize my son's life. I couldn't face my son. Money is not my God.' Redknapp talked much about money. He lived in a palatial house by the sea in Poole near Bournemouth and enjoyed expensive foreign holidays. The contrast between the hang-dog authentic Englishman thanking his 'missus' for making eggs, beans and a cup of tea and the tycoon manager sharing bottles of pink champagne with Ron Atkinson, an idol, suggested a man feeling entitled to take out as much as he put in. Haggling over the price of a player was, in ''Arry the 'Ammer's' opinion, the epitome of astute business. Despite West Ham's limited finances, Redknapp appeared to be obsessed by trading players. One hundred and thirty-four players would be transferred during his seven years of management, an extraordinary number. Like an East End barrow boy, Redknapp loved dealing. No deal was bigger than the sale of Rio Ferdinand, the club's star defender born in November 1978 in Peckham, south London.

In 1999 Ferdinand was in the fourth year of a seven-year contract at West Ham. He was an outstanding product of the club's youth academy, proof that, with proper investment, England could produce world-class players. His annual salary was about £1.5 million. In Redknapp's characteristically outspoken opinion, 'The day I would want to leave West Ham is the day we start wanting to sell the Ferdinands, the Lampards and all them.' Terry Brown, West Ham's chairman, shared his manager's resistance to any suggestion of Ferdinand's departure. The defender was critical to West Ham's recent success, orchestrated by the manager. Redknapp, Brown knew, would vehemently oppose a sale at any price.

Rio Ferdinand's agent was Pinhas 'Pini' Zahavi, a genial and intelligent Israeli with a solid reputation as a discreet deal-maker representing stars. Pini's telephone calls to club chairmen and managers were always answered. He prided himself about his care for Ferdinand and his other clients. 'They're babies,' he laughed. 'They need everything.' Pini had mentioned to Terry Brown in early 1999 a firm offer of £12 million by AC Milan for his player, an offer of £10 million by Liverpool and the 'interest' of Real Madrid. Brown vetoed any sale. 'Could you not delay any move by one year?' asked Brown. Combined with Redknapp's repeated opposition, Pini agreed to defer Ferdinand's move. During those conversations, Pini and Ferdinand also concurred that the player's next move should not be abroad but to one of England's big clubs, possibly Manchester United. Pini and his associate Gustavo Mascardi, an Argentinian who would sell Juan Sebastian Veron to Manchester United, enjoyed excellent relations with Peter Kenyon and Alex Ferguson. 'He wants to come to Manchester United,' Pini repeatedly told Ferguson. 'He dreams of coming to Manchester United. He'll be good for you.' But the Scotsman was emphatic: 'No thanks. I don't want Rio. I've got Wes Brown and he's going to be the best defender in the world.'

On the afternoon of 14 May 2000, Rio Ferdinand proved his value. At Upton Park, West Ham's ground, he helped to humble Leeds in a goalless draw. David O'Leary, the enthusiastic manager of Leeds, was crest-fallen. Leeds was a superior team and he credited Ferdinand's outstanding performance for the humilia-tion. 'Would you be prepared to sell Ferdinand?' he asked Harry Redknapp. 'Don't be daft,' snorted the manager derisively. 'We need Ferdinand,' O'Leary told Peter Ridsdale, the chairman of Leeds, during their return journey to the north of England. Ridsdale nodded wearily. Managers constantly moaned about their wish list, an inevitable burden. 'They'll never sell,' sighed Ridsdale. Unwilling to be rebuffed, O'Leary, a former Arsenal player, pondered how best to breach West Ham's citadel.

A few days later, Rune Hauge, the Norwegian agent, telephoned. His disqualification by FIFA from tem-porarily acting as an agent had caused many English club chairmen and managers to regard Hauge as a pariah. At Everton, Michael Dunford had recently been surprised to receive a telephone call from Hauge stating that he repre-sented Thomas Myhre, a Norwegian goalkeeper who was being offered for transfer after being successively loaned to four clubs. Myhre's agent was Paul Stretford; the player proclaimed that he had severed his connection with Hauge. Inserting himself into deals remained a regular habit for Hauge. Dunford protested but that behaviour did not deter others from continuing their relationship with Hauge, including Alex Ferguson at Manchester United and David O'Leary of Leeds.

Hauge's excuse for telephoning O'Leary at home was Eirik Bakke, a Norwegian attacking midfielder employed by Leeds, whom the agent represented. Hauge knew that O'Leary and Peter Ridsdale were ambitious to compete again in the Champions League. The profit for the club in one year from playing in the competition could be £20 million. In a calculated gamble, Ridsdale planned to borrow £60 million secured against future gate receipts to buy a winning team. A defender was on his shopping list. Hauge was sniffing for business.

'Can I help you with anything else?' Hauge asked O'Leary. 'You can get Rio Ferdinand for me,' laughed O'Leary. Hauge instinctively replied, 'I'm part of the group looking after Rio. I can probably help.' That was untrue. Only Pini Zahavi acted for Rio Ferdinand and he would not share his client with Rune Hauge. O'Leary was unconcerned about the truth. He was receptive to any ruse which overcame the FA's rule forbidding the direct 'tapping' of players under contract.

Despite the agent's notoriety, David O'Leary respected Hauge. Finding and negotiating the purchase of the world's best players required special skills. Not only to fix the price on a commodity lacking any fixed value, but also to massage the vanities and extinguish any outbursts. Above all, Hauge was discreet, not least because of the damnation he had suffered. Unlike other agents, his negotiations rarely appeared in the newspapers. Hauge agreed with O'Leary that Ferdinand was an ideal target and he persuaded O'Leary that he could deliver Ferdinand. O'Leary was aware that the terms for employing Hauge were subject to Peter Ridsdale's agreement. Only the chairman, O'Leary explained, could conclude contracts. 'I never get involved,' he insisted. However, O'Leary could not agree a fee with Hauge but he could authorize the agent to act on the club's behalf to negotiate the terms of a contract. O'Leary says he consulted Ridsdale and, with the chairman's approval, signed on 15 May 2000 the brief authorization submitted by Hauge to Ian Sylvester, the club secretary. A separate letter from Hauge requested 5 per cent commission. Sylvester replied that only 'my chairman' could agree the financial terms but did not offer to secure that approval.

Despite a second letter on 14 July, Hauge failed to receive any written confirmation of the commission from the club. Ridsdale would subsequently insist that he was unaware of Hauge's involvement at that stage, and only discovered Hauge's existence 'a couple of days' before the transfer. But O'Leary and Hauge claim that Ridsdale spoke to the agent at the outset of the negotiations and stipulated that Leeds would offer £12 million for Ferdinand. For his part, Ridsdale offered to pay 5 per cent of the transfer price to Hauge if the deal was completed; and nothing for failure.

O'Leary was unaware of any financial arrangements between Ridsdale and Hauge. After signing the authorization, he rarely spoke to the agent. According to O'Leary, after signing the authorization, 'I was out of the loop'. Sporadically, O'Leary heard from Ridsdale, 'We're pursuing Terry Brown' or, 'West Ham are digging their heels in', but nothing more. Ridsdale, O'Leary had discovered, prided himself on handling financial matters and announcing with a smile, 'I've done the deal. Everything is sorted out.' Potentially, Peter Ridsdale's approval was worth at least £600,000 to Hauge who quickly approached Pini Zahavi.

'Leeds want to make an offer for Rio,' Hauge told Pini. The Israeli was surprised since in his search for a new club, he had never considered Leeds. 'What's your position in this?' asked Pini suspiciously. 'I've got the official authorization,' replied the Norwegian. 'Let me see it,' said Pini. The fax machine produced the evidence. The single sheet was sufficient. 'Talk to Terry Brown,' said Pini. 'We're interested.' For both agents, the potential financial reward was huge, and that alone would excite suspicions. Why, it would be asked, was a transaction between two English clubs initiated between a Norwegian and an Israeli? Could Peter Ridsdale not just telephone Terry Brown? No one could provide a comprehensible answer.

Over the following weeks, Hauge telephoned O'Leary at home to confirm his conversation with Pini, adding a critical ingredient. 'I've spoken to West Ham's chairman,' said Hauge. 'We've got a good chance.' That was incorrect; Terry Brown had been unwilling to speak with Hauge. That rejection did not deter the Norwegian; in football, even the unwelcome could insert themselves into a deal.

Days later, Terry Brown heard disappointing news. 'Rio wants a transfer,' announced Pini Zahavi. Brown was surprised because only recently Ferdinand had mentioned that he would remain at his club. Newspapers had reported that Rio was not for sale; but suddenly the *Mirror* had reported that Rio was being sold to Leeds. Brown recognized the fingerprints. Agents and managers regularly used trusted journalists to promote their lucrative deals. The mischief-makers, however, had forgotten the stumbling block – Harry Redknapp. Brown knew he would oppose any sale.

Hauge's approach to Pini had triggered secret conversations with Redknapp. 'Rio's worth £20 million,' said Redknapp to both Hauge and Pini. That staggering sum, Redknapp hoped, would deter his two friends from further interest. Redknapp's opposition to the deal, the agents knew, would be fatal. That was unwelcome news in Leeds. 'We've got to bid,' urged O'Leary. Ridsdale agreed. The telephone answering machine in Brown's office began to record messages from Ridsdale asking for a conversation about Ferdinand, but the messenger who finally made contact with Brown was unexpected.

Terry Brown was watching cricket at the Oval when Redknapp telephoned. 'I've just had a bid for Ferdinand from Leeds,' he said. 'They're offering £15 million.' Brown was puzzled, not least about why the manager and not the chairman should receive the offer. 'What do you think?' Brown asked. 'I know you can't reject it,' replied Redknapp, 'because it's best for the club.' Brown expressed his astonishment that Redknapp was suddenly so willing to lose a key player: 'This doesn't sound like you to let Rio go.' Redknapp sounded unusually measured. 'No, I think this is best for the club. The transfer market is going to collapse soon.' Redknapp knew that the transfer fee would not only benefit West Ham but also the two agents.

Pertinently, Redknapp's version about those events is sharply different. He portrays himself as an ignorant bystander in West Ham's most crucial transfer and denies making a telephone call to Brown at the Oval. He says that the first he heard of an offer for Ferdinand came from Brown himself. Redknapp says that Pini had told him that Ferdinand was 'happy' at West Ham and never wanted to be sold. And finally, Redknapp expresses amazement that Rune Hauge was involved. 'I never knew,' he says, although in that same period he was in contact with Hauge concerning the transfer of Ragnvald Soma, a Norwegian player. 'There will never be a transfer for me,' exclaimed Soma, explaining his unwillingness to deal with West Ham, 'as long as Rune Hauge is involved in the negotiations. I simply don't trust him.' Irreconcilable contradictions are common in the football business.

On 18 November 2000, West Ham were playing at Leeds. Rio Ferdinand's excellent performance helped the Londoners win 1-0. In the small directors' suite after the match, Ridsdale approached Brown. 'What's the price for Ferdinand?' he asked with some embarrassment. '£18 million,' replied Brown, who had consciously plotted to raise the stakes. Ridsdale nodded and walked through the crowd towards Allan Leighton, the chief executive of Asda and a shareholder of the club. Four minutes later Ridsdale returned. 'OK,' he smiled. 'Fax me your offer on Monday morning,' said Brown.

The £18 million was to be paid in two tranches, £12 million and £6 million. Ridsdale was pleased. Ferdinand would sign a five-year contract. 'He's now worth £35 million,' Ridsdale told his fellow directors. Pini valued Rio at £30 million. On either valuation, Ridsdale was certain of a substantial profit. The final reckoning was the commissions. Pini earned about £1 million, paid by Leeds in stages during Ferdinand's contract. Rune Hauge's payment was considerably more complicated. Hauge had asked for 5 per cent which meant a payment of £900,000 for a few telephone calls. According to the rules at Leeds, Ridsdale was authorized to spend £2 million without reference to the board of directors and he decided not to mention to any non-executive director his agreement with Hauge. Until February 2003, over two years after the transfer, Allan Leighton remained unaware that any payment had been made to the agent, or that the agent had even been retained. Once the payment was revealed, Ridsdale asserted that he had paid Hauge £900,000. In reality, the directors felt that they had not been fully informed.

According to Ridsdale, it was only after the transfer was agreed, during a conversation with Terry Brown with whom he was negotiating Ferdinand's transfer directly, that he discovered Hauge's involvement. The picture is unclear. Firstly, Brown denies that the first approaches came from Ridsdale. Brown says that the first approach was from Hauge – an approach which he rejected. After refusing to deal with Hauge, Brown first discussed Rio's fate with Zahavi. During the long discussions with the Israeli agent, Brown consistently ignored Ridsdale's telephone calls and recorded messages. Only after some weeks, did Brown finally engage in the negotiations with Ridsdale. Brown's version is supported by Zahavi.

More baffling, if Ridsdale's version was correct, Leeds was under no contractual obligation whatsoever to pay Hauge any money. Yet, immediately after the transfer was announced, says Ridsdale, he was warned by the Norwegian that the deal would collapse if Leeds did not pay an increased commission of 10 per cent, or £1.75 million. In Ridsdale's version, he says that he shouted to Steve Harrison, the finance director. 'We've been raped.' Although there was no contractual obligation by Leeds towards Hauge, and Ferdinand's transfer was agreed, Ridsdale says that he felt nevertheless compelled to pay the commission. On Ridsdale's authority, £1.75 million was discreetly transferred to the Norwegian's off-shore account and was not made known to the board of directors of a public company.

In subsequent explanations, Ridsdale claimed that the pressure to pay the extra commission came from Pini Zahavi. The Israeli agent, says Ridsdale, also threatened to undermine the deal unless Hauge's demands were met. Zahavi vehemently denied exerting any pressure on Ridsdale. 'Never in my life,' said Zahavi, 'did I say anything to Ridsdale about Hauge's commission. Never. I never knew what they paid Hauge. I assumed it was 5 per cent. I never threatened to stop the transfer. That is just not true.' According to Ridsdale's version, the Israeli agent had also argued that Hauge had worked hard to achieve the transfer and deserved the extra money. That suggestion by Ridsdale is also vehemently denied by Zahavi: 'I have no idea what Hauge did.'

Ridsdale has also justified the extra money on the grounds that the Norwegian agent mentioned his own need to pay other unnamed people. The link of Hauge with the suggestion of secret payments should have alarmed Ridsdale. After all, Hauge was banned from operating as an agent in 1995 for giving 'bungs' to several British football executives. Ridsdale claims to have been untroubled by that history.

Other exceptional payments were made to complete the transfer. Ferdinand earned an additional windfall. Since he expressed his 'reluctance' to transfer to Leeds and only agreed after his agent's persuasion, Terry Brown agreed to pay the player £500,000 in compensation for the remainder of his contract; and Brown also agreed to pay Redknapp £300,000 for not spending any of the sale money on new players. 'Every business needs a bit of luck,' Brown said to him. 'Your luck was when I arrived,' replied Redknapp with his usual self-confidence. West Ham's bonus to Redknapp proved to be wasted.

The sale caused despondency at West Ham. Without Ferdinand, the team began to slide in the Premier League. Attention was focused on Redknapp. Compared to the cool, professional foreign managers in the competing Premier League teams, Redknapp's volatile temper – smashing bottles and throwing trays of food – matched his self-description: 'In life, I like people to know exactly what I think. I'm an easy-going bloke. But give me a shove in the wrong direction and I have a wicked temper.' Redknapp believed that football was a sport where money bought success: 'If you've got the dough, you've got more of a chance to be the "best" manager.' Money was especially important in Redknapp's life; he was openly dissatisfied with his annual salary of over £1 million. His income was less than that of the foreign coaches employed by British clubs and did not match the phenomenal increase enjoyed by his players. His plight, he complained, was nothing less than 'criminal . . . Us bosses could not book a ticket on the gravy train. Suddenly I found I was getting less than my most ordinary player and that can't be right . . . Surely my pay should be on a par with my top players.'

Redknapp's dissatisfaction irritated Terry Brown; and arguing with Redknapp was unpleasant. 'His moods go down-up-down, so gloomy,' complained a West Ham director. Redknapp was 'up' when West Ham was winning and was buoyant when spending money. Defeats pushed him angrily 'down' and then he blamed West Ham's finances. Terry Brown, Redknapp complained, failed to provide sufficient money to get eleven talented players on the field. In response, the chairman was puzzled by his manager's attitude towards his players' fitness.

In 1999, Redknapp had ridiculed a journalist's description of West Ham players drinking until 4 a.m. on the day of a match. 'I tell you it is absolute rubbish,' scoffed Redknapp, insisting that he forbade alcohol on the coach or in the players' bar on match days. 'That sort of thing does not happen.' Shortly before, however, Redknapp had attacked foreign players in England for undermining the team spirit by refusing to drink. As a player, he admitted, his life revolved around drinking and gambling. 'You could say our motto was "Win or lose, always on the booze."' Redknapp appeared to endorse the light-hearted threat by Peter Reid, the moody manager of Sunderland, to drop any player who was unwilling to become 'legless'. The drinking at West Ham had not enhanced the team's performance. At the end of a brutal humiliation by Swansea, Redknapp admitted his confusion: 'It was one of those days. I can't really explain it. We're short of a few faces and we were all over the show. I tried to fit square pegs in round holes and it didn't work.' His endorsement of drinking had annoyed Ragnvald Soma, the Norwegian player, who complained that some players turned up for training at West Ham smelling of alcohol. 'They don't drink at West Ham,' countered Redknapp. 'The players' bar is completely alcohol free and has been since I've been here – I stopped that years ago.' Soma nevertheless signed for West Ham on 17 January 2001 for £800,000.

Redknapp's inconsistencies about drunken footballers reflected an ambivalence towards the truth. Lying, he believed, was justified to protect his team and his personal interests. Sometimes it seemed that the facts took second place. In October 1998, Duncan Ferguson, a 27-year-old forward, was sent to prison for three months after maliciously biting a player. Redknapp commented, 'I

don't think Ferguson should have gone to prison for that.'
In the same week, John Hartson, a forward for West Ham,
was convicted in Swansea for kicking flower baskets
around a shopping centre and boasting how he '"lamped"
geezers who wound me up in pubs'. Redknapp appeared
to be outraged by the player's punishment. 'I think the
world of John Hartson,' he said. In the same month, he
defended Hartson's aggressive kick of Eyal Berkovic, an
Israeli midfielder, in the face. When his denials were challenged, Redknapp dismissed the attack, 'it was nothing'.
Eventually, asked to justify the violence, Redknapp admitted 'what [Hartson] did was totally out of order,
absolutely terrible'. Redknapp's reluctant admission
prompted the demand for Hartson's instant dismissal.
Redknapp's response exquisitely extolled football's morality, 'No one is going to sack a £10 million footballer are
they? He would go for free to another club.' Redknapp's
indiscretion provoked no criticism, at least not from the
FA. Hartson's agent, Jonathan Barnett, offered newspapers an exclusive interview with his client for £20,000,
while Glenn Hoddle commented, 'there is no longer any
shame for being sent off while representing your country'.

Redknapp's attitude towards the finances of a football
team was shaped during his management of Bournemouth,
a troubled Third Division club. Appointed as manager in
October 1983, Redknapp assiduously toured the country,
watching endless football matches to identify good, inex-
pensive players. By 1987, his new team had defeated
Manchester United and had won promotion to the Second
Division for the first time. Redknapp acted as a big fish in
a small pond with a personality to silence doubters. The
king's demands were never to be resisted.

Ambitious for success, the club allowed Harry
Redknapp to trade players despite the debt increasing

between July 1987 and June 1992 from £150,000 towards £2.6 million. In 1990, despite Redknapp's expenditure, including generous contracts with the players, the club was relegated to the Third Division. The club's debt was destined to increase to £4.4 million.

In 1992, the club's financial troubles compelled another change of ownership. Redknapp resigned. The 'worries and stress' of managing a club, Redknapp complained, prompted his resignation, but he boasted that during his six years, the club had earned £848,000 in profits by his transfers. 'I could spot a player,' he wrote, which proved 'I had a big future in this management game.' That was not the legacy which Roy Pack, Bournemouth's subsequent financial adviser, recognized in 1997. Pack, a former Arsenal and Portsmouth player who became a corporate strategic planner, could only spot horrendous debts. Redknapp had increased the club's costs but not its income. The small profit on his transfers had been swamped by the players' annual wages, which had risen about fivefold to around £1 million. 'Harry made his demands and he got them,' Pack told the *News of the World*. 'There was a degree of irresponsibility in his actions. It has developed into the mess we are now desperately trying to resolve. What has happened is almost unbelievable and in a business sense it is ludicrous.'

Redknapp was infuriated by Pack's criticism, which he dismissed as inaccurate. 'Why did you say that?' Redknapp screamed down the telephone. 'I thought we were friends.' Pack laughed. 'I'm a barrow boy. You're a barrow boy,' he replied. Redknapp escaped any blame for Bournemouth's plight. He arrived as an assistant manager at West Ham without a blemish on his reputation. Trading players remained his vision of management.

'There's no spark,' Harry Redknapp told his wife
about the West Ham team in 1992. Relegated twice in
three years, the players were morose. 'The squad is
hopeless,' he despaired. Two years later, in August 1994,
Billy Bonds, the manager, resigned after a strange succession of events and Redknapp was appointed as his
successor. As he was a devotee of the Hammers, no one
could doubt Redknapp's sincerity. 'Losing means a very
bad Saturday night,' he wrote. 'It is like a personal
injury, like something has gone badly wrong in your life.
Bad results slaughter me. They gut me.' He envisaged
himself as the club's saviour and began a buying spree
of foreign players. By August 1996, although he professed that football was essentially an English game, he
had paid £4 million for eleven foreign players, the
largest collection in Britain at the time. Even for a frequent visitor to the horse track for whom 'betting plays
a large part in my life' the purchase of foreign players
was hazardous. Watching videos or one match was a
poor substitute for consistent reports on the grapevine
about British players.

There were several expensive mistakes. In 1996,
Redknapp bought Florin Raducioiu, a Romanian, from
Espanyol for £2.4 million. 'I followed his career for years
before I signed him,' Redknapp said, 'so I know what he
can do.' The agent was Dennis Roach. A few weeks after
arriving, Raducioiu was shopping in Harvey Nichols
rather than boarding the team bus for Stockport for a
match. Redknapp admitted, '. . . his displays were worth
about two bob'. Raducioiu was resold after six appearances for £1.6 million. Redknapp also admitted that his
purchase of Marco Boogers was 'disappointing' because
'his attitude stank'; and buying Ilie Dumitrescu from
Tottenham proved to be forlorn. 'I have to buy at the

cheap end of the market,' explained Redknapp. 'I was buying second-hand players with no MOTs.'

After two years of Redknapp's management West Ham's record worsened. Defeat followed defeat in 1997. In the stadium, the fans chanted 'What a load of rubbish' and 'Redknapp out'. Outside the stadium, Terry Brown and the other directors were violently attacked, forcing Brown and his wife to flee on foot to the local Underground station to avoid injury. 'Without doubt this has been my worst season as a manager,' confessed Redknapp. 'I don't know where the next goal is coming from.' To placate the fans and avoid relegation, Brown advanced money to buy new players, although the manager's hyperactive trading of players was puzzling. Twelve out of nineteen players photographed for the previous year's official calendar had been transferred. The purchase of Gary Charles, a defender, for £1.2 million from Benfica was one of many mysteries. After just four games, Redknapp abandoned his latest acquisition. 'Is he no good?' Brown asked. 'What do you expect for £1.2 million?' replied Redknapp, adding rhetorically, 'What do you expect for nothing?' 'Well, why buy him, then?' asked Brown. 'We're paying him £1 million a year in wages.' The manager's response was pert: 'Yeah, but they're all getting it.'

Brown was paralysed by that irrefutable snub. Challenging team managers, as all club chairmen knew, was perilous. They were either to be wholly trusted or fired. Since almost every manager would eventually be fired, the sacking culture encouraged Redknapp to spend. Without a normal market rate to fix a player's true value, any valuation between nil and £5 million depended on how much Terry Brown, a property developer who paid £2 million for a controlling stake in West Ham, was willing to spend.

Redknapp's remedy for the absence of unlimited millions was his pride in spotting a young player of quality he could nurture. Three outstanding players enhanced that reputation: Rio Ferdinand, Joe Cole and Frank Lampard. West Ham's loan of Gary Charles to Birmingham only eleven months after his purchase and the other disappointments diminished that renown. The stark variations in his performance baffled the club's directors. And his close relationship with a handful of agents was particularly mysterious. Ignorant of foreign languages, Redknapp relied on agents, in particular Dennis Roach and Willie McKay, whom he described as 'my representative in France'. Redknapp appeared to encourage those agents to use the club's training ground as their base, chatting to players about transfer fees and wages in other clubs. In turn, those agents regarded Redknapp as an ideal manager. Willie McKay was seen hosting Redknapp in Scalinos and other expensive Italian restaurants in London, not least to celebrate the transfer of Marc-Vivien Foe, a Cameroonian midfielder. Dennis Roach was equally close. 'I don't know how an agent can be dishonest,' Redknapp exclaimed when challenged about that relationship. The FA's allegations against Roach for taking money from both sides in a transfer did not disturb Redknapp. 'It's not a big deal if an agent earns from both sides,' he explained. 'If you want a player, it doesn't matter what happens to the money. All that matters is I think the deal is good value for the money.' The value for money in Redknapp's deals was occasionally questionable. Peter Storrie, the club's managing director, explained Redknapp's relationship with agents to Terry Brown. 'Harry likes the turnover of players because he always wants to freshen up the dressing room.' 'But does Harry take money?' Brown asked

Storrie. 'Absolutely not,' Storrie replied. Reassured, Brown refrained from mentioning his irritation that he was personally earning the money for someone else to waste.

The question about Redknapp's financial ethics was provoked by his attitude towards football's worst cases of corruption: the allegations against Terry Venables for dishonesty, and George Graham and Brian Clough for accepting 'bungs' from agents for transfers. In Redknapp's opinion, their denials of wrongdoing were unquestionably true. Despite their long friendship and the notoriety of Venables's admission of dishonesty to the DTI, Redknapp professed complete ignorance 'about Terry's business'. Redknapp's opinion about Brian Clough's dishonesty at Nottingham Forest was conditioned by the disgraced manager's adamant denials and Redknapp's mistaken assumption that the FA had failed to prove any transgression. 'What did he do wrong?' asked Redknapp, adding, 'Brian Clough never confessed. Cloughie was totally innocent. He was a hero for the absolutely incredible thing of winning the European Cup.' By contrast, George Graham's admission to taking 'bungs' from an agent proved that the manager was 'greedy' and 'stupid to risk everything'. 'Honesty, morality, decency,' Redknapp proudly announced, was his mantra. Like most of England's football professionals, Redknapp had not read the Reid report about 'bungs'.

Redknapp's views were, arguably, commonplace among the football fraternity. Infringements of society's customary code were tolerated so long as the teams were victorious. But the aftermath of Rio Ferdinand's sale and West Ham's deteriorating performance had strained Redknapp's relationship with Terry Brown. 'He's not a proper coach,' Brown complained to his fellow directors, irritated by his manager's indiscipline. Redknapp's demands for money and the gossip about the Ferdinand deal itself were disquieting. 'I'm an accountant,' Brown said to Redknapp, 'and I'm very suspicious of everyone in football.' Among football executives, Brown knew, there were no friends, merely rivals and employees back-stabbing to a greater or lesser degree. His unease was understood by Redknapp. 'Eventually,' admitted the manager, 'everyone gets the sack, that is obvious in this game.' At Upton Park, Westminster and the FA's new headquarters in Soho Square the battle for football's honesty was approaching a new climax. The target was the agents, accused of unscrupulousness and the sleuth hunting the suspected villains was the FA's compliance officer.

10

THE AGENT: DENNIS ROACH

Graham Bean was the symbol and substance of the FA's self-regulation. Two years after his appointment, the Premier League chairmen described their compliance officer as 'a disappointment'. Choosing a policeman, lamented David Davies on behalf of the FA, had suggested that the FA was 'a police force with considerable resources and that the game will be cleared up in five seconds'. In public football's regulator mournfully regretted that too much had been expected too quickly; among themselves senior FA officials admitted their reluctance to become involved in more than nominal regulation. Bean's enthusiasm had become embarrassing for them.

The detective constable was unaware of any hostility; rather, he was proud of several successes. First, he had exposed a tickets scam organized at Wembley stadium for the Worthington Cup Final in 1999 between Leicester City and Tottenham. Each player had been allocated twenty complimentary tickets and could buy a further seventy-five tickets. Some players had 'recklessly' resold their tickets to Tottenham supporters. Bean had traced the source of each ticket and the offending players had been fined by the FA.

In a second success at Chesterfield, Bean had unexpectedly arrived at the ground and found evidence of the club under-reporting gate receipts to pay the players unregistered cash bonuses. To his disappointment, the FA had only fined the club £20,000 and deducted nine points, but the leniency of the punishment had not detracted from his achievement.

His third success had been the investigation of fraud at Hull. Nick Buchanan, the chairman of Hull, had urged Bean, 'Perhaps you should spend less time here?' But Bean had persisted once he heard about the involvement of Stephen Hinchcliffe, a controversial businessman, in the club's purchase. 'Either you want the job done or you don't,' Bean had challenged Nic Coward, his superior. 'The club seems to be riddled with corruption.' Within two years of Tom Belton brokering the club's sale, its debt had grown from £100,000 to £2 million. Coward had relented. Six directors had been questioned by the police for using the club for their financial benefit, taking unauthorized expenses and loans, but no action was taken.

Those successes had been tempered by the atmosphere in the FA's headquarters. Like other traditional employees, Bean sensed discrimination against those working for the pure love of the game. While Bean's annual salary was stuck at £43,000, young marketing girls recruited by Paul Barber, formerly employed by Barclays Bank, earned double. Those young women were travelling across the world, often on first-class tickets, enjoying the privileges denied to the older employees. The FA had become swamped by the Saatchi culture, turning football into showbiz. Running costs had doubled from £43 million a year to over £90 million. Grudgingly, Bean agreed with Ken Bates that the new faces in the Soho headquarters were more like 'television presenters, beansuit manufacturers and advertising executives' than seasoned football aficionados. While the impression of Adam Crozier's revolution transforming the FA from an edifice steeped in tradition and blazers into a swish corporate brand was accurate, the casualty was the enforcement of regulations to save football's soul. The ultimate battle would be to defeat the dictatorship of the Premier League chairmen: their self-interest threatened the entire sport. Before undertaking that contest – the litmus test of the FA's authority – Bean sensed there should be moves to root out chicanery among the agents.

Lured by easy money, the number of football agents in England had proliferated. In 1995, agents had been legalized but were required to be registered by FIFA. To qualify, applicants were required to deposit £100,000 in a Swiss bank account, complete an application form and answer twenty multiple choice questions. The questions included 'What does FIFA stand for?', 'Tick the qualities required to be an agent', and explain whether 'an impeccable reputation' was desirable. By 2002, there were 179 licensed agents in England, compared to 82 in Germany, 88 in France and 54 in Italy. Hundreds of others fluttered around as unofficial agents. Sharp dealers, operating from mobile telephones, encouraged players to initiate a transfer by feigning unhappiness or illness, with the assurance that the agent's fees would usually be paid by the clubs, not the players.

'All agents,' quipped Graham Taylor, the unsuccessful England manager, 'should be lined up against a wall and shot.' Ever since the 'Bosman' ruling by the European Court of Justice in September 1995, players had been allowed free transfers at the end of their contracts, removing them as assets from the clubs' accounts and permitting an unlimited number of foreign players to be employed in English teams. The Bosman ruling had encouraged transfers, spiralling wages for players and the reluctance of clubs to train young players. Since there were no controls, the finances of football clubs had destabilized. Supporters loyal to a century of tradition found that their clubs were more like anonymous businesses. At one end of the widening gap, smaller clubs had sunk into financial trouble, while the star clubs sought glory on the foundations of transient wealth. The principal beneficiaries of the jungle were the agents. Of all the agents earning millions of pounds from that mayhem, Dennis Roach was the most notorious and the natural target of Graham Bean's pursuit.

Graham Bean opened his investigation of Dennis Roach in August 2000 with notable optimism. Joe Royle, the manager of Manchester City, and Freddie Shepherd, the chairman of Newcastle United, had complained about Roach's alleged unethical behaviour. Within two weeks, Roach had allegedly sought separate payments from four English clubs for the transfer of two English players, a clear breach of the FA's rule forbidding payment by more than one party to an agent. Under the FA's rules, Roach should have asked for his fee from the players, his clients, rather than the clubs. But that fundamental rule was invariably ignored. Football agents in England usually received their commission from the clubs, even though they were representing the players. That remarkable contradiction legitimized a conflict of interest, a common practice in the football business, despite the risk of unscrupulousness. Targeting Roach attracted sensational headlines and even glee among some chairmen of Premier League clubs, the same people who had bought his services. 'FA versus Roach' might be billed as a defining moment for football and the enforcement of Adam Crozier's 'fit and proper test', but that was a misunderstanding of English football and Roach's career. Investigation of his conduct rarely troubled Dennis Roach. Roguishly sharp and humorously articulate, Roach had become accustomed throughout his twenty-five-year career to scrutiny by the FA and the Inland Revenue.

In 1992 and 1993, Inland Revenue officers seized documents from 'PRO International', Roach's offices. They focused on Star Sports, the company based in the Channel Islands which had organized the soccer tour of South Africa. 'The dodgiest deal I have ever done,' confessed Richard Tessel, a participant in the tour. The deposit of £261,000 into a bank account in Guernsey had not been declared to the Inland Revenue, but the ownership of the account was disputed by Roach. 'It's not my account,' insisted the agent. He nevertheless admitted, 'I came to a compensation agreement with the Revenue.'

Roach had suffered an earlier brush with the Inland Revenue. During his career, he had accumulated many enemies, especially rival agents. In his paperless business, some of his 'agreements' with other agents had been misunderstood, provoking grudges. Among his enemies was Ludwig Kollin, a Croatian agent living in Switzerland.

In December 1989, Ludwig Kollin arrived at the Swallow Hotel in Waltham Abbey with Ludek Miklosko, a Czech goalkeeper owned by Banik Ostrava, a Czech club. Kollin possessed a letter signed by the club's manager and general secretary bequeathing the authority to negotiate a sale on the club's behalf. Kollin was optimistic about West Ham's interest. Seeking instant success,

England's leading clubs were increasingly buying foreign rather than English players. Kollin's disadvantage was his vulnerability as an unknown agent and trader.

To Kollin's surprise, he was telephoned in his hotel room by Roach. 'I'm representing West Ham to negotiate Miklosko's purchase,' said Roach. Kollin was puzzled. Roach's presence, according to Peter Storrie, was required because Kollin was not 'a registered agent', but in that period agents were not allowed by the FA or registered by FIFA. Roach was no different from Kollin, except that the Englishman enjoyed a friendly relationship with the club's management. 'Why is West Ham using Roach as its representative?' Kollin asked Lou Macari, West Ham's manager. 'Roach telephoned and said he's representing you,' Macari replied. Kollin was puzzled but not surprised. Impenetrable contradictions were a staple diet of football. The transfer was agreed and Kollin was reassured that Roach would share the commission.

The transfer price was deposited in an account of the Credit Suisse bank in Zürich. Shortly after, the manager of Banik Ostrava complained that £138,000 was missing. The air was full of claim and counter-claim. Kollin, the Czechs believed, had taken the money. Kollin vehemently denied any wrongdoing and alleged that the missing money remained deposited in Roach's Swiss bank account. Roach ignored Kollin's repeated requests to share the commission and claimed, 'I brought Miklosko to West Ham. I was never paid by West Ham.' To discover the fate of the money, Kollin filed an official criminal complaint in Switzerland. The investigation by Erich Leimlehner, a Swiss judge, did not trouble Roach. His eloquence and charm usually persuaded foreigners of his innocence. 'Kollin's the full shilling,' smiled Roach, suggesting that the Croat was an unreliable witness. Leimlehner unearthed the deposited money in a Credit Suisse bank account number 175664 marked 'KOL Attn 39 To Thomas Finn', suggesting that Kollin had appropriated the money. 'Roach opened the account using my name,' countered Kollin. Roach denied the allegation. 'The whole matter is disgusting,' concluded Leimlehner, closing his investigation. Those involved in the football business, he decided, deserved each other. Roach was ebullient. Antagonism towards him was tempered by his indispensability. Few, it appeared, including the owners of football clubs, could resist his involvement in transfers, or his profits.

In February 1996, Ludwig Kollin returned to West Ham to sell Slaven Bilic, a Croatian defender. Kollin, representing the player, anticipated negotiating directly with Harry Redknapp, but unexpectedly Roach telephoned Kollin and announced his involvement as the representative of Karlsruhe, Bilic's club. 'I'm the only agent West Ham will deal with,' insisted Roach, 'and you're not registered.' Kollin protested to Redknapp: 'That's not what we agreed.' 'I can't do anything,' replied Redknapp. 'Peter Storrie insisted. I've made too many mistakes buying foreign players.' Kollin appealed to Terry Brown, West Ham's chairman. Even Brown favoured Roach. Any deal for Bilic, confirmed Brown, must be negotiated with Roach. Resignedly, Kollin told Roach, 'I've lived for six years under suspicion of being a crook,' referring to the accusation that he had secretly deposited money in a Swiss bank account. 'Oh that's normal in football,' replied Roach. 'But I suffered,' countered Kollin. 'I always pay the money I owe people,' said Roach proudly, 'so I'll pay some compensation.' The belated payment was not indicative of Roach's changed

behaviour. In June 1997, Kollin complained that he had
not received any money from Roach for Bilic's £1.4 million transfer to West Ham. Roach ignored Kollin's
demands. Kollin complained to Graham Kelly, but the
FA ignored the letter. In revenge, the Croatian agent contacted Graeme Young at the Special Compliance office of
the Inland Revenue in Princess Gate in Solihull. 'Roach
has a Swiss bank account,' confided Kollin in a bid to
damage his rival. Roach shrugged off the allegation. He
denied owing the Inland Revenue any money and
obtained an injunction to prevent Kollin making personal
threats or approaching within 250 metres of his property.
He appeared immune to embarrassment. Roach's problems with the Inland Revenue aroused little interest in
either the Premier League or the FA. Neither believed
that the finances of the agent ought to be controlled by
their organization, not least because their members
eagerly hired his services and his profits were discovered
only by accident. At West Ham, Peter Storrie would
decide to return Florin Raducioiu to Espanyol of Spain
and asked for the return of the £2.4 million transfer fee.
He was told that Roach's commission of £300,000 would
be deducted. 'I dread to think how many took cuts from
that money,' sighed Storrie.

Even Alex Ferguson fell before Roach's intransigence.
Ferguson had banned Roach's involvement in the negotiations for the sale of Paul Ince to Inter Milan. 'The deal's
dead if Roach is involved,' said Ferguson. 'Over my dead
body, he will not go.' But Martin Edwards had been compelled to use Roach to negotiate with Massimo Moratti.
In the transfer of Mark Hughes from Barcelona,
Ferguson had again swallowed his anger and negotiated
with Roach. Similarly, Peter Ridsdale relied on Roach to
deliver Olivier Dacourt, a French midfielder from Lens,

to Leeds. During the flight to Lens, Roach had demanded a fee of £200,000 for his efforts. Ridsdale was outraged but judged that annoying Roach was counter-productive. 'Leeds could not have got Dacourt without me,' said Roach. 'I was the only one in the room who could speak French so I deserved that for translations.' Ridsdale reacted scathingly. 'I spoke English to Lens's manager. Roach didn't translate.' Roach was familiar with disputes about the truth. 'I asked for £200,000 on the flight out,' he explained, 'and I got £200,000.' The detail was more complicated.

During the six months after Dacourt's transfer, Roach and Ridsdale had argued about the payment. 'What did you do for the money?' asked Ridsdale. 'Why should we pay you £200,000?' Roach was insistent: 'I came at David O'Leary's request. He insisted I come. That's my fee for arranging everything.' Reluctantly, Ridsdale agreed to pay for the tip-off but only on receipt of a proper invoice. To his surprise, Roach sent two invoices, both for £100,000. Seeking an explanation in the Byzantine world of football was pointless, not least because Roach would casually insist that Ridsdale had requested two invoices!

Notoriety and disputes stimulated Roach's persistence. Through Roach clubs received information about foreign players who were cheaper, better disciplined and less trouble than British players. In his bid to find those players Roach formed a partnership with Vincenzo Morabito, an Italian he met at a match in 1992 in Switzerland. Morabito, Roach suggested, should be his representative in Italy.

Morabito, like Roach, had become an agent by accident. While living in Sweden as a football journalist, he had been reporting a UEFA match between Inter Milan and Gothenburg. The Italian manager needed a translator and Morabito, intelligent and fluent in several languages, offered his assistance. That relationship introduced the journalist to the notion of selling Scandinavian players to the major European clubs. In 1993, he moved to Copenhagen from Germany. 'I've had trouble with the tax authorities,' he told Geir di Lange, a football scout living in the north of Denmark. Over the next year, Morabito used di Lange to find young players and forge relationships with other European clubs. Di Lange was impressed by Morabito's close relationships with several managers, especially Walter Smith of Glasgow Rangers. After a friendly match between FCM and Rangers in Herning, di Lange sat with Morabito and Smith at the Hotel Eude. He claims to have seen Morabito hand Smith an envelope. 'Just routine paperwork,' explained Morabito. The Dane broke the relationship with Morabito after the Italian refused to pay for his work. 'You're a gangster,' di Lange accused Morabito. The Italian vehemently denied any wrongdoing. Di Lange, he explained, circulated defamatory stories in revenge for Morabito protecting a local player from a pernicious contract favouring di Lange. Amid the wild allegations and mutual recriminations that characterized relations between agents, no one could be certain of the truth.

Unconcerned, the Italian built a partnership with Boorge Jacobson, another Danish journalist turned unofficial scout who was willing to identify local footballers to be sold by Morabito. Within four years, the Dane also argued with Morabito about the payment of commissions. By then, Morabito had returned to Italy, developing a close relationship with Massimo Cragnotti, the son of Lazio's owner. Living in the Umbrian hills with his Danish wife, Morabito was regularly asked to negotiate the transfers for the Roman club, especially to

Chelsea and other English clubs. Like Roach, the Italian involved himself in deals and offered clubs his services to sell players, taking his profits in commission and whatever extra he obtained above the price requested by the selling club. His success provoked more arguments with Jerome Anderson and Paul Stretford, two equally ambitious and young English agents, amid accusations of failure to share commissions and attempting to snatch players. In Stretford's version, denied by Morabito, they met by chance at Heathrow airport and Stretford launched himself forcibly on to the suspected predator.

Agent wars were the background to Morabito's decision to forge a partnership with Dennis Roach. Using Roach's relationships with British club managers and chairmen, Morabito would find European players willing to transfer. Among their first joint deals was the sale of Mark Fish, a South African defender. Lazio's price for the player was $1.8 million. Anything above that sum was pure profit for the agents. Roach and Morabito sold the player for $2.5 million, a healthy 40 per cent commission. While both agents professed loyalty to clubs and players, their credo was to earn on the transfer, making their own interests paramount. That formula influenced their joint operation to transfer Klas Ingesson from PSV Eindhoven to Sheffield Wednesday. Ingesson's agent was Morabito, who told Roach that his client wanted a transfer. Roach approached Trevor Francis of Sheffield Wednesday. 'I can get you Klas Ingesson,' said Roach. Eindhoven paid Roach £100,000 for the sale, which he shared with Morabito. The transaction revealed Roach and Morabito as freelance traders rather than caring agents embracing loyalties to either a club or a player. To clothe their activities with respectability, they created the International Association of Football Agents, promoting themselves as the leaders of agents adhering to the highest moral standards.

Morabito, however, had doubts about his latest partner. Frequently, in dividing the commission received from transfers, Roach would deduct a percentage, explaining, 'I need this to give to the manager.' Morabito agreed, although he was uncertain about exactly what was happening. His only encounter with gifts in England had been at the end of his negotiations in 1989 with Ron Atkinson, then the manager of Sheffield Wednesday, for the transfer of Roland Nilsson, a Swedish player. Morabito's commission, it was agreed during their celebration at a local hotel, would be £15,000. 'I'll want a good drink out of this,' Atkinson told Morabito. The Italian stuttered. 'I don't buy drinks,' he replied. Atkinson refused to deal with Morabito ever again. By contrast, Roach freely revealed that he did buy Atkinson drinks. During tours with the manager, he happily paid for a good hotel suite and supplied cases of pink champagne, Atkinson's favourite drink.

Dennis Roach laughed about Morabito's experiences, but the Italian was puzzled. He had worked hard to arrange the transfer in 1997 of Andrei Kanchelskis, a forward, from Fiorentina to Rangers. Roach had, as usual, negotiated with Walter Smith, his close friend, the Rangers manager, while Morabito took care of the Italian club. Their commission to be equally divided was £500,000. Roach offered Morabito £150,000. 'There are lots of expenses,' said Roach, 'and I need £30,000 for someone at Fiorentina.' Morabito was outraged. No one in Fiorentina had asked him for any money. He was doubtful about Roach who, for his part, reasoned that if anyone would transfer money to an Italian club official, it would be his Italian partner. As usual, there were recriminations and no conclusions as to the truth. Their partnership fractured after Roach protested that others had argued with Morabito on similar grounds. In their dog-eat-dog environment, Roach was unconcerned that Morabito was a victim of football's lawlessness.

Disputes among agents did not trouble football executives. Rick Parry, responsible for formulating the rules of the new Premier League, had discovered that football executives 'are not uncomfortable about the conflicts of interest. It's easy for people to compartmentalize.' Parry was neither 'upset' by the blurred rules concerning agents nor disturbed by Roach's receipt of money for arranging transfers from clubs rather than the players he apparently represented. 'It's not wrong,' Parry believed, reflecting the particular tolerance towards Roach among the senior executives of the FA, especially during Graham Kelly's era.

In 1996, Roach had negotiated Glenn Hoddle's contract as England's team coach with Graham Kelly. 'Dennis was straightforward and reasonable,' announced Kelly. Two years later, in August 1998, Kelly was grateful to the agent for managing the furore during the publication of Hoddle's World Cup diary (written by David Davies, the FA's director of communication, for a fee negotiated with Roach). Hoddle's indiscretions had damaged the FA. The following year, the image of the FA was damaged by the publication of Hoddle's opinions on reincarnation and the idea that the disabled were being punished for sins in a former life. National esteem appeared to be secondary to profit. Once again, Kelly was impressed by the loyal agent who sat beside Hoddle on 6 February 1999 during the excruciating press conference after negotiating his client's resignation. The omnipresent Roach sought to protect Hoddle from malice and ridicule. During that process, Graham Bean believed, the agent had gained sufficient insight into the FA to embarrass the senior officials if necessary. 'He'll use all his powerful friends to escape,' said Bean.

Dennis Roach blessed himself as unassailable. Judged on his personal wealth – even 'Cockroach's' rivals spoke of an agent with over £10 million in the bank – no one within football appeared willing to offer serious evidence against him. The result was a rich man profiting by his wits and personal relationships. Since the club chairmen never formally complained about losing money, discovering the backgrounds to Roach's deals was beyond Graham Bean until summer 2000.

Joe Royle, the manager of Manchester City, was negotiating with West Ham for the purchase of Paulo Wanchope, a Costa Rican striker, for £3.65 million. Wanchope's reluctance to move north irritated Royle. 'Get him fucking up here tomorrow,' Royle told Wanchope's agent, Dennis Roach. Eventually, Wanchope arrived and Royle, to his own irritation, agreed to pay Roach £250,000 for allowing the transfer on Roach's assurance that he was receiving no other commission. Suspicious of Roach, and angry that the lengthy dispute had contributed to Manchester City's relegation from the Premier League, Royle asked Wanchope whether his agent would receive a commission from the player. '£250,000,' replied Wanchope. If Wanchope was correct, a double payment would be a clear breach of the FA's rules and a breach of Roach's agreement not to ask the player for payment. 'The transfer of Wanchope was the first time I have ever dealt with Dennis Roach,' said Royle. 'Suffice to say it will be the last.' Roach denied asking Wanchope for a payment. 'It was a misunderstanding because of his poor English,' explained the agent.

Graham Bean read Joe Royle's complaint in a newspaper and opened an investigation to formally discipline Roach. That announcement provoked a second complaint against Roach.

Bobby Robson, the respected manager of Newcastle United, revealed that Roach had demanded a 'sweetener' of £760,000 to facilitate the transfer of Duncan Ferguson from Newcastle to Everton, a transfer which Ferguson desired. The compensation was payable, Roach had stipulated, because Ferguson's sale to Everton was a premature breach of the player's contract by Newcastle.

Twenty-nine-year-old Ferguson was an unexceptional striker, except that in 1995 he had been jailed for three months for an assault on a rival player. Despite his imprisonment, he had been bought by Newcastle in 1998 for £8 million and signed a five year contract to be paid £38,000 a week. Ferguson's choice in 2000 was either to remain at Newcastle for a further three years, collecting £6 million in wages without playing again, or agreeing to his transfer to Everton. The player wanted to move but sought compensation for the lower fees Everton would pay. Newcastle refused to pay any compensation despite the breach of contract. 'I won't transfer unless they pay me the £700,000,' stipulated Ferguson. Roach had asked Robson for £700,000 to 'make the deal happen' which included £60,000 for himself. 'You're getting nothing from us,' replied Freddie Shepherd, the club's chairman, 'because you're not acting for us.' Under the FA's rules, Roach should have asked for his fee from Ferguson rather than Newcastle, although many interpreted that distinction as unrealistic. Roach told Robson about the impasse. In the agent's opinion, he was fulfilling his instructions to 'screw Newcastle'.

In Bobby Robson's opinion, Roach's intervention was outrageous. Robson alleged that the agent knew Newcastle were negotiating to buy Peter Lovenkrands from a Danish club. That deal could only be completed once Ferguson had been sold to Everton. Robson waved a fax from Roach saying the deal would 'not take place unless we have reached agreement on our outstanding problem – which I am sure we can do'. Robson's concern was aggravated after hearing that David Murray, the chairman of Rangers and a friend of Roach's, also wanted to buy Lovenkrands. It seemed that Roach was deliberately interfering both to help Murray and to earn an unreasonable commission on Ferguson's departure. Ferguson's continued intransigence stymied Robson's plans. Lovenkrands signed for Rangers and Robson publicized his complaint against Roach after selling Ferguson to Everton for £6.3 million.

Graham Bean opened a second investigation into the agent. Bean became puzzled by the friendship between Roach and Walter Smith. Over the years, Walter Smith, the manager of Rangers, and his chairman, David Murray, appeared to favour Roach's insertion of himself into transfers. In October 2000, Roach was unexpectedly allowed to broker the transfer of Raul Tamudo, a striker playing for Espanyol, to Rangers, while Tomas Duran, the player's agent, was sidelined. During those same weeks Rangers was receiving offers from Jim Smith, the manager of Derby County, for Jonatan Johansson, a Swedish striker. Smith offered David Murray £2.75 million. To Smith's surprise Roach telephoned to say that the transfer would be approved if Smith also paid the agent £250,000. Smith declined and increased his offer to £3 million. Again Roach telephoned to say that the sale would be approved but only if Smith paid Roach £250,000. Smith was puzzled because Roach was not Johansson's agent (who was Gordon Smith) and he could not understand why Derby should pay Roach if he was acting on behalf of Rangers. In Jim Smith's version, Roach claimed to be in charge of all transfers at Ibrox, although that was denied by David Murray: 'That is simply not true.' Smith increased his offer to £3.25 million and once again Roach insisted on his fee. 'Roach wanted £250,000 for sending a fax,' Smith complained. Eventually, Johansson was sold to Charlton. Roach denied Jim Smith's version: 'I wasn't involved in any shape or form. I'm not Johansson's agent.'

Dennis Roach's relationship with Walter Smith continued after the manager moved from Rangers to Everton. Instead of conserving the club's dwindling funds, Walter Smith had indulged in a spending spree, buying foreign players with Roach's help. Among these players who proved to be disappointing was Ibrahim Bakayoko, a striker from the Ivory Coast, bought for £4.75 million from a French club and resold for £2.5 million. Without a complaint Bean could not investigate Roach's relationship with Everton. He had not, however, anticipated the response to his investigation of the two other transfers.

Dennis Roach accused the FA of hypocrisy, arguing that they had ignored the secretly recorded boasts of Freddie Shepherd and Douglas Hall in a brothel in 1998. On the tape, recorded by the *News of the World* they had talked about their sexual conquests, describing Newcastle girls as 'ugly dogs', and boasting about their club's sale of shirts to fans for £50 which cost £5 to manufacture. Those revelations had brought the game into real disrepute. Moreover, he argued, since he had never received a fee from Newcastle, his request and the alleged irregularity were redundant. Roach was bullish about it all. 'I believe this is a Mr Crozier witch-hunt and I'm confident that he'll fail with these charges,' he said. 'As chairman of the International Association of Football Agents, I have worked closely with FIFA and the FA to improve the reputation of agents. I would have thought I'm the last person to face charges but I'm quite happy to defend myself.' Joe Royle and Freddie Shepherd began to reconsider their public criticism of Roach. They reasoned that perhaps irritating Roach was not the best plan. The chairmen of other Premier League clubs, rather than pledging unity against Roach, were searching for an advantage. Royle sought to withdraw his complaint. 'Roach hasn't done anything wrong,' Royle told Bean. There had been, he explained, a misunderstanding, because 'Wanchope only speaks 50 per cent English.' Any recantation, however, was too late. 'We'll be the judge of all that,' Bean replied, unmoved. 'I think there's a case.'

Spurred on by newspaper reports, in December 2000, Bean formally interviewed Roach at the FA's headquarters on charges of acting on behalf of more than one party, taking money from people other than the principal, behaving unethically and bringing the game into disrepute. Accompanied by his lawyer, the agent met Bean, who, he carped, was 'over-promoted as a constable'. During the recorded interview, Roach excitedly denied that the FA had jurisdiction over himself as he was registered by FIFA. Wagging his finger at Bean, he warned the official to 'lay off'; while the FA's lawyers scoffed at the agent and his defence. FIFA, said Nic Coward, had promised to send a letter declaring that the FA was empowered to enforce the rules. Roach was unintimidated. He anticipated that Coward was certain to become lost in the labyrinth of FIFA's machinations and Bean's pursuit would begin to flag.

In March 2001 Roach's self-confidence was emboldened by the unexpected opportunity for more wealth. Daniel Levy, the new chairman of Tottenham, dismissed George Graham and sought to hire Glenn Hoddle as the manager of his 'spiritual home'. Roach welcomed the new blessing. Once again, he could perform as agent and father figure of his best friend.

In the previous months Hoddle's managership of Southampton had not been profitable for Roach who was also a season ticket holder at the club. Every week, the agent telephoned Rupert Lowe, the chairman, whose fortune was earned developing retirement properties, with offers. This hustling, often preceded by newspaper reports that 'Lowe should buy a player', usually concerned foreign players. Southampton could not afford expensive English or west European players. Latvia, Ecuador and the former Yugoslavia were useful sources of players to compete with the Big Five's escalating transfer fees. But those purchases were perilous. In November 2001, Lowe had spent £3.5 million buying Agustin Delgado, an Ecuadorian, from another agent, and the player remained unused. 'We should buy on merit,' cautioned Lowe, concerned by Hoddle's partiality to treat Roach's offers more seriously than other agents. Hoddle agreed but nevertheless suggested, on Roach's initiative, a four year contract with Patrice Tano, a striker from the Ivory Coast. 'He looks superb,' said Hoddle. Tano returned to France, cast off without playing, blaming 'passport complications' as an excuse.

To lure Hoddle from Southampton, David Buchler, the new vice-chairman of Tottenham, approached Roach on the board's behalf. The agent's reputation was unknown to Buchler, an insolvency expert, whose previous football experience at Millwall, Swindon, Barnet and Oxford United had not exposed him to top agents. During the two days of negotiations to secure Hoddle's employment, Buchler was particularly impressed by Roach's concern over the manager's interests. Smooth and affable, Roach presented himself as reasonable and reliable, speaking eloquently about his many contacts in Europe. 'A digger,' concluded Buchler, 'cutely matching supply and demand.'

Buchler's judgement was appreciated by Daniel Levy, the new 39-year-old chairman of Tottenham, who preferred avoiding the spotlight. Since leaving Cambridge, Levy had managed or owned ten businesses, trading in cutlery, shoes, health food and a low-cost clothing chain, Mister Byrite. In 1995, he joined ENIC, the English National Investment Company, an offshore company initially involved in textiles. ENIC was financed by Joe Lewis, a 58-year-old former restaurateur who is reported to have earned billions of pounds by currency speculation from his home in Lyford Cay in the Bahamas. Lewis employed Daniel Levy, a family friend, as an investment manager at ENIC. With access to huge wealth and attracted to football's new fortunes, Levy persuaded Lewis that together, as partners, they should become substantial investors through ENIC in the business across Europe. The strategy was to build an international sports and entertainment group to profit from the media's interest.

In January 1997, ENIC bought a 25 per cent stake in Glasgow Rangers for £40 million. 'We were not just looking for a business growing at 10 per cent per annum,' said Levy, 'we were looking for something that was also exciting.' The excitement was purely the gamble to earn

millions. 'There is no passion here,' said Levy, admitting
that neither Lewis nor himself was particularly keen on
football. 'This is purely financial.' Football, he believed,
was commercially under-exploited, particularly in television and merchandising. Rangers' true value, he
predicted, was £325 million, more than double the
market price. 'We chose football,' Levy explained,
'because it is the most popular sport on earth and the
biggest money spinner.' To enhance the dream of those
potential profits, ENIC bought stakes in other European
football clubs: Vicenza, FC Basel, Slavia Prague and
AEK Athens. The strategy rapidly soured.

On 19 May 1998, to prevent match-fixing, UEFA
barred clubs with common ownership entering the same
European tournament. ENIC's clubs were prevented
from entering the lucrative competitions. ENIC's shares
fell 50 per cent. Levy's woes increased. Corruption in
Italian and Greek football, he discovered, was rampant
and, two years after his original investment, the value of
their investment in Rangers fell by a quarter to £30 million. Levy blamed David Murray for ignoring their
agreement to limit borrowings and plunge the club into
debts of £100 million. 'You're running Rangers as a huge
loss-making entity,' said Levy, aghast how a beloved
chairman could ruin a club by ignoring any financial controls, an accusation that Murray vigorously disputed.

Enough confidence remained for Levy and Lewis to
respond with interest to one major opportunity. In
December 2000, Alan Sugar agreed to sell ENIC a 29.9
per cent controlling interest in Tottenham for £22 million. Sugar retained a 13 per cent stake. Levy was pleased
with the deal. At 80 pence per share, he was paying 20
pence less than he had offered, and Sugar had rejected,
one year earlier. Sugar's timing was still judicious. His

original £8 million investment in 1991 had quadrupled in value and, soon after the sale to ENIC, the share price halved to about 43 pence. Levy had bought a tired property. During Sugar's chairmanship, Tottenham had won few trophies and its team had included few stars. The new chairman planned to invest over five years for the club's recovery. Dennis Roach was happy to assist. To the agent's advantage, Levy was 'grateful' that Roach had not 'ruined the deal' to lure Hoddle back to Tottenham. 'Glenn's heart is in the club,' agreed Roach. 'He understands the sport and the business,' added Levy, searching for the agent's agreement. Roach nodded eagerly. Levy, taciturn and unaggressive, was unlikely to challenge the agent's established methods of business. Without concealing his anger, Rupert Lowe agreed that Hoddle could leave Southampton.

Glenn Hoddle had arrived at White Hart Lane pondering the purchase of Goran Bunjevcevic, a 29-year-old defender playing for Red Star Belgrade. The attraction to Levy was that Bunjevcevic would be available on a free transfer in June 2001, at the end of his four year contract. Levy heard that critical information from Phil Spencer, a registered agent searching for business.

Glenn Hoddle did not want Phil Spencer involved in the deal. The new coach suggested to Daniel Levy that Roach should be retained to negotiate Bunjevcevic's transfer with Dragan Dzajic, the president of Red Star. Roach's retainer was agreed at £200,000. On his return from Belgrade Roach reported to Levy that Bunjevcevic was not after all available on a free transfer. He had just signed a new five year contract. Levy was confused over whether Roach had mentioned that the new contract had been signed three or nine months earlier. Some suspected that on 'the initiative of the Yugoslavs' the contract had been signed only days after Tottenham expressed its interest. The consequence was unavoidable. To secure the player's release from the contract, said Roach, the Yugoslavs were asking for £1.4 million. Notwithstanding the discrepancies, Daniel Levy agreed to deposit the money in a Moscow bank.

To finalize his own contract Bunjevcevic flew to London on 18 May 2001 and met John Alexander, Tottenham's secretary. The footballer was accompanied by Dragan Ruvavac of Red Star and Peter Baines, a solicitor at Pictons in St Albans. For many years Baines had acted as Roach's trusted representative. Bunjevcevic was using Baines at Roach's suggestion. Sporadically, during the negotiations at White Hart Lane, Baines left the room to make a call on his mobile telephone. Alexander became puzzled. As a check, he telephoned Roach's mobile telephone each time Baines left the room. The line was engaged. On Baines's return Alexander telephoned Roach's mobile telephone and it was no longer engaged. To seek an explanation, Alexander immediately telephoned Dragan Dzajic of Red Star. 'Who is representing Red Star in this transaction?' asked Alexander. 'We're represented by Roach,' the Yugoslav replied. Twenty minutes later, Roach telephoned Alexander. 'Why are you probing?' he asked. 'To fulfil FA rules,' replied Alexander. One hour later, in a telephone call from Belgrade, a Yugoslav secretary speaking on behalf of Dragan Dzajic told Alexander, 'No one, including Dennis Roach, is representing us in this deal.' Temporarily, Alexander suppressed his suspicions and completed the contract with Bunjevcevic, mentioning afterwards the peculiar circumstances to Daniel Levy. 'Strange,' agreed Levy on reflection. 'But the deal's OK, isn't it?' 'Yes,' replied Alexander. To ensure there was no breach of the

FA's rules, Levy telephoned Roach. 'Have you represented two parties?' he asked. 'It's just a coincidence,'
Roach told Levy, 'that my lawyer was acting for the other
side. I was just making sure that both parties came
together.' Like so many club chairmen in the same situation, Levy was pleased with the deal and preferred to
'turn a blind eye' to any doubts.

The circumstances of the disappearing 'free transfer'
encouraged Roach's enemies to publicize their suspicions.
Their suggestion, Graham Bean heard, was that Red Star
had completed a back-dated long contract to obtain a
larger fee from Tottenham, to be used for various commissions.

Bean travelled across Europe to gather the evidence.
The signed testimony of Gianluca Nani, the managing
director of Brescia football team, on 29 November 2001
was incriminating. Before Roach's journey to Belgrade,
Nani revealed, he had been told by Ian Radford, an agent,
that Bunjevcevic was available on a free transfer. Nani
wanted to employ the player, but Brescia's team coach
had refused. 'We were offered Bunjevcevic on a free
transfer,' insisted Nani, puzzled that Tottenham had
shortly after paid £1.4 million.

In his further quest for evidence, Bean resisted visiting
Belgrade. The directors of the Yugoslav club had signed
a letter to the FA asserting that Red Star had not paid
Roach. Since the club was also the political and military
authority for football in Yugoslavia, Bean decided that the
capital was 'too dodgy' for an independent investigation.
Failing to unearth the conclusive evidence frustrated the
investigator, but there was no echo of that sentiment at
White Hart Lane. Bean was told by Tottenham's new
directors that the 'rumour machine' of foreign witnesses
lacked credibility. The notion that football was a 'rogues'

business' was dismissed. 'Does football pass the smell test?' Levy asked rhetorically. 'I've never come across corruption during the actual game in England.' In the past, Levy conceded, some agents and managers had 'played at the edges' and there was 'no doubt there are dishonest agents in England', but dishonesty had become recently harder under the FA's new rules. Nevertheless, to ensure probity, Levy introduced an 'aggressive' new contract for agents retained by Tottenham. They were to undertake not to accept payments from any other party. That contract was in force when Roach embarked on his next mission for the club.

The painful departure of Sol Campbell, Tottenham's outstanding defender, prompted a frantic search for a replacement. A candidate, José Antonio Chamot, was suggested by Roach and Hoddle endorsed his agent's recommendation. Chamot was a 32-year-old Argentinian contracted for one more year at AC Milan. Roach told Levy in July 2001 that, after discussion with Antonio Braida and Adriano Galliano at Milan, Chamot would cost £1.5 million, and Roberto Settembrini, the player's agent, would expect $300,000. Roach was retained as a consultant by Tottenham for £200,000 to represent the club in the transfer negotiations.

The gossip about Roach's imminent arrival in Milan was picked up by Vincenzo Morabito, his erstwhile partner. Morabito had been involved with the transfer of Chamot himself, except on very different terms. Since arguing with Roach, Morabito had forged a close relationship with Jon and Phil Smith of First Artist. Together they had offered Chamot to Colin Hutchinson, the managing director of Chelsea. Morabito's terms reflected his instructions from Milan: Chamot, he was told by the club, was a free transfer but would expect a substantial salary. Hutchinson nevertheless rejected the offer. Disappointed, Morabito searched for other clubs and then heard of Roach's involvement and the £1.5 million transfer fee demanded from Tottenham. Jon Smith telephoned Daniel Levy. 'Chamot,' said Smith, 'is a free transfer. Milan will ignore the remaining one year of his contract.'

Daniel Levy was puzzled. Roach had personally reported that the price was £1.5 million and that had been confirmed in a letter. After Jon Smith's telephone call Levy challenged Roach. 'I don't believe you,' said Roach. 'He's just trying to get into my deal.' Levy was confused and told Hoddle, 'I think we should let Jon Smith negotiate.' 'Absolutely,' replied Hoddle.

On 18 July 2001, John Alexander, Tottenham's secretary, was dispatched to Milan with Jon Smith. To their surprise, Roach was still in the city negotiating Chamot's transfer. After easing Roach out, Jon Smith negotiated and signed the contract for the free transfer for a commission to be paid by Tottenham of £150,000. The final version of the deal on 19 July 2001 demonstrated the vicissitudes of the business: two agents could offer a different deal for the same player. Roberto Settembrini, the player's agent in the Roach deal, had disappeared from Milan, leaving a puzzling fax (from Roach terminating their negotiations) in his room at the Excelsior Hotel. More bizarre, in the contract negotiated by Jon Smith with AC Milan on 19 July, Claudio Vigorelli, an Italian agent, was named as Chamot's representative rather than Roberto Settembrini. However, after some discussion, Vigorelli's name had been crossed out. In its place, Jon Smith was included as the 'player's agent'. That presented another puzzle. Jon Smith had been sent to Milan to represent Tottenham, not the player. Nevertheless, on behalf of the club and the player, Smith agreed that Tottenham would pay Chamot $1.5 million per annum for a two year contract and provide four return business-class tickets to Buenos Aires and a 'suitable' car. Resolving those irregularities became irrelevant after Chamot's medical examination in London pronounced that the player was unfit. The directors of AC Milan, Levy was told, had not disclosed that their player was receiving injections for an injured ankle. The transfer was cancelled. To nearly everyone's bewilderment, Chamot returned to Milan and continued to play for the club before joining the Argentinian squad in the World Cup.

Vincenzo Morabito was not slow to whisper his concerns about Roach and no one was more interested than Graham Bean. At first it seemed to Bean that Roach might have been hoping to share the £1.5 million fee with Milan, a conflict of interest because Roach had been retained by Tottenham. But the investigator discovered a conflict of evidence which appeared to exonerate Roach. Contrary to Morabito's evidence, Antonio Braida at Milan told Bean that Chamot was not free. Milan had originally expected a transfer fee. The contradiction with the contract negotiated by Jon Smith in Milan on 19 July for a free transfer was baffling. 'Braida's provided an explanation for Roach,' thought Bean. The inconsistencies shocked Daniel Levy. His latest conversation with Roach was not pleasant. 'These agents are nightmares,' Levy told his colleagues. 'Although,' he added swiftly, 'rumours don't prove anything.' Unaccountable and unprincipled, the agents might be the most influential group in football, he realized, but were also potential rogues with no 'set criteria' and the potential to destabilize the business. Since the evidence against Roach did not stack up, Levy was uninterested in seeking any further explanation. Pursuing the matter was pointless. Glenn Hoddle was crucial to ENIC's successful ownership of the club and he was certain about Hoddle's integrity. If Roach was not playing straight, Levy reasoned, Hoddle would have terminated their twenty year friendship. Accordingly, he refrained from discussing the debacle with his coach.

There was also good reason to question the motivation of Jon Smith and Vincenzo Morabito in provoking suspicions about Dennis Roach. Both agents cast Roach as a 'dinosaur' to be slayed in the new saga, 'Agent Wars'. Smith was ambitious to inherit Roach's favoured relationship with Tottenham and was encouraged by a morsel proffered by Levy. To replace Sol Campbell, Hoddle wanted to buy Dean Richards, an uncapped defender at Southampton. Still smarting from Hoddle's desertion, Rupert Lowe refused to take Daniel Levy's telephone call. Levy's solution was to hire Jon Smith. By chance, the agent encountered Lowe at Brighton Football Club on the night of 11 September 2001. As the tragic events in New York unfolded, the two men discussed business. 'He's not leaving,' scowled Lowe. Shortly after, Lowe complained to Dave Richards, the chairman of the Premier League, that his player was being destabilized by Tottenham. Lowe's obstinacy was profitable. Since Hoddle insisted on the player, Levy was obliged to pay Lowe's price for Richards, £8.1 million. The inflated fee was to be paid in one instalment. Lowe was chortling. Jon Smith received £300,000 in commission. Daniel Levy had discovered that the controls exercised by a chairman of a football club over his business's expenditure were limited.

The aftertaste for Roach was intended to be hurtful. Graham Bean, dedicated to unravelling the truth, was convinced that the evidence of the two foreign transfers combined with the previous two English deals would aggravate Roach's situation. On 27 July 2001, the FA formally charged Roach, alleging his receipt of double payments for the transfers of Wanchope and Ferguson. The announcement was intended to herald another major scandal similar to the Clough and Graham 'bungs' inquiry.

Roach was defiant. After thirty years wheeling and dealing, he would not succumb to the FA's hapless bureaucrats. His fortune had financed the creation of InterNetClub, an internet operation managed by his son, Nick, alias 'Little Roach', providing subscribers with information about every football player in the world. His self-confidence was reinforced by the FA's decision on 12 April 2001 to subscribe to InterNetClub. The FA's commitment to invest £4 million a year for five years was extraordinary, not least because it was approved by Nic Coward, the FA's lawyer, responsible for the investigation of Dennis Roach. The agent was unabashed that the FA soon discovered that the system failed to perform and, despite extra costs, the FA lacked any recourse against the Roaches. Hilariously, Roach felt, the same association was also levelling serious charges against himself. Regardless of their lawyers' opinions, he was certain of finding loopholes and mistakes. Firstly, the FA's allegations about his receipt of double payments for the transfers of Wanchope and Ferguson were untrue because he never received the money; secondly, the FA's regulations about agents had not existed when the transfers occurred; and thirdly, the FA lacked any jurisdiction over agents registered by FIFA. In October 2001, in response to the FA's charge, he applied to the High Court to declare that the FA was acting unlawfully.

Four weeks later Nic Coward realized the weakness of the FA's position. As Roach contended, the FA lacked the authority to discipline agents and the regulator's sole sanction was to compile a report for FIFA. Fifteen months after starting the investigation, Coward told Graham Bean, 'There are problems about getting Roach.' The FA's lawyers began preparing to withdraw their complaint; the only recourse was to send the dossier to Gianpaolo Monteneri, FIFA's director of legal services. Roach was ecstatic. Days earlier, Monteneri had spoken warmly about Roach at a seminar in London; and FIFA, plagued by allegations of Sepp Blatter's corruption, would, he hoped, be disinclined to pursue him. His consolation was brief. The real threat to his business was posed by his rivals.

During his career, Dennis Roach had made many enemies, few worse than Vincenzo Morabito, who was still outraged by Roach's refusal to share commissions. Those disputes had not damaged Morabito's business success. On the contrary, his football agency, FIMO, went from strength to strength. 'Globally, Vincenzo's the biggest agent,' enthused Jon Smith, the chief executive of First Artist, an exaggeration but nevertheless important for Smith's plans to become the chairman of Europe's biggest football agency, at Roach's expense.

In December 2001, Smith's search for a foreign partner to transform First Artist into a global agency ended. Vincenzo Morabito, boasting relationships in Italy, Spain and Scandinavia matched Smith's requirements. First Artist paid £15 million for FIMO to become its equal partner in a public company quoted on the AIM stock exchange. Morabito received £6.7 million in cash, deposited in his Swiss bank account. Combined, Smith and Morabito claimed to represent over 400 players.

'We're now the biggest management agency in Europe,' said Smith, 'the engine room of the biggest market in football, which is the biggest sporting industry in the world and also the biggest entertainment industry on God's planet.' In June 2001, the company's turnover was just £1.8 million with profits of £700,000. The projected pre-tax profit within one year, for the company capitalized at £19.3 million, was £2.6 million. Jon Smith anticipated that First Artist could be worth £40 million by the end of 2002 and £100 million one year later. On flotation in December 2001 shares in the company rose from 33 pence to 71.5 pence. 'The bubble hasn't burst,' said Smith in December 2001. 'Football is healthier than it has ever been.' Smith's ambitions depended upon acceptance of his credibility. In his telephone calls to the chairmen of Leeds, Charlton, Chelsea and other Premier League clubs, he asked, 'Can we help you in any way?' Repeating his mantra that First Artist had become 'the world's biggest football agency', he mentioned offices in eight countries and that he represented 120 players in Britain. Size, he preached, was all-important. 'We manage the heroes of the zeros,' he gushed about the high-income players his agency represented. 'First Artist is the biggest on the planet,' he repeated. 'We agents will control football.'

To suggest a huge business, the prospectus of First Artist paraded its involvement in hundreds of deals involving dozens of players every year. But only a handful of players were named and the prospectus omitted the truism that once a player had signed a four year contract, the opportunity to generate more business was limited. First Artist could only neutralize the hazard of 'no deal, no income' by forging close relationships with the chairmen of Premier League clubs. Expanding their business in that direction depended upon eliminating other mavericks, the one-man agencies who, Smith hoped, would be squeezed into oblivion by the new regulations. In particular, Smith anticipated the obliteration of Barry 'Silky' Silkman, an amiable former footballer for Crystal Palace, a friend of Terry Venables and Harry Redknapp, and an unsuccessful greyhound trainer living in Barnet. 'Silky', mischievously personified by his critics as an experienced agent knowledgeable about managers and rivals involved in the old 'bung' culture, irritated Smith. Silkman was certainly vulnerable. Squeezed between the agents in Europe enjoying close relations with foreign clubs and the publicly quoted English agencies, Silkman was financially endangered – relying on an unusual number of transfers to Cambridge United – and occasionally powerless.

In October 2000, Silkman had opened negotiations with Freddie Shepherd for the transfer of Clarence Acuna, a Chilean midfielder, to Newcastle United, expecting a commission of £1 million for the introductions. Unannounced, Silky was cut out of the deal. Shepherd dispatched his own representative to Chile and refused to pay the agent any fee. For months Silkman had contemplated suing Shepherd but feared that Shepherd or his competitors would encourage an investigation by Graham Bean, similar to Roach's. 'I hear that you're investigating me,' Silkman said, entering Bean's office at the FA's headquarters in London. 'You'd better stop or else.' 'Or else what?' snorted Bean. 'Get out of my office, into the lift and fuck off out of the building. I've taken on bigger men than you. I wasn't investigating you but I am now.' Bean was joking but in truth he could only challenge the small agents. Those agents operating abroad, like Carlos Gustavo Mascardi, Pinhas 'Pini' Zahavi and the two English agents, Willie McKay and Mike Morris based in Monaco, were beyond his control. Similarly, First Artist and the other publicly quoted agencies were also immune. But there was a convergence of interest between Bean and Jon Smith towards Dennis Roach.

Jon Smith and Vincenzo Morabito had embarrassed Roach over the transfers of Goran Bunjevcevic and José Antonio Chamot to Tottenham. They chortled about the accumulated damage inflicted on his reputation by Graham Bean's investigation, which restricted the agent's opportunities. Smith's ambition was to inherit Roach's privileged access to Tottenham. 'I'll help you rebuild Spurs,' Jon Smith promised Daniel Levy. In early June 2002, Morabito found a third possibility to fluster the older rival.

Roach had negotiated on Tottenham's behalf the purchase of Milenko Acimovic, a Slovenian midfielder playing for Red Star Belgrade, for £500,000. With some zest, Morabito had delved and reported that Acimovic had been available on a free transfer. Jon Smith telephoned Daniel Levy, the club chairman, to relay their hopefully disturbing revelation that the payment of £500,000 was unnecessary. Levy was surprised. 'I was told that the money was needed to repay Acimovic's debts to the club,' Levy told Smith. From Roach, Levy heard another version. 'The player's contract,' the agent said, 'would expire on 30 June and he would have been snapped up before the expiry if Tottenham didn't pay.' The Slovenian newspapers reported a third account: they quoted Srecko Katanec, the Slovenian national coach, telling Acimovic that the £500,000 had been pocketed by a foreigner. The truth was irrelevant to Levy who needed to reinforce his team. 'The agents can sort it out between themselves,' he smiled. To maintain the club's financial stability, he was limiting the money available to rebuild his ageing squad, and Acimovic was cheap. The value of a player was the amount the club felt inclined to spend if the agent could deliver the player. As a last resort – concerned about possible dishonesty – Levy unexpectedly pulled Acimovic to the side just before the contract was signed. 'Where's the money going?' he asked. Acimovic's reply was reassuring: 'To the club.' Whether the player was telling the truth or not was irrelevant. Acimovic was the choice of Glenn Hoddle, and the coach trusted Dennis Roach.

Dennis Roach understood the ultimate consequences of Jon Smith's tactics. In Smith's contest to become a giant, his methods to extinguish Roach's livelihood were brutal. 'Big Cockroach' was being cast as an unfavoured matchmaker. Disdainful of Roach's history as a master among agents in football's cut-throat world, the newcomers were treating the pathfinder as a dinosaur. Roach felt the squeeze. Just as the influence of agents over the future of English football was increasing. His younger competitors were forging relationships with club executives which were denied to himself. Compounding his predicament, the young footballers were becoming increasingly fickle and greedy. In their lust for the new millions, the players' loyalties were evaporating, and they criticized his failure to offer the twenty-four-hour mollycoddling housing-to-haircuts service provided by his rivals. Poignantly, Roach's aspiring heirs remained, like himself, outsiders. None were invited for social or professional reasons to the FA's glass edifice in Soho. The revolution transforming agents into decisive brokers disgusted the panjandrums, but the FA's executives were powerless eyewitnesses of the competition among the agents.

Rather than deal with some of the problems that Bean had unearthed, Adam Crozier decided to demote or even sideline his investigator. In May 2002, Bean discovered that his job was to be advertised. His replacement had been identified – Steve Barrow, an insurance regulator without much experience in football, was to become Bean's superior, although he was expected to adopt a low profile. 'The market will decide what happens to clubs,' ordained Nic Coward. And the same arrangement, Coward implied, would banish unwelcome agents.

Dennis Roach began searching for a lucrative exit, just as others of his generation were similarly cast as dinosaurs.

11

TURMOIL AND TRASH

Blind to his fate, Harry Redknapp arrived at Upton Park on 9 May 2001 understandably ecstatic. The manager had negotiated a new four year contract worth £10 million with Terry Brown, West Ham's cautious chairman. His annual salary would rise from £1 million to £1.6 million, plus lucrative benefits. Redknapp was confident that the contract – printed and on his desk – would be signed that morning despite West Ham's recent run of poor results. 'It's been a massive blow,' he had admitted about the team's defeats. 'Deeply disappointing. It's hard and very frustrating because you haven't got the players and can't afford to buy them.' The team had been destabilized by the sale of Rio Ferdinand, an additional aggravation after the earlier sale of John Hartson for £7 million to Wimbledon. Six defeats had followed that transfer. His despondency had been relieved by Terry Brown's reassurances. 'Harry, I want you for ten years, not four,' Redknapp recalled hearing.

Lean and undemonstrative, Terry Brown's true sentiments were well concealed. Like a poker player, Brown regarded every opportunity with caution. In the unglamorous world of London's East End, the trade of football players organized by agents aroused suspicions. Only recently, Pierre Ducrocq, a French midfielder for Paris St Germain, had been offered to West Ham for £1 million, yet shortly after the player had been offered to Derby for £3 million, and was finally transferred on a loan. Brown had been puzzled; some circumstances about the world of agents were inexplicable. Sitting in a windowless office while the stadium at Upton Park (sponsored by Doc Martens) was under construction, the master of balance sheets was unable to disentangle the rumours about Redknapp's extraordinary trade in players. 'We've never found any evidence of anything untoward but also we've never investigated Harry,' Brown told his confidants.

Despite Redknapp's faults, West Ham owed much to the manager's skills, although his pontification in newspapers revealed his intellectual limitations. A particular player, Redknapp had recently written, was 'dangerous' because 'he's good with the ball at his feet'; but it was 'important', he stressed, that players, 'stay on their feet'. There was an endearing naivety about Harry Redknapp compensating for his faults, but the tolerance disappeared in May 2001. A seismic change had occurred in English football since Arsène Wenger's arrival at Arsenal in October 1996. The cool, analytical approach of the new breed of managers, especially foreigners like Gérard Houllier at Liverpool and Sven-Göran Eriksson as England's coach, branded Redknapp as a symbol of a bygone culture. His strained relations with West Ham's directors since Rio Ferdinand's sale had aggravated the manager's plight.

Redknapp had received £300,000 as a share of the Ferdinand bonanza on condition that he did not agitate a

buying frenzy. That understanding had been ignored. 'We
need a defender,' Redknapp moaned as West Ham lurched
into freefall down the League table, its worst short-term
performance in 105 years. Six million pounds had been
spent before Redknapp suggested that West Ham buy Titi
Camara and Rigobert Song, French-speaking Africans,
from Liverpool for £4.7 million. 'Titi had a great season
at Liverpool,' gushed Redknapp. Brown understood the
agent would be Pape Diouf, a French former football
journalist who specialized in trading players from
France's former colonies. Diouf's associate in England
was Willie McKay, Redknapp's friend. McKay
approached Rick Parry, Liverpool's chief executive. 'Will
you pay me a fee if I can place him?' McKay asked Parry.
Unaware that McKay had been asked by Redknapp to
seek out Titi, Parry agreed, pleased that McKay had
found no difficulty organizing the transfer of a disruptive
player. Parry was doubly delighted that McKay also set
up the sale of Rigobert Song to West Ham. Terry Brown
paid McKay a commission for the purchases. Redknapp
hailed the transfer of Titi Camara as a coup: 'I've got a
£10 million striker for £1.5 million.' Both players proved
to be disappointments and Camara's wages, £30,000 per
week, added to West Ham's soaring expenditure: £23
million for wages in 2000 and rising to £30 million in
2002.

Redknapp was unrepentant about the impression of a
wasteful manager dependent upon close relationships
with agents. 'I want £12 million for new players,' he
announced after West Ham was defeated 3-2 by
Tottenham at home. The record of his expenditure since
Rio Ferdinand's sale was alarming. He had spent £10.3
million for ten players. Five of those players, costing £5.3
million, had made a total of just forty-eight appearances.

Titi Camara's three appearances had cost £486,000 each. The benefit of Rio's sale had evaporated. Instead of Rio's single salary, there were ten salaries and not one of those new players, mostly foreigners supplied by Willie McKay, was worth retaining. All were candidates for transfer. Redknapp was unabashed by those costs. West Ham's directors were aghast. On the verge of committing the club to a £10 million contract with Redknapp, their solution was his dismissal.

By arrangement, Harry Redknapp was sitting in Terry Brown's office on the morning of 9 May to sign his contract. Brown dropped the bombshell: 'Harry, we've decided to let you go.' Redknapp stared in disbelief and began to cry. Tears rolled down his cheeks. There was little more to say. His compensation was agreed at £1.6 million over twenty months, sufficient to dry the tears of a man who once wrote, 'I learned about life in the school of hard knocks.' After the announcement Redknapp was honest, 'Leaving the club was the last thing on my mind when I went over this morning. I never dreamt it would happen.' Finding a new job, Harry Redknapp hoped, would not be too difficult. He met the chairmen of Leicester City and Southampton, both Premier League clubs, but his applications seem to have foundered on his reputation for spending and his relationship with agents. He retired to 'Waterside', his mansion with landscaped gardens running down to the harbour in Poole. The house was reported to be worth £3.5 million. Nearby, he had bought another house which would be worth over £5 million. He had decided to sell his magnificent flat in Hornchurch. While he cared for his property portfolio, he negotiated to become director of football at Portsmouth, planning to buy players for the depleted team through his friend, Willie McKay.

Harry Redknapp's replacement at West Ham was Glenn Roeder. The 45-year-old former player and a coach under Redknapp was a clean-living, quietly spoken executive fashioning himself on the model management of Arsène Wenger. The Frenchman's example, combined with the influx of foreign players, had focused attention upon the relationship of dependency between particular English managers, including Redknapp, and the agents who were determining the fate of the national game. Despite the importance of that transformation, the FA and the Premier League preferred to rely on the clubs' chairmen to unravel the menace and their approach was confused.

Doug Ellis, the chairman of Aston Villa, observed Harry Redknapp's demise and wondered about his own relationship with John Gregory, the club's fiery manager. Ellis had welcomed Gregory, a former Villa 'utility player', in 1998 with the same enthusiasm as for his nine predecessors. Six managers had been sacked by Ellis and three had departed voluntarily. 'I believe John is the best one for the club,' said Ellis, the owner of a demoralized team who limited the money available to buy new players. Skilfully, Ellis also limited the salary for Gregory. Until he proved himself, Gregory would receive just £50,000 per year. Thanks to his vigorous agent, Paul Stretford, that income would rise within two years to £400,000, although Gregory was heard to complain that he deserved every penny and even more.

Ellis cursed that deals with foreigners were frequently fraught. Benfica, the Portuguese club, had refused to pay Villa the agreed fee after the transfer of Gary Charles, a defender; and a representative of an Italian club had threatened Ellis after refusing to pay for another transfer. 'I suggest you drop this issue for your personal safety,'

Ellis was told after repeated requests for his money. No foreign deal excited Ellis's misgivings more than the purchase by John Gregory of Juan Pablo Angel, a striker from the Argentinian River Plate club. South America provided some of the world's best football players, but their agents were also the source of unusual arrangements.

Juan Pablo Angel, undoubtedly a good player, was half-owned by Siglo XXI, a company controlled by Carlos Gustavo Mascardi, his agent. Regularly Mascardi, like his competitors, bought a 50 per cent stake in the ownership of nine-year-old footballers for £100, speculating on their future performance. Although that arrangement was an offence under FIFA's rules, the Association refused to implement any ban. 'A player,' rued Ellis wisely, 'is just an instrument used to his own advantage.'

Without telling Doug Ellis, John Gregory had flown at his personal expense in summer 2000 to Argentina to watch Angel play. Mascardi ensured that his guest enjoyed himself. On his return, Gregory persuaded Ellis that Angel was ideal for Aston Villa. Initially, Gregory said the price was $16 million. As the days passed during November, the price fell to $9 million. By the time Ellis met Mascardi's representative and lawyer in London in January, the price had risen to $12.5 million. 'My nose told me it was suspicious,' complained Ellis. He suspected that the gyrations between dollars and sterling were to pay 'bungs' to some of the participants. Nevertheless, Ellis agreed to pay £9 million (converted by the club at $11.9 million) with the unusual proviso that £1.6 million was for Angel's image rights, not a property that would be of any value in Britain. To Ellis's irritation the payment was also split. Just over £2 million was paid to a bank in Medellín, in Colombia, while the remainder was transferred to Trinicom Holdings BV, an offshore account at the Citco Bank registered in the Dutch Antilles. Ellis believed that the money would be divided between four people in three countries, who all owned a share in Angel. The player himself would receive 15 per cent of the fee, and declared himself to be 'rich and happy'. In a fruitless attempt to protect his club from any ethical breach, Ellis arranged for the FA to transfer the money to South America but his behaviour annoyed the agents, Carlos Gustavo Mascardi and Pini Zahavi. The Israeli expected his normal fee of 10 per cent of the original purchase price of $16 million. Eventually, he reduced his commission to an 'agreed' £350,000. Ellis disputed the existence of any agreement for that sum and paid £300,000 spread over Angel's contract. The confusion and arguments prompted Ellis's suspicions about everyone involved, including John Gregory.

In Mascardi's version, Gregory was 'absolutely not involved in the deal. Ellis did everything.' The agent did not warm to Ellis's manner, alleging that £1 million was missing. There was no evidence for that allegation. The discrepancies and bad feeling prompted Adam Crozier to criticize the transfer as 'corrupt'.

Crozier's suspicions were aroused by the revelation that Mascardi represented another client, Juan Sebastian Veron, the famous midfielder, who had obtained an Italian passport although he was an Argentinian national. Forged documents, based upon a dead man's identity, invented Veron's great-great-grandfather in Italy and allowed Lazio buy a non-EU national. The agent had shared with Pini Zahavi a commission of £2.4 million for arranging Veron's sale to Manchester United.

Ellis's suspicions about Mascardi erupted again soon after Angel's arrival. Passing through the dressing rooms after a match, Mark Ansell, his deputy, spotted Gustavo Arribas, Mascardi's partner, and Gregory in conversation. Soon after, Gregory began suggesting that Villa should buy a succession of foreign players through foreign agents. His suggestion was unexpected; on his arrival at Villa, Gregory had boasted that he would only employ English players. 'Our team is ten Englishmen and a convict,' Gregory had laughed. The 'convict' was Bosnich, the former Australian. But in September 2001, Arribas possessed a letter signed by Gregory stating that he could represent Villa to buy Diego Forlan, a Uruguayan striker, from Club Independiente of Argentina. Ellis had not approved the letter. The price for Forlan, Ellis was told, was $8 million. Ellis rejected the proposition and Forlan was sold to Manchester United for $10 million. The escalating price suggested to the suspicious that the extra cost was for 'bungs' distributed in South America, and, unusually, Forlan personally received £500,000 as an incentive from Manchester United for signing a contract.

Ellis's suspicions were exacerbated by his own purchase of Ozalan Alpay, a Turkish defender recommended by Gregory. Alpay had cost $8 million (£5.6 million). Two payments for the transfer had been deposited by Ellis in two Swiss bank accounts: $1 million was for Rolf Mueller in the Hypobank in Zurich, and $7 million for Fazul Akgunduz in the Catrada Private Bank in Zurich. In retrospect, Ellis could not understand why those payments had been made in Switzerland. Mascardi also had a Swiss bank account which, Ellis suspected, was shared with Englishmen. Ellis was particularly perturbed that at least five agents had become involved, including Pini Zahavi and Mascardi. He could only speculate about the final destination of Aston Villa's money, deposited in a Swiss bank.

Football was not clean, as Ellis knew so well, although his anger about agents depended upon the success of his team. In 2001, his dissatisfaction with his team's performance shifted to suspicions of 'Honest John' Gregory, a fan of Terry Venables and George Graham, who relied upon a handful of agents. Ellis focused on his manager's friendship with one particular agent, Paul Stretford, the chairman of Proactive Sports Management, and a potential conflict of interest.

Paul Stretford, an assertive former salesman of vacuum cleaners lacking any personal participation in professional football, had started his agency in the basement of his home near Manchester in 1987, seeking clients by offering a better service than established agents. He promoted his talents after the transfer in 1995 of Andy Cole for a record £7 million, a major coup which he had never repeated, and his brief fame as the agent for Stan Collymore, an occasionally notorious celebrity. Collymore was subsequently concerned that he was unable to establish precisely how much Stretford earned in commission representing his interests. This lack of transparency characterized the football business, undermining its credibility. To correct that tarnished image and to parade the fact that he represented 240 players and employed seventy-two staff in nine countries as a legitimate sector in a billion-pound business, Stretford floated his company, Proactive, on the stock exchange on 17 May 2001 for £24.5 million. 'There are stringent safeguards and controls on plcs,' the chairman enthused to those questioning the probity of football agents. 'Plc,' he suggested, was proof of honesty. Public companies, he emphasized, unlike one-man-band agents working on mobile telephones, were transparent. This faith in plcs is contradicted by the frauds perpetrated under the guise of public companies such as Maxwell, BCCI, Polly Peck and Barings Bank; experiences which, sadly, had not occurred to Stretford, a dealer rather than a sage.

Proactive's ownership was constructed by Stretford on close relationships. Kevin Keegan, the manager of Manchester City, Peter Reid of Sunderland, Bobby Robson of Newcastle, Michael Dunford of Everton and Graeme Souness of Blackburn Rovers were invited to become founding shareholders of Proactive. In the real commercial world, the flotation of Proactive made little financial sense. But Stretford personally recovered about £1 million from the company's flotation, and anticipated a rising share price as the football boom continued. To assist his expansion, he would hire Jamie Hart, the son of Paul Hart, the manager of Nottingham Forest, and Kenneth Shepherd, the son of Freddie Shepherd, the chairman of Newcastle United. Both Hart and Shepherd earned commissions selling players to their fathers' clubs. Stretford understood the value of those relationships and flatly rebutted any challenge. 'Nepotism is not a crime,' he believed. A conflict of interest was acceptable and not a 'problem', he sought to delude critics, 'so long as it's conducted professionally'. Proactive's share price moved between 25 pence and 40 pence, encouraging its shareholders in the football clubs to use Proactive's services and increase their company's profits. Those circumstances, especially football agents operating under the cover of public companies, excited Doug Ellis's suspicions.

In recent months, Paul Stretford had supplied four players to Aston Villa and simultaneously also acted as John Gregory's personal agent, managing Gregory's private company. In his autobiography, John Gregory paid many compliments to Paul Stretford, although the manager omitted to mention the earlier bankruptcy of

FrontLead Ltd, the agent's company, an insolvency which cost Stretford's creditors £128,000. Paul Stretford admitted the existence of suspicions but denied any wrongdoing. Keen to portray himself as the opposite of Eric 'Monster' Hall, an agent criticized by the FA for taking and giving secret payments, Stretford commented in an interview titled 'Paul Stretford the honest football agent', 'I can honestly say in eight years, I've never been even asked by any manager to make a payment to him for a transfer to go through. Or when a deal's complete, asked to pay him something. Never . . . So if it's going on, I don't know how or who with.' Irritated by the shabby image of agents, he paraded his own probity: 'I don't think we live in a bung culture as such.' He did, however, admit the existence of suspicions about his relationship with John Gregory: 'I could be accused of having a conflict of interest but I have acted in a proper manner throughout.' Stretford was, however, critical of his peers: 'I'm really worried about the lack of professionalism and I am frankly appalled at the behaviour of some of the so-called agents that certain players have signed with.' While praising his own empathy with players, he highlighted those who 'leave themselves open to attack. I've managed to be successful because I've made sure all parties are satisfied.'

'You're too close to Stretford,' Ellis told Gregory after paying £1.475 million to agents during 2001. Doug Ellis prided himself that any deal involving Paul Stretford was closely scrutinized, especially after the agent was paid £250,000 for negotiating Peter Schmeichel's 'free' transfer to Aston Villa. The goalkeeper was a mixed success. 'That's the last time you use Stretford,' ordered Ellis. Some of Stretford's deals, Ellis believed, were unsuccessful.

During a trip together to Denmark in 1998, Stretford had persuaded Walter Smith, the manager of Everton, to buy Peter Degn, a midfielder from Aarhus. Michael Dunford, Everton's chief executive, exploded in an unusual challenge:'Bloody hell, Walter, what a waste of space' . . . 'Degn's useless.' Four years later, after four appearances, the player was transferred back to Denmark. Michael Dunford's opinion about the forceful-talking Stretford was explicit: 'He wants his pound of flesh but I wouldn't buy a second-hand car from him.' Stretford's rebuttal was explicit: 'I didn't pull one over them. I believe the person who decides to buy the player is the manager.' To prove his credibility, Stretford sold Everton four more players after the Degn debacle.

At Sunderland, Peter Reid, the club's abrasive manager, had also relied on Paul Stretford. Criticized by newspaper columnists in the 1980s as 'stupid', Reid, a combative midfielder who won thirteen England caps, had demanded too much money for himself as a player. 'I don't think footballers are greedy,' he said. 'What I've got to do is cash in on myself while I can.' Labelled by a tabloid newspaper 'Peter Greed', he became manager of Manchester City in 1989 but was fired in August 1993 after bad results and questions from Robert Reid QC, the chairman of the Premier League's 'bungs inquiry', about two transfers. In particular, Robert Reid QC could not understand the circumstances of the purchase of Kare Ingebrigtsen, an Austrian player represented by Rune Hauge, and Ingebrigtsen's receipt of £50,000 after his transfer to Manchester City. Having interviewed Peter Reid, the Premier League's inquiry decided that no money had passed to the manager. Despite the complete exoneration, Reid spent two years in the wilderness until he discovered his fortune. In March 1995, the mercurial

browbeater was recruited as the manager of Sunderland
by Bob Murray, the club's surly owner, whose fortune
had been earned manufacturing bathroom fittings. His
latest choice proved to be inspired. Peter Reid, the fifth
manager in four years, saved Sunderland from relegation
from the First Division and masterminded their promotion in 1996 to the Premier League; and, after a second
relegation, managed their return to the Premier League
in 1999. To maintain the club's position, with limited
finance, Peter Reid adopted a similar strategy as Harry
Redknapp, buying foreign players. Like Redknapp, the
pattern and quality of his purchases through selected
agents aroused controversy.

Reid bought Kim Heiselberg, a defender who returned
to Denmark after hardly playing; and he bought Jan
Eriksson, a defender from Sweden who played for forty-
five minutes and was released. From Mechelen of
Belgium, Reid bought Tom Peeters, a midfielder, who
arrived and departed without one League appearance.
From Argentinos Juniors, Reid bought Julio Arca and
Nicolas Medina, both for £3.5 million. Reid had watched
Medina play before the transfer, but after his arrival in
Sunderland he declared the player to be unusable. He
bought Edwin Zoetebier for £325,000 on a three year
contract and six months after his arrival allowed him to
leave without playing one game in the League. He bought
Eric Roy from Marseilles for £200,000, whom he praised
as 'my best ever signing'. During the second season, Roy
was dropped. The purchase of Stanislav Varga, a centre
back from Slovan Bratislava, was particularly unusual.
Varga was offered to Reid by Ludwig Kollin. 'His contract ends in June 2000,' said Kollin. 'He'll then be free.'
'Send him for a trial,' replied Reid. After two days Reid
was persuaded and he arranged to meet Kollin, Scott

McGarvey, the player's agent, and Roman Duben, the representative of Bratislava, in Zürich to conclude the deal. The negotiations collapsed after Sunderland refused to pay £800,000, the price stipulated by Duben before leaving Bratislava. Shortly after, Mike Morris, an agent based in Monaco, reopened negotiations on Reid's behalf and offered £850,000. 'I couldn't understand what was happening,' admitted Duben, bewildered by Sunderland reporting Varga's transfer fee as £875,000. After a few months playing for Sunderland, Reid spoke of selling Varga for £3.5 million, but in March 2002 he went on loan to West Bromwich Albion.

Mike Morris, based in Monaco, was counted among Reid's favourite agents. Regularly seen at Sunderland's training ground, Morris was a broker rather than an agent caring for individual clients. Adopting the role of adviser or lawyer, he had perfected methods to cope with the FA's and FIFA's rules. Frequently he was summoned by club managers as a trusted expert to overcome the FIFA regulation forbidding agents to approach players under contract. In May 2001, Morris offered Lilian Laslandes, a 31-year-old striker playing for Bordeaux, to Sunderland. Reid bought the Frenchman for £3.6 million despite reports of his poor performance and his availability, the previous year, for £2 million. During the 2001–2 season, Laslandes never scored for Sunderland. To save his salary, he was loaned by Reid to Cologne. Laslandes's purchase had followed Reid's purchase through Morris of Lionel Perez from Bordeaux for £200,000. Perez departed on a free transfer two years later.

The losses for Sunderland were not only the purchase fees but also the wages. The accumulated losses for English football were the millions of pounds which should have trickled down through the Football League to the grass roots, to improve the national game. English football was haemorrhaging its seedcorn to enrich foreign clubs and agents but the executives of neither the FA nor the Premier League showed any resolve to protect the sport's future.

In the absence of any official restraint, Peter Reid showed no caution about buying foreign players through other agents, including Paul Stretford. In March 1999, relying on Stretford, Reid had bought Carsten Fredgaard, a Danish forward from Lyngby, Sweden, for £1.8 million. Fredgaard played just once against Walsall and was discarded. To save his wages, the player was loaned to West Bromwich for one month, then loaned to Bolton for two months, and finally he was resold to Copenhagen for £500,000. Paul Stretford felt no embarrassment about the debacle. He explained that the player had been 'watched by scouts for some months' before the transfer was agreed. 'Football is not an exact science. Some deals work and some don't. It's swings and roundabouts.' The club, and not the agent, he insisted, should bear the responsibility for any bad deal. 'My relationship with Reid is excellent,' confirmed Stretford.

The trade in Danish players to English clubs was nevertheless curious. With a few exceptions, a succession of undistinguished Danish footballers had been transferred to England, seemingly for the benefit of the agents and not the clubs. Among the players were Jorgen Nielsen, a goalkeeper, bought by Liverpool, who never appeared; Krishie Pausen, bought by Trevor Francis for Birmingham City for £5 million, although worth, according to Scandinavian agents, at most £500,000, who only played in twelve First Division matches; and Morten Hyldgaard, a Danish goalkeeper, bought by Coventry for £200,000, who remained unused. Danish agents suggested that the attraction for their footballers was England's low taxation. After two years' absence, Danish citizens returning home paid 25 per cent income tax rather than the standard 65 per cent. The advantage for the English clubs was less comprehensible. There was a similar pattern of purchases from Latvia. Imants Bleidelis had been purchased from Skonto Riga by Southampton in 1999 and played once in two years. There were similar 'mistakes' about players from Ecuador, but Peter Reid and other managers still trusted the judgement of their favoured agents, especially Paul Stretford.

To prove his professionalism to Sunderland, Aston Villa and other Premier League clubs, Stretford boasted, 'If the club is interested we do our due diligence and look into the background of the player. Then we find out who he belongs to and what agents are involved.' Stretford particularly extolled his shrewd research about South American players. In March 2000, he was especially proud about Sunderland's purchase of Milton 'Tyson' Nunez, a Honduran striker. 'I saw Nunez play for Honduras in the Gold Cup,' Stretford explained after the purchase, 'and when Sunderland said they were keen I went into researching him.' Nunez was described by Stretford as a former player for Nacional of Uruguay, a major team, who had been transferred to PAOK Salonika.

To establish Nunez's ability, Stretford had travelled with Andy King, Reid's scout, to watch Nunez play in an international match in Honduras. They were accompanied from Miami by Pablo Betancour, Nunez's agent. Andy King was unimpressed, not least by the chalk quarry where the match was played. 'Truly mafia,' he reported, 'but Stretford was pushing. He said Villa would "dive" for Nunez if we didn't buy.' The two Englishmen returned to Miami with Betancour and Stretford outlined the final deal. The initial fee for Nunez would be £800,000 and would increase to £1.6 million after his arrival in Sunderland. However, the financial benefit of the transfer seemed to be tilted in favour of the agents. Stretford's finding fee from Sunderland would be £150,000 and the two agents would share a further $1.5 million based upon Nunez's performance. Stretford returned to England to finalize the contract. During the exchange of faxed messages, Stretford's references to 'Nacional', the First Division team, were corrected by Betancour to 'Uruguay Montevideo FC', a Third Division team. Stretford appeared to believe that the two teams were identical and 'Uruguay Montevideo FC' remained in the final contract. In March 2000, on the basis of Stretford's representations, Sunderland's representative signed the contract and bought Nunez.

Over the following year, Nunez played just once for Sunderland, appearing as a substitute. He became the forgotten player until Reid discovered that Nunez had never played for Nacional. In self-defence, Stretford explained his belief that Nacional and Montevideo were the same club. His famed diligence was flawed. Stretford blamed Betancour for perpetrating a 'sting' and suggested that Andy King, the scout, was responsible for approving Nunez. Stretford explained he was a 'victim', who nevertheless, for taking no responsibility, expected to earn nearly $1 million from the deal. Sunderland refused to pay the second tranche of the fee. Pablo Betancour and the Uruguayan club sued for the money. In reply, Stretford accused Betancour of perpetrating a fraud. Stretford's allegation was rejected by a judge in the English High Court. 'Mr Stretford,' the judge declared, 'wasn't directly told any lies, but gradually given the wrong impression.' There was no evidence, emphasized the judge, that Betancour had been dishonest.

In June 2001, Nunez returned to South America on a free transfer. Bob Murray, Sunderland's chairman, never publicly criticized Stretford or Peter Reid for the Nunez debacle, or for the succession of other inexplicable transfers of players. He tolerated a manager who detested criticism, so long as he produced success. Reid, who owned 5.5 per cent of the club's shares, detested his critics, especially local journalists. They were banned by the club from the press box in the stadium. But one damning statistic could not be concealed: Reid had spent £67.5 million on sixty-six players and recouped only £19.5 million from sales. He had splashed out £48 million, a phenomenal amount for a club worth less than £8 million on the stock exchange.

John Gregory at Aston Villa did not enjoy similar protection, not least because he openly criticized Doug Ellis for being 'small time', 'a penny pincher' and 'stuck in a time warp'. 'People do consider me brash and arrogant,' admitted Gregory, 'but I don't give a damn.' Considering that Aston Villa was a publicly owned company, the manager's behaviour confirmed football's uniqueness. During 2001, Ellis wondered about his manager's purchases. In four years, he had spent £71.5 million on players and recouped £46 million. He had bought Bosko Balaban, a Croatian forward, for £6 million despite an unenthusiastic report by Brian King, Villa's scout, based upon one match in Latvia. Unusually, Balaban's agent, as part owner, received 50 per cent of the price, but the payments to other agents became confused. Graham Smith of First Wave billed the club for £125,000 in commission, firstly as the player's agent and then as a representative of Aston Villa. The club did not protest about the contradiction. Ellis only admitted that he was perplexed by his manager's increasing interest in foreign players. Balaban made just eight substitute appearances.

'You're intelligent but selfish,' Ellis told Gregory, suspecting that his manager, to extract money to trade players, was instigating anti-Ellis chants among the fans and inserting critical stories in the newspapers. 'It's easy to buy players with money you haven't got,' Ellis barked at Gregory in what he called 'naval language'. Aston Villa's financial problems reflected the plight of most clubs. Just as Manchester United's value had fallen in less than two years from £1 billion to £340 million, Aston Villa's value had crashed. On flotation in May 1997 for £126 million – 'against my better judgement', according to Ellis, who wanted more – its shares were three times oversubscribed, but the price had since fallen from £11 towards £1. The club's pre-tax profit in 1999 of £22 million had become a loss in 2001 of £151,000, despite receiving £16 million from Sky TV. Those loyal fans who bought shares were also hit by rising entry charges. Ellis was puzzled how Leeds, worth about £35 million on the stock market, could own players which the club valued at £200 million. Football's finances were senseless. In common with most Premier League clubs, Aston Villa could not retain any money or pay a respectable dividend from its non-existent profits. Borrowing like Peter Ridsdale to buy players in the hope of competing in Europe was, said Ellis, 'a risk I can't take'.

On 24 January 2002, Ellis had tired of Gregory's public criticism, especially the accusation that the chairman lived in 'a time warp' for refusing to buy more players. The manager was also weary of the incessant conflict and suddenly resigned. 'John's resignation is sad,' sighed Ellis. 'It was most unexpected but has been amicable.' Gregory himself explained how he 'needed a break to consider his future', but three days later he was named as the new manager for Derby County. The contract had been negotiated by Paul Stretford. Ellis was appalled; he had tolerated too many embarrassments from Gregory. Quietly, Mark Ansell, his deputy, compiled a file on his former manager. Initially, he considered retaining Kroll, the corporate investigators, to pursue Gregory but on reflection he preferred the FA to bear the cost and responsibility. On 15 April 2002, Ansell presented a dossier of evidence against Gregory to Adam Crozier in London. Also present were Nic Coward, Richard Scudamore and Dave Richards of the Premier League. The evidence against John Gregory, Ansell hoped, would be used against a man who had traduced the club's trust. 'We're going to investigate this,' Crozier promised.

Ellis was pleased by the FA's reaction, although he would have been appalled had he known that his file would only be forwarded to Graham Bean for investigation in early December, eight months later. Ellis would be loath to admit that he lacked any hard evidence against Gregory to substantiate his suspicions. The FA was not presented with more than, at most, a hint of any wrongdoing committed by Gregory. Ellis's two bulging files simply echoed his anger against the agents involved in three transfers – Angel, Balaban and Alpay – and Ellis's irritation that his millions had been deposited in inaccessible, offshore accounts. To the detriment of the game, managers and agents were blighting his beloved sport. Football was apparently beyond the control of the clubs' owners. The agents held sway.

To Jon Smith and Paul Stretford, Ellis was as much a dinosaur as Dennis Roach. Although neither agent could boast one client who had been selected for England's

World Cup squad in 2002, the future growth of their
companies depended upon club chairmen and managers
committed to aggressive trading of players through an
intimate relationship with a particular agent. By securing
attachment to a club, with access to privileged information, Smith and Stretford would be relieved of the
uncertainties, especially lost income from unsuccessful
transfers. A nepotistic or exclusive relationship with
Premier League clubs guaranteed profits. Their exclusion from the giant deals involving Manchester United's
purchase of Juan Sebastian Veron for £28 million, Jaap
Stam's transfer from Manchester United to Lazio for
£16.5 million, Ruud van Nistelrooy's move to
Manchester United for £19 million, and Rio Ferdinand's
sale to Leeds for £18 million compounded their vulnerability. Foreign agents had earned millions of pounds from
those deals and, pertinently, a sweetheart arrangement at
Manchester United involved Elite, an agency employing
Jason Ferguson, the son of Sir Alex Ferguson.

In a unique manner, Sir Alex Ferguson seemed subject
to helpful dispensation from the normal rules preventing
conflicts of interest. In 1999, he admitted in his autobiography to have received five years earlier a brown parcel
containing £40,000 in cash from Grigory Essaoulenko,
the vice-president of Spartak Moscow. The parcel was
handed over at the end of transfer talks about Andrei
Kanchelskis. The money had been returned after remaining for one year in the club's safe. After interviewing
Ferguson, Graham Bean recommended that Manchester
United be disciplined under the FA's rule 26 for
'improper behaviour and conduct likely to bring the game
into disrepute'. His recommendation had been ignored to
avoid embarrassing Maurice Watkins and other directors
of England's leading club.

Football agents recall Sir Alex's partiality towards his twin sons, Jason and Darren. Mark McGhee, a former player for Aberdeen, had moved, with Alex Ferguson's active encouragement, as a manager from Reading to Leicester to Wolves. McGhee's misfortune was to drop Darren Ferguson from the Wolves team. McGhee's relationship with Alex Ferguson ceased. Jason Ferguson, the other twin, was equally protected. Agents discovered that Sir Alex encouraged Manchester United players seeking transfers in or out of the club to abandon their established agent and engage Jason Ferguson for transfers to clubs of the manager's choice.

Jonathan Greening, a 21-year-old forward, had wanted to transfer to West Ham, but Sir Alex opposed Greening's choice and urged him to move to Middlesbrough. 'He doesn't want to move to Middlesbrough,' Mel Stein, the player's agent, told Ferguson. Sir Alex was irritated; he urged Greening to abandon Stein and appoint Elite as his agent. Ferguson hinted that the alternative was to 'rot in the reserves'. Stein threatened Sir Alex with writs and eventually brokered Greening's transfer to Middlesbrough himself. Jason Ferguson lost that business but he did broker, with the help of Mike Morris, the transfer in September 2000 of Jaap Stam from Manchester United to Lazio. Stam was unaware of the sale until the deal was completed and he had been flown in a private plane to Rome. The urgency and secrecy suggested that Sir Alex had tipped his son about his desire to sell the defender, and Jason had activated other agents. The agents' commission was £1.4 million. Jason Ferguson was also party to the negotiations to buy Stam's replacement, Laurent Blanc. Zealously, Jason Ferguson entrenched his special relationship with Manchester United by representing Roy Carroll in his transfer from Wigan to Manchester United in

summer 2001; and in creating a unique offer of a
Manchester United shirt, similar to the shirts available at
the official shop for £30, for £275. The extra cost was for
the signature of the chosen player, a certificate of authenticity and a frame.

Protests about Sir Alex's apparent nepotism were
ignored, although Manchester United was a publicly
quoted company subject to statutory regulations. The
FA, Premier League and the regulators failed to query
Jason Ferguson's possible access to privileged information and ignored accusations of conflicts of interest. The
complaints encouraged other sons to seek a similar advantage. Darren Dein, the son of David Dein of Arsenal,
Kenneth Shepherd, the son of Freddie Shepherd of
Newcastle United, Craig Allardyce, son of Sam Allardyce
of Bolton, and Mark Redknapp, son of Harry Redknapp,
the manager at Portsmouth, all became involved in the
football business with the possibility of benefiting from
privileged information.

Denied that privileged access, Jon and Phil Smith of
First Artist struggled to establish special positions in
other clubs. Every three months Phil Smith telephoned
Alan Curbishley at Charlton to offer First Artist as the
manager's agent. 'We must do some business,' said Phil.
'Very pushy,' said Curbishley, aware that the Smith brothers wanted to secure him as a gateway to supply players to
the club, similar to the relationship First Artist had established at Crystal Palace.

Crystal Palace, the same troubled club Jon Smith had
known under Terry Venables's management, was an
incubator. In July 2000, Simon Jordan, a 32-year-old,
brash self-made millionaire who sold his half share in the
Pocket Phone Shop to One2One for £36.5 million,
bought Crystal Palace from the administrators for £9.6

million. Known by his red suits and silver Ferrari, Jordan attracted publicity by giving Rolex watches to his players and taking his new team to a lap-dancing club in central London. The articulate new chairman did not believe 'there is a great deal of difference between telephones and football if you approach football as a business and not as an ego trip'. In buying and selling players, he relied on First Artist. 'I see agents as an evil curse on football,' he pronounced in a bitter tirade. 'They are parasites. They drive up the price of transfers and salaries, and make and break deals at will. They are duplicitous and a menace as far as I am concerned. I hate them, but it's supply and demand. There's a lot more money involved, so players feel more comfortable with an agent. I'm a deal-maker and always happy to reach a common ground with players but agents have shifted the balance of power, so that all the power is now with the players. Agents have also forced up the cost and price of everything, so the finances of clubs are far more precarious than is commonly realized.'

To ease his financial burden, Jordan bought shares in First Artist worth £250,000 as 'an investment opportunity'. With the help of Phil Smith, Crystal Palace had hired Trevor Francis, a client of First Artist, as the team manager, replacing Steve Bruce, another client of First Artist. To cement the relationships, Matthew Francis, the son of Trevor Francis, was employed by First Artist. Four Crystal Palace players were also represented by the agency. Like the Smith brothers, Jordan dismissed the notion of a conflict of interest. 'I don't accept that at all. It's purely a personal investment in First Artist, nothing to do with football or Crystal Palace.' On reflection, he admitted, 'Clearly, it's nice to have a rapport and relationship when some of our players are represented by them.' The 'rapport' allowed Jordan to influence the agents supplying his players, which was not a handicap while negotiating the footballers' contracts. The advantage, however, was limited. After two years, he found his ownership 'unrewarding, disappointing and demoralizing', not least because his annual wages bill had quadrupled from £2.5 million to £10 million.

Crystal Palace was a small prize for Jon Smith compared with the prospect of establishing a close relationship with Chelsea. To fulfil Ken Bates's ambitions, the London club had bought many foreign players. Twice during 2000, Gianluca Vialli, Chelsea's Italian coach, did not field one British footballer. After Vialli's dismissal, the agent enjoying the best relations with Claudio Ranieri, the club's ninth head coach under Bates's ownership, was Vincenzo Morabito. Ranieri was Morabito's client. Over the years, Morabito had sold many players to Chelsea and Jon Smith expected First Artist to be crowned Chelsea's favoured agent. The plan was materializing just as the fortunes of football, and especially Ken Bates's, lurched downwards.

In May 2002, Stanley Tollman, Ken Bates's partner, was accused by the New York prosecutor of thirty-three separate charges of fraud and tax evasion. Since the 1980s, Tollman had allegedly presented false accounts suggesting irrecoverable losses to the banks and, in anticipation of bankruptcies, was accused of secretly transferring assets to other companies ultimately owned by Tollman. Banks in New York, which claimed to have lost $42 million, sought to seize all of Tollman's assets. Among their targets were shares in Chelsea registered under Swan Management in Guernsey. Bates denied a financial crisis, but Chelsea's quandary was indisputable. Swan had sold its remaining 26.3 per cent stake in the

club, principally to Bates. The chairman increased his
stake from 17.7 per cent (he had sold 15 per cent of his
original shares since 1996 at a profit) to the maximum
29.9 per cent. The share price was 18 pence, a costly drop
for those, including BSkyB, who had bought the shares
two years earlier at £1.47. Bates was tarnished by the
association with the two architects of Chelsea's revival –
Stanley Tollman and John Papi – who had both been
accused of dishonesty involving bankruptcies, and he was
under pressure to pay £7 million every year until 2007 on
the £75 million Eurobond loan. For a company which
consistently lost money, the burden was onerous. Chelsea
could not afford new players and European clubs could
not afford its rejects. The finances of the clubs were
squeezed and the agents, especially Jon Smith, who had
relied upon a relationship with Chelsea, were among the
casualties.

That month, May 2002, the Smith brothers were fearful of failing to produce the profits promised to the City
banks which had invested in First Artist. At their offices
in Wembley, Phil Smith, a robust trader who justified his
frequent use of expletives as a manifestation of 'wearing
my heart on my sleeve', was setting his staff high targets
to sign new players. During their regular Monday morning conference, the young recruits claimed to have heard
Phil Smith urge them to 'get alongside the club managers', bend the truth to obtain business and even boast
that some managers required bribes. Smith would vigorously deny those claims but his aggressive demands
caused several of the agency's younger staff concern.
They were especially worried that Phil Smith was expecting them to breach the FA's code of conduct.

Rule 12.4 of the FA's professional code in the 'Players'
Agents Regulations' stated that the contract between a

player and a club should explicitly identify who was
paying the agent's fee. A second rule stipulated that an
agent could only be paid by one party in a transaction –
either the club or the player – but not both. 'Paying at
both ends' was forbidden.

Two transfers completed by First Artist concerned
some employees. The first involved the transfer in June
2002 of Steve Robinson, a 28-year-old midfielder, from
Preston North End to Luton Town. First Artist obtained
£5,000 in commission from Luton Town and subsequently asked Robinson to also pay £5,000 commission,
although he only paid £1,000.

The second transfer raising concern was Nicky
Eaden's from Barnsley to Birmingham City. Eaden, a
defender, had signed a contract with First Artist in 1997.
In 2000, he became a 'free' player under the Bosman
rules. Phil Smith finalized Eaden's employment by
Birmingham City and invoiced the club on 10 July 2000
for a commission of £50,000. Eight weeks later, after the
contract was finalized and the club had paid the commission, First Artist asked Eaden to pay £15,000 commission
over three years for negotiating the transfer. 'We are not
earning enough money on these deals,' Eaden recalled
Smith saying. Unaware that First Artist had received as
much as £50,000 from the club, Eaden paid the first
instalment but later protested, firstly, after he was told
about Birmingham City's payment to First Artist by the
club's chief executive; and secondly, in early 2002, after
he was actually shown First Artist's invoice by Steve
Bruce, the club's manager. Eaden's complaint of the
double payment only became known to First Artist's
young employees during 2002, after a heated argument
between Eaden and Phil Smith. According to Eaden,
Smith had said that Birmingham City had only paid

£20–25,000 in commission for his transfer and the remainder was for other work. Furthermore, Phil Smith allegedly told Eaden that the agency had 'done a favour' to the player by not recording the fee, which would otherwise have attracted income tax. Eaden received advice from an accountant contradicting Smith's suggestion. Their bitter argument about illegal double payments became known to everyone at First Artist's headquarters.

In the opinion of First Artist's disgruntled employees, their agency was breaking the FA's rules. Eaden's transfer to Birmingham could only be completed after the player's own contract was finalized. Therefore, approaching Eaden for a commission for work completed eight weeks earlier, and taking fees from both sides simultaneously broke the FA's rules.

The Smiths disagreed. They believed that they were innocent of any wrongdoing and vehemently argued that Eaden's transfer was two separate transactions. The first transaction was the transfer between clubs, in which First Artist was acting for Birmingham City, and the second transaction was the negotiation of the player's contract with the club. That arrangement, the Smiths argued, was accepted in the football industry. Their view was that Eaden was not contracted to First Artist at the time the agency was negotiating his transfer, but only after the agency obtained its commission from the club. Hence, they insisted, the FA's rules had not been breached. That explanation was rejected by the agency's dissatisfied employees. The letter and the spirit of the FA's rules, requiring an agency to possess a written contract with either the club or the player during the negotiations, had, they argued, been broken.

The combination of the Smiths' aggressive pursuit of profits and the disquiet within the Wembley headquarters about the agency's treatment of several other players transformed the increasing antagonism into a crisis in July 2002.

Neil Miller, the agency's general manager, told the Smith brothers that he was resigning. He blamed the general culture of the Smiths' business; despite their pleas, Miller departed. Miller's departure prompted the resignation of Steve Wicks, and, to the brothers' surprise, nine of their staff also offered their resignations. Six joined Miller to establish Grassroots, a rival agency representing several First Artist players. The Smiths feared catastrophe and sought an injunction to prevent their former employees soliciting the agency's clients. On the eve of the trial, First Artist settled the case on undisclosed terms which permitted the former employees to continue to run the rival agency. This settlement meant that the allegations were never resolved in court. The crisis had passed. First Artist had not immediately lost any valuable clients but endured a very damaging experience. The Smiths' football dream was souring.

Restricted by what he perceived to be football's declining fortunes, Jon Smith looked with envy at the close relationship of Jerome Anderson, the chairman of Sports Entertainment and Media, a rival publicly quoted agency, with Arsenal and in particular with David Dein. Anderson, a former estate agent and insurance broker from Cockfosters in north London, is a lifelong supporter of the club and boasts 'a love affair with Arsenal'. A relationship with England's champions was every agent's dream.

12

'THE DREAM-MAKER': DAVID DEIN

Paul Walsh was bitter. 'Gutted' and 'angry' were his sentiments about David Dein, the vice-chairman of Arsenal and architect of the club's remarkable success.

During the first days of July 2000, Paul Walsh had telephoned David Dein and offered Igor Stepanovs, a 23-year-old Latvian striker eager to play for an English club. 'I think you'll find him good,' urged Walsh, a former Premier League footballer turned agent, registered by FIFA. Understanding the pedigree of the telephone call, Dein agreed to consider Stepanovs. The risk would be borne by Paul Walsh. If Dein was not interested, Walsh's time and expenses would be wasted; but if Arsenal were prepared to buy the Latvian, Walsh would expect a commission. The ultimate beneficiary would be Skonto Riga, a Latvian football club. In common with the owners of the world's minor clubs, Guntis Indriksons, the club's president, regarded the English Premier League as a source of rich profits. Several of his players had been bought by English clubs, including Marian Pahars by Southampton. Latvian footballers were fashionable commodities that year.

To sell more players to English teams, Indriksons had
sent a squad under Gary Johnson, their British manager,
to play against Stockport, Woking and Sheffield United.
By the end of July, David Dein, relying on reports from
Arsenal's scouts, decided to buy an option on Stepanovs
and another player. To negotiate with Arsenal,
Indriksons required the services of an English agent. He
was recommended to use Jerome Anderson, an agent he
had never employed before. In Jerome Anderson's opinion, 'It was a complete coincidence that Indriksons came
to me.' There was some evidence that Indriksons had
been advised to retain Anderson by Alex Kozlovski, a
Belorussian agent, unregistered by the FA and FIFA,
whom Jerome Anderson called 'my representative in
Riga'. Indriksons gave Anderson a power of attorney
which was valid between 2 and 11 of August. That was
Anderson's first contact with the Latvian player, about one
month after Walsh's telephone call to Dein.

On 2 August, David Miles, Arsenal's secretary, signed
an agreement with Jerome Anderson to pay the Latvian
club £100,000 for a two-month option on Stepanovs.
The final decision on the purchase, as Dein frequently
reaffirmed, would be taken by Arsène Wenger, Arsenal's
manager. 'Arsène Wenger decides which player he
wishes to acquire, and indeed sell,' David Dein has said,
insisting that the manager and not the vice-chairman
decides.

By the end of the option, Wenger had made no decision. On Indriksons's behalf, Kozlovski telephoned
Jerome Anderson frequently to discover the fate of the
deal. His own commission depended on the club signing
Stepanovs. In turn, Anderson called Arsenal. He was told
that the club would wait until Stepanovs played again.
During that period, Kozlovski promised Jerome

Anderson that he would persuade Stepanovs to retain Anderson as his agent.

On 2 September 2000, Wenger flew in a private jet to Riga to watch the national team play Scotland. Wenger had undertaken the journey only after a trusted French scout had agreed that Stepanovs was a good purchase for the London team. Wenger returned to London and reported to Dein that Arsenal should buy the player.

At Gary Johnson's request Paul Walsh again telephoned Dein. 'I hear that you're interested in Stepanovs,' said Walsh. The vice-chairman's answer was a bombshell. 'Yes, but Jerome Anderson is dealing with it,' replied Dein. Walsh was puzzled. 'What's Jerome Anderson got to do with it?' he asked. 'I'm Stepanovs's agent, not Jerome Anderson.' 'Have you got any paper to prove it?' asked Dein, anticipating the answer. In his Highbury headquarters, Dein had assessed Walsh as just another aspiring one-man-band agent, operating from a mobile telephone. Those peripheral lightweights, offering unknown foreign footballers in the hope of earning fortunes in commission were, in Dein's opinion, best sidelined. Even if, like Walsh, they were agents registered by FIFA. Before Walsh could obtain the written authorization from Johnson in Latvia, the vice-chairman moved fast. In a telephone conversation with Johnson, Dein declared his interest to buy Stepanovs immediately for £1 million. Indriksons was delighted. In an exchange of faxes, the sale was completed on 4 September 2000, just two days after Wenger's flight. The pertinent omission from that deal was Stepanovs's contract with Arsenal. Although the player had been sold to the club, he had not signed a contract and remained technically unrepresented. Wishing to avoid any accusations of a conflict of interest and a breach of the FA's rules, Jerome

Anderson suggested that Alex Kozlovski, his own representative, advise Stepanovs. Arsenal, nevertheless, would be invoiced to pay the commission fee to Jerome Anderson. Two hours after landing at Heathrow on 4 September, Stepanovs signed a formal contract with Jerome Anderson to act as his representative. The timescale was bewildering, even though everyone involved was satisfied. At the outset, Anderson had represented Skonto Riga; then through Kozlovski, he represented Stepanovs; and finally, he was paid by Arsenal. Potentially, the allegation could be made against Jerome Anderson of a conflict of interest which favoured Arsenal and the agent.

Soon after, with Kozlovski's help, Stepanovs signed a contract with Arsenal. There was, according to Anderson, little negotiation about the salary of about £7,000 per week, low for an Arsenal player. That did not displease Dein.

In David Dein's opinion, 'Stepanovs was brought to Arsenal by Jerome Anderson and Paul Walsh was not involved, although he did try to involve himself in the transaction.' Dein is scathing about aspiring agents chasing small commissions, shouting 'I was there first.' He wants them smoked out. In his air-conditioned office, Dein has the authority to pronounce, 'The first call does not matter.' Walsh was the forgotten loser, another casualty of David Dein's trust in Jerome Anderson, an intruder disliked by many as a wealthy enigma who had first represented the Latvian club and then became the player's agent. The contradictions caused no unease for the principals involved. Gary Johnson's verdict about Anderson was definitive: 'He's very good for players and he's trusted by Arsenal, who do the right thing by the players.'

Suspicion and accusations by rivals nevertheless dram-
atized the relationship between Arsenal's vice-chairman
and Jerome Anderson. Football and its billions magnified
the sentiments. Unravelling their relationship, inextricably
linked to fortunes and sensation, could explain several
mysteries, but there was no evidence of a paper trail.
Regardless of their insistence that their relationship was
wholly honest, the perception of a conflict of interest was
used by critics to create controversy.

Football's secrecy was endemic. With little effort and
no public criticism, football's finances were intentionally
concealed behind the public image of an undisputed success. Arsenal Football Club ranked among England's
best, and was poised to challenge Europe's giants. The
lure was historic glory and unprecedented profits. The
vice-chairman justly claimed credit for the club's success
as a football team, his advocacy of new stands and corporate boxes at Highbury and, supremely, the recruitment
of Arsène Wenger as manager. But the financial hinter-
land to those triumphs remained a riddle, complicated
by the inclusion of a new ingredient: Darren Dein, the
vice-chairman's son. Darren Dein, a 28-year-old solicitor,
was retained as a consultant to Jerome Anderson, appearing to his critics to draw on the patronage of his father
and the self-interest of the trusted agent. David Dein
described his son's relationship with Jerome Anderson
as 'freelance'. As a lawyer, Darren Dein did not require
registration by FIFA as an agent.

The question to David Dein by Sir Roger Gibbs at a
board meeting of the Arsenal directors during 2001 was
direct. Gibbs, a respected banker whose family had been
active as bankers in the City since 1808, is the former
chairman of The Wellcome Trust and had been a director of Arsenal since 1980. He had become concerned by a

newspaper report about Darren Dein's financial relationship with Jerome Anderson. Gibbs asked David Dein
directly if the report was accurate. Dein's reply, it
appeared to Gibbs, denied the existence of a relationship.
'We must avoid conflicts of interest,' said Gibbs. 'Yes,'
agreed Dein. The vice-chairman may not have understood precisely the City banker's interpretation of what
constituted a conflict of interest. As a trader, and, like all
those involved in football, Dein had not encountered the
City of London's strict rules forbidding conflicts of interest. In the opinion of the football community, the City's
rules for business were irrelevant to their sport.

Soon after that exchange, Gibbs obtained the prospectus issued by Jerome Anderson to float his agency in
November 2000. Anderson had listed Darren Dein as the
'Group's legal consultant'. The banker again asked David
Dein for an explanation. 'My son,' insisted Dein accurately, 'has never represented Arsenal in any transaction
and has never negotiated with the club on any transaction.' The directors also received a personal letter from
Jerome Anderson stating that Darren Dein only provided
a limited amount of legal advice to the company. Gibbs
was completely satisfied with Dein's assurances, although
neither David Dein nor Sir Roger Gibbs were aware of
the disputed events which had occurred one year earlier
in Rotterdam.

On 27 September 2000, Darren Dein was sitting with
Frank Sedoc, a 35-year-old Dutch agent, in the Arsenal
directors' box at Highbury. In that intoxicating atmosphere they watched Arsenal defeat Lazio. Unlike Paul
Walsh, Frank Sedoc was not registered by FIFA to act as
an agent, but Sedoc was not ignored as Walsh had been
by David Dein. The Dutchman had been instrumental in
introducing Celestine Babayaro, a Nigerian defender,

Roberto Di Matteo, an Italian midfielder, and Frank
Leboeuf, a French defender, to Chelsea; and pertinently,
for guiding Nwankwo Kanu, a striker, to Arsenal.
Steeped in the football business, Sedoc ranked among
those unofficial European agents whose expertise was
required to satisfy the ambitions of the Premier League's
chairmen.

'My father's worried about Seaman,' said Darren
Dein, referring to Arsenal's ageing goalkeeper. David
Seaman was suffering from a shoulder injury. 'We need a
new goalkeeper.' After many years in the business, Sedoc
understood Darren Dein. The young lawyer, brought up
by a father devoted to the club and the sport, was eager
to profit from the same business. There was glamour,
excitement and greater riches in football than operating
from a soulless solicitor's office. Darren had represented
Thierry Henry, Arsenal's French striker, regarding various sponsorship contracts, and appeared to Sedoc to be
ambitious to expand his involvement with football.
Sedoc was equally interested in forging a closer relationship with the vice-chairman's son. 'I know just the
goalkeeper for you,' replied Sedoc, noticing Darren
Dein's eyes suddenly sparkle. 'Come with me, at my
expense, to Rotterdam and I'll introduce you to him. See
if you like him and if he's interested.' 'Who is he?' asked
Darren Dein. 'Jerzy Dudek,' replied Sedoc, referring to
a 28-year-old Pole playing for Feyenoord, the Dutch
club, and acknowledged as one of Europe's best goalkeepers. The following day, Darren Dein telephoned
Sedoc. 'Jon Smith of First Artist,' said Dein referring to
a football agency in north London, 'represents Dudek.
They've already offered him to my father.' 'That's not
correct,' countered Sedoc. 'First Artist have nothing to
do with Dudek.'

That brief exchange highlighted the misunderstandings and half-truths uttered by those desperate to grab a
share of football's millions, especially the agents and
fellow intruders.

Two weeks earlier, Jon Smith had arrived at the stadium of Feyenoord Football Club in Rotterdam with
Roman Manachefevsky, a Pole claiming to know Dudek.
In reality, neither man knew Dudek and neither was formally contracted by Arsenal to make an offer to the
goalkeeper. They had travelled to Rotterdam in the mere
hope of initiating a multimillion-pound deal. Their commission would be at least £200,000. 'Roman nagged and
nagged me to go,' recalled Smith, 'but I knew it was a hit-
or-miss effort. A flyer. At worst, a pleasant day out.'
Naturally, the two men expected to share the commission with Jan de Zeeuw, Dudek's agent. 'We can arrange
Dudek's transfer to Arsenal,' said Manachefevsky, speaking on their joint behalf in the cafeteria inside
Feyenoord's stadium. The three men, sitting around a
table, could be stigmatized as vultures – all intending to
profit from the skills of a young footballer who was still
unaware of their discussion.

Jan de Zeeuw had discovered Dudek at a sports club
in Poland in the winter of 1995 and, with pride, had
secured a four year contract with Feyenoord. Two years
of that contract remained, but binding agreements in
football were tradable commodities. Transferring Dudek
to Arsenal was exceptionally attractive. Dudek's
inevitable new fame and extra income were a spur to Jan
de Zeeuw's dreams. The agent appreciated, however, his
own vulnerability. He was unregistered by FIFA and
could be ignored by David Dein. To protect himself, he
needed an ally, but that certainly would not be Jon
Smith and his Polish accomplice. 'I'll get Jerzy,' said de

Zeeuw. Minutes later, the goalkeeper entered the room. 'Do you know these people?' asked de Zeeuw. 'No,' replied Dudek. 'Do you want them to represent you?' 'No,' replied Dudek. 'Goodbye,' said de Zeeuw after ten minutes.

Jon Smith's exit was the opportunity for Frank Sedoc's entrance. Unlike Smith, Sedoc knew de Zeeuw and deployed a more subtle approach. Before leaving London, he visited Arsène Wenger at his home in Totteridge, north London. 'Are you interested in Dudek?' he asked. 'Yes,' replied the coach. Sedoc telephoned Darren Dein saying, 'Come and meet de Zeeuw.' Sedoc calculated that this would assure Arsène Wenger and Darren Dein that he, unlike Jon Smith, did have access to Dudek. Simultaneously, he could persuade de Zeeuw that Arsenal was interested in the goalkeeper. The vice-chairman's son agreed to fly to Rotterdam.

The three men sat in the coffee shop of the Novotel Hotel, near Rotterdam's airport. All three faced the possibility that a successful outcome might be a breach of Dudek's contract with Feyenoord, a ploy which David Dein, as a senior member of the board of the FA, had repeatedly condemned. Darren Dein wanted to break into the football business; Jan de Zeeuw glimpsed his first opportunity to earn serious money from an international deal; and Frank Sedoc, as an experienced broker, expected to reap a healthy commission. Pertinently, de Zeeuw had not notified Jorien Van den Herik, Feyenoord's president, about his plan to arrange the transfer of the club's goalkeeper. After just forty minutes of meandering conversation, Darren Dein stood up to return to London. De Zeeuw claims Darren said, 'Good. I'll talk to my father.' Darren Dein vehemently denies uttering those words. He makes it clear that he has never

'made any attempt to represent Dudek in a possible transfer to Arsenal'. David Dein unequivocally confirms his
son's denials. 'My son,' he says, 'who is a qualified lawyer,
has never represented Arsenal in any transaction and has
never negotiated with the club on any transaction. There
is no conflict.' David Dein insists that his son never spoke
to him about Dudek.

On 1 October 2000, four days after Frank Sedoc had
watched Arsenal defeat Lazio, he was sitting with de
Zeeuw in the Arsenal directors' box watching the home
team beat Manchester United by a spectacular goal
scored by Thierry Henry. 'Fly with me to London on
Sunday,' Sedoc had said, 'and I'll introduce you to David
Dein and Arsène Wenger. I'll pay for everything.' Sitting
nearby was David Dein. Sedoc believed that he had
proved his relationship with David Dein by arranging
Kanu's transfer to Arsenal from Inter Milan for considerably less than Dein had considered paying. 'David
always thinks he can negotiate better,' Sedoc had confided to a friend, 'but he's not as good as he thinks.'
Sedoc's ability to arrange an invitation for himself and de
Zeeuw to the directors' box, and de Zeeuw's introduction
to Arsène Wenger in the boardroom after the match, confirmed his trusted status. While de Zeeuw discussed the
possibility of Dudek's transfer with Wenger, Sedoc
arranged for Dennis Bergkamp, the Dutch forward, to
sign a shirt for de Zeeuw's son. That evening de Zeeuw
returned to Holland convinced of Arsenal's interest. Two
important steps remained: Arsenal would make an official
offer to Jorien Van den Herik, and de Zeeuw would negotiate the goalkeeper's contract. De Zeeuw waited for
Darren Dein and Sedoc to send Arsenal's offer.

Over the following months there was no progress. Jan
de Zeeuw's version of events, sharply denied by Darren

Dein, mentions a telephone conversation with Darren Dein. 'My father is fed up,' Darren Dein allegedly said. 'So many different people are offering Dudek. Send me a written authorization that I can represent Dudek.' Darren Dein denies that conversation, describing de Zeeuw and Sedoc as 'mischievous', but, in any event, whatever may or may not have been said, the relationship was irrevocably terminated. According to de Zeeuw, he feared that someone else wanted to represent Dudek. The Dutchman's reply to Darren Dein was explicit: 'No one is authorized to represent Dudek except me.' To reinforce his authority, de Zeeuw claims he sent Darren Dein a letter also signed by Dudek, confirming that authority.

Frank Sedoc was also excluded from any future negotiations by de Zeeuw. Baffled and angry, Sedoc lamented that wasting time and money was normal but this was unusual. 'There are only friends in football,' lamented Sedoc, 'when they need you. That's when David Dein is my friend.' De Zeeuw had protected his property and, after establishing direct contact with David Dein, he recruited Bas van Noortwijk, a respected Dutch agent registered by FIFA, as his new associate. That, he believed, would satisfy David Dein's requirement.

In mid-May 2001 a fax from David Dein expressing Arsenal's interest in Dudek arrived at Jorien Van den Herik's office in Antwerp, the centre of his engineering business employing over 2,000 people in factories and offices on both sides of the Atlantic. It was a surprise to the hard-faced entrepreneur renowned for his straight talking. 'Out of the blue,' was his description. Compared with Arsenal, Feyenoord was a minor club owned by a non-profit-making trust. Van den Herik's unpaid involvement was a time-consuming 'hobby'. Dein's approach highlighted the disparity: Dein arrived in Rotterdam on

Sunday, 20 May 2001, on a private jet with Danny
Fiszman, the club's chairman, and Arsène Wenger for
lunch and to watch a match against Utrecht. Dein and
Van den Herik had seen each other at the regular meetings of UEFA, but had not established a relationship. Van
den Herik's impression was of a man busy networking in
the corridors and whispering into a mobile telephone.
Dein was a less successful businessman compared to Van
den Herik, but in the world of football Dein was the
architect of Arsenal's colossus while Feyenoord was small
and suffered from over-stretched finances. Selling Dudek
had become vital to repay the club's considerable debts.

During the simple meal in an office, Dein asked jocu-
larly, 'How much do you want for Dudek?' Van den
Herik's reply was deliberately non-committal. 'No player
at Feyenoord has a price tag,' he replied. As a respected
businessman negotiating with major car manufacturers
and building contractors, he did not enjoy the theatre of
haggling before reaching an agreement. 'Well, give us an
idea,' urged Dein, smiling. 'OK, I'll pluck one from the
air,' replied the host. '£12 million.' 'You're joking,'
laughed Dein. 'We'd only pay £4 million.' There was a
pause while Van den Herik gauged the seriousness of his
guests, but that was interrupted by Dein. 'We can't conclude anything now. We'll have to think about it. Can we
meet the player and agent now?'

Jorien Van den Herik summoned Jan de Zeeuw to the
room and watched carefully the Arsenal team shake the
agent's hand. From their manner, he remained totally
unaware that Wenger had ever met de Zeeuw. He would
have been outraged had he known that the agent, contrary
to all football's regulations, had visited Arsenal and discussed Dudek's sale with Wenger over the previous
months without his agreement. Just as Dein would be

outraged that an approach had been made to Patrick Vieira, his captain, without his knowledge. 'Can Dudek come to London tomorrow and see the facilities?' asked Dein. 'No problem,' replied the club's president. 'I'll wait to hear from you with a firm offer.' Van den Herik anticipated an offer of about £7 million.

Arsène Wenger had the authority to offer Dudek a contract. In de Zeeuw's version, the manager verbally offered Dudek a five year contract and promised to double his salary, conditional on a transfer agreement between the two clubs. Arsenal disputed that suggestion, although everyone was certainly optimistic. De Zeeuw and Dudek were invited to watch Tuesday night's match, a testimonial for David Seaman. The famous goalkeeper's anticipated retirement confirmed Arsenal's interest in Dudek, but the invitation was declined to avoid embarrassment. All that remained was for Arsenal to settle the transfer fee with Feyenoord. The Pole's dream appeared to be fulfilled.

The following day in Rotterdam, Van den Herik saw a large photograph in Dutch newspapers of Dudek visiting Arsenal. He assumed that the personal terms had been agreed and awaited an e-mail from David Dein with a firm offer. In his experience over the previous eleven years, everything would be concluded within twenty-four hours. Instead, there was silence. On Thursday 24 May, he telephoned Dein. 'Are you making a firm offer?' he asked. 'We've got a board meeting tomorrow,' replied Dein, deliberately playing for time, 'and I'll call you afterwards. But I must tell you that we are considering two other goalkeepers.' Van den Herik was not disturbed; no other goalkeeper, he believed, could rival Dudek and the events on the previous weekend confirmed Arsenal's intent. The Dutchman, however, was unaware of the

implications of Dein's familiar phrase, 'I'll come back to
you.' Haggling and keeping his options open was natural
for the former food trader.

One week later, there was still no word from Dein. Van
den Herik was puzzled. On 31 May, he sent Dein an ultimatum to send an offer by the following day or he would
assume the transfer was cancelled. Dein's reply was to
offer £5 million. Van den Herik regarded the offer as
meaningless. Europe's best goalkeepers were selling for
£10 million, and if Dudek was sold to Arsenal,
Feyenoord would need a replacement. There would be
nothing left from £5 million. Dein's offer was rejected
with a counter-demand of £8.5 million.

Jan de Zeeuw had also become impatient; the deal, he
feared, was teetering. Dudek was anxious. Arsène
Wenger's offer and the subsequent publicity had convinced him of a certain transfer. The silence was
unsettling. De Zeeuw flew to London to confront David
Dein. An invitation for lunch at Dein's home in
Totteridge reassured the agent despite his host's complaint, 'Van den Herik isn't discussing a serious price.' De
Zeeuw was unaware of Van den Herik's contradictory
complaint that Dein was refusing to send a 'serious firm
offer'. However, the agent was placated. 'Don't worry
about Jorien Van den Herik,' said Dein reassuringly. 'I
know him well. We both have boats in the south of
France.' But Dein's comforting words were meaningless.
Despite Van den Herik's pleas and letters, Dein never
contacted the Dutchman again. The stalemate was unresolved. Arsène Wenger flew to Tunisia for his summer
holiday, Dein began sunbathing on his yacht on the Côte
d'Azur, while Van den Herik, in America, was becoming
outraged. 'I can't do anything,' admitted Wenger in
repeated telephone calls with de Zeeuw. In desperation,

de Zeeuw telephoned Dein who declared, 'I am committed to another deal.' De Zeeuw was paralysed; he was unaware that Dein had negotiated with David Sheepshanks, the chairman of Ipswich, to buy Richard Wright, a 23-year-old, for nearly half the price of Dudek. Two days before the deal was announced, Jonathan Barnett, the goalkeeper's agent, was told. Barnett, a former casino executive, was an unusual agent. Proud that he had only visited four or five training grounds in his life, he explained, 'I wouldn't know where to go. It's a waste of time. I just sign players on word of mouth and recommendation. They come to me.' Wright's transfer to Arsenal was, the agent declared, 'a great opportunity for Richard'. By any measure, it was an extraordinary purchase, not least because Barnett earned £520,000 in commission.

Unlike most outfield players, goalkeepers can continue to improve into their thirties and Jerzy Dudek ranked among the world's best. By comparison, Richard Wright was inexperienced and arguably an unsuitable replacement for Seaman. Some could not believe that Wenger, ambitious to win all the trophies, would choose Wright. 'Are you in charge or not?' de Zeeuw asked Wenger. 'There's nothing I could do,' replied Wenger, denying that Arsenal's negotiations for Dudek had been worthless.

The news outraged Van den Herik. 'There had been no misunderstandings with David Dein,' he declared. 'Dein was possibly pursuing an unknown agenda.' The consequences were unfortunate. The collapse of the transfer unsettled Dudek and Van den Herik had no choice other than to sell the goalkeeper. His sale to Liverpool for £4.5 million was less than Arsenal's offer, while Richard Wright, after the transfer, sat on the bench at Highbury practically unused. In July 2002, Arsène Wenger showed his lack of confidence in Wright and the goalkeeper was sold to Everton for £4.5 million. In the aftermath, Dein explained that, although he had wanted a deal, Van den Herik had asked for too much. Nevertheless Dein felt obliged towards the Dutchman. In reconciliation and to compensate the club, Dein agreed to play Feyenoord in a friendly match, but that event never materialized. De Zeeuw was also bewildered and could only rue Frank Sedoc's trenchant obituary: 'If you had dealt with Darren, there probably would have been no problem.' De Zeeuw assumed that his mistake was to have rebuffed Darren Dein or failed to consult Jerome Anderson.

That judgement was vigorously rejected by David Dein, complaining about a familiar backlash from all those who got squeezed out. Arsène Wenger made the decision, Dein explained, and Richard Wright was cheaper. And, critically, David Seaman remained as Arsenal's goalkeeper.

The circumstances of Stepanovs's and Dudek's transfers were quoted by those resentful of David Dein's considerable influence in English football. The appointment of Adam Crozier as the chief executive of the FA; the appointment of Richard Scudamore as the chief executive of the Premier League; the appointment of Sven-Göran Eriksson as the England coach; and the dismissal of Ken Bates as chairman of Wembley stadium's reconstruction could all be traced to the leverage and energy of David Dein. He was undoubtedly a modernizing influence in English football who had even introduced displaying the names of players on their shirts. All that activity had spawned enemies. Their weapon was the revelation of a financial relationship between Darren Dein and Jerome Anderson. Publicizing that potential conflict of interest alerted Arsenal's directors to formally request

a statement from David Dein at a board meeting. David
Dein's assurances were accepted but the publicity was
unwelcome. The embarrassment did not detract from the
evidence suggesting a man of undisputed ability, vision
and utter devotion to Arsenal and English football. Yet
like many in the game Dein's record outside football
influenced his reputation.

Born in 1943, Dein dropped out of university and
developed a flourishing business as an importer of
Caribbean foods under a railway arch in Shepherd's
Bush, branching out later to become a sugar trader. In
1983, Peter Hill-Wood, the chairman of Arsenal, offered
a 17 per cent stake in the club to several City friends, but
all rejected the chalice. Football was in crisis, attendances
were falling and some of England's best players were
employed by European clubs. Dein, a passionate supporter of Arsenal, bought the stake for £290,000. By
1991, he had increased his shareholding to 30 per cent
despite a meltdown of his personal fortunes. His sugar
business had been hit by a third-party fraud and was
threatened with insolvency. Despite his misfortune as a
businessman, he promoted himself as the representative
of the new commercial thinking in English football,
although occasionally his judgement proved to be faulty.
In 1991, he supported ITV's bid rather than Sky's higher
bid for the exclusive rights of Premier League; and after
1991 he promoted the notion that multinational corporations would invest in the new Premier League clubs. That
sponsorship, he argued, would 'bring the lower divisions
more than they have now . . . the lower divisions will
probably be better off'. Those predictions proved to be
mistaken. In 1995, Dein lost a personal court battle to
recover £13 million from the fraud. His food, sugar and
haulage business collapsed. To settle his debts, he

reduced his shareholding in Arsenal after 1996 to 16 per cent. The purchaser of his shares was Danny Fiszman, a diamond and property dealer, content to allow Dein to occupy the spotlight as the continuing mastermind behind Arsenal's success. Fiszman paid less for his shares than Granada's investment in 2000 of £47 million for a 5 per cent stake.

Dein's triple ambition to be elected the chairman of the FA, to become England's representative at UEFA and to occupy a seat on FIFA's executive. His election campaigns for power in the FA embraced a notably moral tone, particularly targeted against agents. A polite, gentlemanly manner bestowed credibility on his repeated criticism of agents for destabilizing and even poisoning his club's relationships with players. One headache for Dein was the activities in June 1999 of Claude Anelka, the brother of Nicolas Anelka, a French striker contracted for four years to Arsenal. Claude Anelka had discovered that Real Madrid were willing to pay a huge sum for his brother. The incentive to provoke a breach of contract with Arsenal and arrange his brother's transfer was a reported commission of £6 million from Real Madrid. According to Dein's complaint, Claude Anelka, helped by Marc Roger, an unregistered agent, sought to induce the premature release of Nicolas Anelka from Arsenal's contract by issuing barbed remarks about the footballer's impending 'illness' and need for a 'rest'. Real promised Nicolas Anelka a gross annual salary of about $8 million. 'Life is a jungle,' explained Claude Anelka. 'So I have to do what we want to do.' Dein's informant was Vincenzo Morabito, who represented Lazio's interest in Anelka, and had seen Real Madrid's unsigned contracts. 'That's the usual way they work,' commented Morabito. 'We feel as if we are being blackmailed by Anelka,' complained Dein, who nevertheless awaited a counter-offer from Juventus of Italy.

On 2 August 1999, Dein succumbed to the so-called 'blackmail' and Arsenal accepted £22 million from Real Madrid for Anelka. Dein's public protestations of outrage were criticized by those who recalled how Dein had originally spirited the 17-year-old Anelka away from his Paris team in February 1997, albeit paying £500,000 in compensation for the breach of Anelka's contract. In Dein's opinion the purchase of Anelka was entirely legitimate. Two years later, Dein said that the £22 million received for Anelka had established his club's astute identification of an outstanding young player. Yet, in the same breath, Dein reinvigorated his campaign against agents. 'I have been on a crusade,' Dein announced, 'since the Anelka saga to ensure agents act in a proper, orderly and dignified manner.' Both Anelka and Marc Roger questioned whether Dein himself always abided by those same standards towards agents. Mel Goldberg was an agent voicing similar doubts.

In autumn 1994, Mel Goldberg, a solicitor, was seeking a club for the forward Dennis Bergkamp who was anxious to transfer to an English club. Before telephoning David Dein, a personal friend, Goldberg travelled to Milan with Kevin Keegan, the coach of Newcastle United, and two directors of the club. The group had been greeted in the Palladian apartment of Massimo Moratti, the president of Inter Milan, a renowned titan in the football world. During a formal lunch served by white-gloved waiters from silver platters, Moratti, speaking in English, had promoted the value of Bergkamp.

Mel Goldberg's presence at the lunch provided a glimpse of the Byzantine nature of the football business.

The lawyer from north London, anxious to earn a commission from the player's transfer, did not represent Newcastle, Inter Milan or the footballer. His introduction had been prompted by a telephone call from Giuseppe 'Pino' Pagliara, an Italian agent living in Manchester. 'Milan want to sell Bergkamp,' Pagliara had said. 'Can you put a deal together? They want £5.5 million.' At his own risk, Goldberg faced the middleman's dilemma of matching the buyer and seller without the promise of exclusivity. His success was to arrange the lunch and, in the event of a transfer, he would expect to be paid by both clubs. Significantly, Rob Jansen, the player's Dutch agent, was not invited to the lunch and had not even been informed about the meeting. His involvement would only become necessary after the two clubs agreed on a transfer and the player assented to move to Newcastle. Jansen would then negotiate the player's personal contract and would expect his commission from Newcastle.

Keegan returned home and eventually decided to buy Les Ferdinand rather than Bergkamp. Goldberg sighed and recommenced his search for a buyer. To his glee, Doug Ellis, the chairman of Aston Villa, agreed to buy Bergkamp for £5.5 million but Bergkamp declared, 'I don't want to live in Birmingham.' Goldberg sighed again and, in February 1995, telephoned David Dein: 'Are you interested in Bergkamp?' 'Yes,' replied Dein. Over the following two weeks, Goldberg negotiated and agreed the terms for Bergkamp's transfer for £5.5 million with Ken Friar, Arsenal's trusted managing director and 'well known' to Goldberg. The agent was certain that the deal was on the verge of completion when, at 4 p.m. on Friday 16 June 1995, Friar telephoned Goldberg. 'I'm sorry,' said Friar, 'Arsenal are not going to buy Bergkamp.' 'Why?' asked Goldberg. 'Because we do not wish to break our wage structure. His salary is too expensive.' 'Is that final?' the agent asked. 'Yes,' replied Friar. Further discussion, Goldberg understood, was pointless.

The following Saturday morning, a journalist telephoned Goldberg and asked, 'What's Bergkamp doing at Arsenal?' 'I don't know,' replied Goldberg, 'but he's not going to sign for them. I spoke to Ken Friar only yesterday.' 'Well something's going on,' said the informant.

Unknown to Goldberg, Rob Jansen, the player's agent, had decided on his own initiative to find a London club for his client. He asked Jerome Anderson for help, who in turn telephoned Bruce Rioch, Arsenal's manager. Specifically, Anderson denies discussing Bergkamp's transfer with Dein, although in the usual course of events only Dein could have approved the transfer. Dein himself says, 'I might well have spoken to Jerome but my negotiations were with Rob Jansen.' The Dutch agent suggested that Dein speak to Count Gianmaria Visconti di Modrone, the club's vice-president. In effect, the Italians had been backing two horses into Arsenal.

Over the following three days Goldberg telephoned Dein and Friar. Unusually, neither man was available. On Wednesday 28 June, Arsenal announced the purchase of Bergkamp for £7.5 million, substantially more than the offer five days earlier. Sitting alongside the player during the presentation was Jerome Anderson, described as the player's agent. Goldberg was surprised; until that moment, Jerome Anderson had never featured in Bergkamp's career and had not featured in his negotiations. Clearly, both he and Jansen would receive a commission from Arsenal. Goldberg was, according to his own account, cut out of a deal which was worth £2 million more than during the previous months.

Some weeks later, at an Arsenal shareholders' meeting, Peter Hill-Wood was asked why Arsenal paid £7.5 million for Bergkamp if the original demand had been only £5.5 million? Before Hill-Wood could answer, Dein snatched the microphone: 'I know you're talking about Mel Goldberg. But a fee of £5.5 million was never mentioned. We've paid the proper price.' Dein was embarrassed and outraged. 'Goldberg could never deliver Bergkamp for £5.5 million,' he protested. 'Inter Milan would never have sold him for that price. They wanted £7.5 million.' Dein added later, 'I believe that £7.5 million, the agreed price, was very fair.' Rob Jansen offers a different interpretation: 'Milan did a good job getting more money from Arsenal. Dein should have been more sharp.' Dein insists that agents like Goldberg often suggest low sums as an enticement but cannot deliver what they offer. Goldberg, a trustworthy lawyer, rejects that interpretation.

Mel Goldberg was upset by David Dein's behaviour, but he did not protest. The football world was small and annoying Dein, he decided, would be a self-inflicted wound. Rather, he would try again; he telephoned Dein. 'Why don't you consider Bixente Lizarazu?' asked the agent in his precise language. 'He's an excellent defender and he also scores several valuable goals each season. He would be an ideal replacement for the ageing Winterburn.' 'No, I'm not interested,' replied Dein. 'He leaves too many gaps at the back.' Days later, Goldberg heard that an Arsenal scout was visiting Bordeaux to watch Lizarazu play. Goldberg quickly telephoned Dein. 'I tipped you off about Lizarazu,' said Goldberg. 'I'm not so sure,' replied Dein. 'So many agents have called. I need to check my records.' Goldberg believed that Dein had never heard of Lizarazu until his call. The news Goldberg heard from Bordeaux was familiar – Jerome Anderson had become involved through a partner in France. Goldberg intervened and, using his influence, ensured that the player was sold to another club.

The pattern appeared to Goldberg to be obvious. David Dein, he believed, had often favoured Jerome Anderson, a scenario vehemently denied by Dein. But rival agents interpreted the evidence to match their suspicions. Players transferred to the club by one agent were persuaded, they believed, to change their loyalties to Jerome Anderson. Years earlier, Charlie Nicholas, a Scottish striker playing for Arsenal, had also decided after a dispute to abandon Mel Goldberg as his agent and switch to Jerome Anderson. Other players had also changed agents in anticipation of or after their arrival at Arsenal to Jerome Anderson's Sports Entertainment and Media. Among Anderson's recruits were David Seaman, Ian Wright, Emmanuel Petit and Edu, a Brazilian midfielder. The most surprising recruit was Francis Jeffers, a 20-year-old rising star at Everton. Jeffers was persuaded that he would find his transfer to Arsenal easier if he switched to Jerome Anderson's agency.

In a fortunate coincidence, Anderson negotiated Arsenal's purchase of Jeffers from Everton for £8 million, for some an unexpectedly high price, coinciding with the flotation of his agency on the stock exchange. One year later, Jeffers abandoned Anderson and appointed Paul Stretford as his agent. 'Jeffers didn't think the cosy relationship between you and Dein would help him,' Stretford told Jerome Anderson on the telephone, a call which Anderson disputes. In any event, Anderson did not protest. He had become involved in an unpleasant argument with Jeffers's father about money and he knew that the player's future at Arsenal was uncertain. Above all, Anderson understood predators and one defeat did not undermine his self-promotion as the club's unofficial agent representing among the club's other stars Tony Adams and Thierry Henry. Of the forty-five players in Arsenal's squad in 2001, he represented eight, more than any other agent. In 2001, his gross profits were £1.5 million on a turnover of £2.6 million. Football agents, he appreciated, conducted their business on unusual terms. Their clients, the players, were not always guaranteed the right to know their agent's commission while working on their behalf. Transparency was not common in the football business, which had helped Anderson within a decade to become a wealthy man and identified as an agent who understood everyone's requirements.

Anderson certainly understood the needs of Arsenal's footballers. They were young, ultra-fit men, idolized by the fans and countless girls, and earning more in a week than the average Briton in one year. With limited education and no financial experience, they were grateful to Anderson for his patience in caring about their homes, cars, electricity bills and even hairdressers. Above all, the agent provided soothing reassurance about their uncertain destiny with fame. On Saturday and Sunday nights, the agent received a stream of telephone calls from his players, anxious for sensible advice about their performance, their relationships with club officials and their prospects. In a fickle business flaunting physical fitness and emotional vulnerability, Anderson was a trusted friend, offering a round-the-clock babysitting service to men damned by some for the 'fathomless void between their ears'.

Similarly, Anderson was a reliable partner with foreign agents operating in England. In the transfer of Dmitri Kharine, a goalkeeper from CSKA Moscow to Chelsea in October 1992, Anderson had partnered two

Russians agents. According to Robert Reid's inquiry, the £400,000 commission for the agents was paid by Chelsea into Anderson's account in London. Jerome Anderson had retransferred the first £200,000 to the Russians' account in Jersey and handed over to the Russians a suitcase containing £175,000 in cash. He was allowed to keep £25,000 for himself.

Anderson was an agent who understood how to satisfy his clients and the sentiment was mutual. 'There are people in this industry,' David Dein said during a Dow Jones conference on 23 April 2002 while Jerome Anderson sat smiling nearby, 'who are not as honourable as you.' Anderson, bearing a remarkable physical resemblance to his friend, unsurprisingly agreed: 'It's always visible who we are acting for. There's never a conflict of interest.' His uniquely close relationship with Arsenal, Anderson said, was 'just an appearance'. Other agents enjoyed similar access, insisted the agent, although he was unable to name one other. Through his access, Anderson had also become the club's representative for the players' valuable 'image rights'. Representing a club was less hazardous and more profitable than acting as the agent of players. There was always the guarantee of deals and acting for both a club and the players increased the profits.

Jerome Anderson agreed to share his representation of Thierry Henry with Darren Dein. In order to further that cause, Anderson had invited Freddie Ljungberg, the Swedish midfielder, to his office in Finchley to discuss the player's 'image rights'. To Ljungberg's surprise, Darren Dein was also present. Anderson suggested that the Swede allow the two Englishmen to negotiate his 'rights'. Ljungberg was wary; his first contract was due to expire in eighteen months and negotiations for the renewal would soon start. 'You know,' said Ljungberg, 'I'm very happy with my present agent, Vincenzo Morabito. I don't think I want to change.' Nothing more was said. Morabito and Jon Smith understood the challenge, so familiar to other agents in London.

The allegation of a special relationship – a potential conflict of interest – between David Dein and Jerome Anderson was vigorously denied by David Dein, who denies any knowledge about Anderson's methods for inserting himself into deals or persuading players to transfer their business after their arrival at Arsenal to his agency. Publicly, Dein has expressed his 'trust' of Anderson. 'He's not an agent looking for the next transfer,' he told a public audience. 'He's been a great help to the club.'

The 'help' to the club, praised by Dein, exactly illustrates the potential conflicts of interest at the heart of football. Jerome Anderson is an agent representing footballers to their manifest satisfaction, yet Dein, on behalf of Arsenal, is pleased to pay Anderson for the work he does for the club. In Dein's description, the agent delivers the player and makes sure the transfer happens. Since the club has benefited, Arsenal is prepared to pay the agent. In particular, Dein is grateful to Anderson for ensuring that Ian Wright, the club's famous record goalscorer, never transferred away. The player's interest might not in those circumstances be paramount although Anderson insists, 'I make every effort to ensure my client's wishes are met.' Jerome Anderson cared for Arsenal, and, in anticipation of the club's requirements, he had unexpectedly become the agent of Paul Robinson, a goalkeeper at Leeds and a candidate if David Seaman should retire. 'You're tapping my goalkeeper,' Ridsdale accused Dein after a Premier League meeting in October

2002. Dein was puzzled by this. Anderson had provoked the loss of a valuable ally.

David Dein has emphatically denied any favouritism towards Anderson. 'Since Arsène Wenger's arrival at the club in October 1996,' he says, 'there have been eighty-six player movements – in and out. Jerome Anderson has been directly involved in eight of the transfers. Ninety per cent of the transfers have been through other agents. Every agent is treated equally.' That statistic inevitably omits the players recruited by Anderson after their arrival at the club.

In the interests of his club, David Dein has campaigned against the appointment of an independent regulator of football and rejected stringent controls over the clubs' chairmen while advocating control over agents. In the interests of England, he had approached Sven-Göran Eriksson, employed as Lazio's manager, in the middle of the season. Eriksson's abrupt departure was England's gain but annoyed Lazio's managers. Dein's ambition to become chairman of the FA, the regulator of all English football, and the supremacy of Arsenal in the Premier League magnified the controversy. The FA was an ineffective regulator and if Dein, antagonistic towards regulation, became chairman, the FA's weaknesses would not be remedied.

The unease coincided with the first trembles of the financial earthquake everyone feared would shatter English football. Despite the fact that Arsenal won the Double – the FA Cup and the Premier League Championship – the club's financial director was predicting losses of £22 million in 2001–2, proof of unusual management of the club's finances. The cause was Arsenal's wages bill, a problem familiar to the club's rivals in the Premier League. Clubs in the lower divisions – beleaguered by worse woes – feared bankruptcy. Keeping the dream alive for the vain and greedy had risked the entire business. And not a murmur had been uttered by Professor Fraser, the chairman of the Independent Football Commission. Football's own regulator was silent as the game moved towards an unprecedented crisis.

13

ANATOMY OF DREAMS

'I've made a mistake,' Sir Alex Ferguson blasted. In February 2002, the manager of Manchester United uttered his rare confession to a trusted friend at the end of a depressing week. His ambition to win another championship title at the end of that season was evaporating. Despite spending record sums for new players, Manchester United was being trounced by inferior teams. 'I should have bought Rio. That was my mistake,' confessed Ferguson.

Rio Ferdinand, the 23-year-old defender, was dazzling admirers at Leeds United. His £18 million transfer from West Ham in November 2000 had proved to be a valuable investment. Every week his reputation was enhanced and his place in England's squad for the World Cup in the Far East was assured. Ferguson rued his stubborn rejection of the entreaties of Pini Zahavi, Rio's Israeli agent. 'He wants to come to Manchester United,' Pini had urged repeatedly in the year before the sale to Leeds. 'And you need a good defender.' Ferguson rejected the advice, relying upon Wes Brown and eventually Laurent Blanc, an ageing Frenchman past his prime. Millions were eyewitnesses to Ferguson's punishment that season. Standing on the edge of pitches across the country, flapping his arms in rage as shots passed Manchester United's defenders into the net, Pini's exhortations echoed around Ferguson's head: 'He wants to come to Manchester United. He dreams of coming to Manchester United. He'll be good for you.'

Ferguson's conversion coincided with his decision to reconsider leaving Old Trafford after fifteen years. Over Christmas lunch, Kathy, his loyal wife, had asked, 'What are you going to do after you retire?' By New Year's day, Ferguson had persuaded Peter Kenyon, Manchester United's chief executive, to defer his retirement. Four weeks later, Kenyon heard the confession: 'Not buying Rio was one of my biggest mistakes. We've got to buy him.' Nothing had changed in the football world. Money was the chosen solution to every problem, even at the risk of plunging a club's finances into disarray.

As Manchester United's fortunes tumbled over the following weeks, Ferguson pondered his strategy to fulfil his dream. Fortunately, his relationship with Pini was close. Ferguson had recently flown to Israel and, in recognition of his fame, had been honoured by an introduction to the Mistaharim, a top secret Israeli undercover army unit who specialized in posing as disgruntled Palestinians in the West Bank. Ferguson was excited by his glimpse into Israel's secret war and, a few weeks later, returned the compliment by welcoming the commander of the Mistaharim and his son at Old Trafford and introducing them to the team. Counting on that bond, Ferguson phoned Pini to evoke reassurance about Ferdinand's continued enthusiasm for a transfer. 'Talk to Leeds,' urged the agent, dreaming of the £2 million commission. Ferguson was grateful. 'We have the right to be the best of the best,' he reaffirmed. 'There's nothing wrong with that.' His club's profits would be £34 million that year; they could afford to buy the best to fulfil his own dream.

Peter Kenyon waited for his opportunity to approach Peter Ridsdale. During those weeks the finances of English football deteriorated. The bankruptcy of ITV Digital in March 2002, depriving the seventy-two clubs of the Football League of £315 million for the three year deal, was crippling; and the Premier League clubs, despite earning £937 million in 2000–01, could not recover from the previous years' haemorrhage of money in transfers and wages. The illusion that football, earning £1,269 million during the current year, was a ceaselessly money-making machine had soured. Crippled by the players' wages, Chelsea's accumulated debt was £97.7 million. Bates sought to sell players but there were no buyers. His bankers ordered a search for a buyer of the club. Four miles away, Mohamed Al Fayed's bid for Fulham to keep up with the stars had produced a net debt within two years of £61.7 million and the certainty of another surge in debts. The backlash from the financial plight plaguing Italian and Spanish football, abandoning players without pay for five months, was that Premier League clubs were struggling to survive. Below the Premier League things were worse; across the English League wages were being cut and redundant players, abandoned by agents and chairmen, were hunting for work. The excitement of promotion and the fear of relegation – the sport's emotional motor – had been replaced by the threat of bankruptcy and worse. Suspected dishonesty at Swindon, the unpopular relocation of Wimbledon to Milton Keynes, the uncertainty at Fulham, the unresolved perils of Gillingham and the prospective bankruptcy of Nottingham Forest, the debatable legacy of

Brian Clough, were among the casualties of a sport struggling to survive, bereft of inspired leadership by the FA.
Their investigation of Dennis Roach had made no
progress and Aston Villa's dossier about John Gregory
remained unexamined. The panacea for the sport, the
Independent Football Commission, had disappeared. As
Richard Scudamore had anticipated, the 'independent'
regulator was ineffective while the FA's own independence had been compromised.

Agents could not avoid the consequences: the three
new publicly quoted football agencies owned by Jerome
Anderson, Jon Smith and Paul Stretford were bleeding
from the lack of activity. Their profits were dismally low.
Smith's pre-tax profit was just £640,000 compared with
his predicted £100 million; Stretford's pre-tax profits
were £7.8 million; and Jerome Anderson issued an earnings warning, albeit that his profits would rise threefold to
£1.27 million thanks to non-football activities. All their
share prices slumped. Stretford's was down from 50
pence to 7 pence and Smith's from 52 pence to 9 pence.
Fear was creeping across the sport and the official
response was absurdities and internecine warfare.

A symbol of football's malaise was the decision to
rebuild Wembley stadium. On 26 September 2002, the
FA concluded its negotiations and signed the contracts to
construct a stadium for 90,000 spectators and the surrounding infrastructure for £757 million. A German
bank provided a £426 million loan at market rates of
interest over sixteen years. When completed in 2006, the
stadium would be the most expensive in the world with
the probability of opening in the midst of a financial
crisis in football.

Leeds United was a particular example of the common
threat. The club had borrowed £60 million on a gamble

that buying star players would secure the championship, bringing lucrative rewards. But the strategy had failed; during 2002 Leeds would not earn £20 million from European matches. In common with most other Premier League clubs, Leeds was operating at a loss and the bankers, wary of the club's £77 million debt, were demanding the repayment of loans. Ridsdale was pledged to recoup £15 million by the sale of players by July 2002. Reducing the debt was preoccupying Allan Leighton, the club's deputy chairman and the owner of 7 per cent of the club's shares. 'This is a watershed year,' he predicted. Leighton was intolerant of the notion that unidentified benefactors with £20 million to spend on vanity would inevitably ride to a club's rescue. 'The fundamentals are askew,' Leighton realized. Clubs depended upon trading players but FIFA's new rules banned transfers for many months every year. 'No normal business can survive by banning sales to raise cash,' complained Leighton. Selling players was imperative for Leeds.

The news on 21 May 2002 was encouraging. At the end of the Premier League's two-day summer meeting in a country hotel in Northamptonshire, Peter Ridsdale was approached by Peter Kenyon: 'I wonder whether we could talk about your players for sale?' 'You can have Lee Bowyer,' replied Ridsdale, referring to the midfielder who was popular with the fans but notorious as a racist and for associating with thugs. 'No, I'm talking about Rio Ferdinand,' said Kenyon. 'No way, for any money,' countered Ridsdale. 'We'll pay £20 million,' continued Kenyon. 'Is that for one leg or half a leg?' scoffed Ridsdale.

Despite his repudiation, Ridsdale was obliged to report the offer to the club's directors. To his surprise, the reaction was not dismissive. 'We'll sell him for £30 million,' said Allan Leighton decisively. 'We need the money. £12 million profit in less than two years is too good to miss. It'll be the deal of the century.' Ridsdale's disappointment was ill concealed until David O'Leary spoke: 'I couldn't oppose a sale at £30 million, so long as we can spend some to replace Rio.' Ridsdale hoped the sale wouldn't happen. He had agreed with Leighton to raise £30 million by selling Olivier Dacourt, Lee Bowyer and Robbie Keane, and he anticipated no problems. He thought Rio would not be moving. Leighton had a different opinion: not only might Rio be sold, thought Leighton, but O'Leary would also be fired.

The supermarket executive, recently appointed to save the Royal Mail from collapse, was impatient about failure. Like any business, the fortunes of football clubs either rose or fell, the momentum was never static. Over the previous two years, O'Leary had tried for success but Leeds had fallen short of their ambitions. 'He's a 60:40 man,' judged Leighton, 'who's not delivering.' The dream of a young British-born team nurtured by O'Leary had been sustained until the end of 2001, but had been shattered after the criminal trial of Lee Bowyer and Jonathan Woodgate for assaulting an Asian youth. O'Leary had condemned Bowyer and Woodgate for 'disgracing' their club, and simultaneously criticized the FA for 'political correctness' for disqualifying the two from the England squad. Since O'Leary attracted derision for that warped judgement, Leighton understood the manager's limitations. O'Leary was culpable for too many mistakes, the author of too many lame excuses, a source of endless contradictions and a man who blamed everyone, including his own players, but never himself. The embarrassment about the insensitivity of his autobiography, *Leeds United on Trial*, published just after the end of the

criminal trials in December 2001, was compounded by
his comments to promote his book that Bowyer and
Woodgate should both have been imprisoned. Bowyer,
O'Leary seemed to have overlooked, had been acquitted.
The club, Leighton concluded, had spent £93 million on
players and won nothing except appalling publicity and
ridicule for defeat in the third round of the FA Cup by
Cardiff, a minor club. Millions of pounds had failed to
buy success. 'Football is a simple game made complicated
by people who ought to know better,' Bill Shankly once
said. The complications, Leighton realized, were caused
by those who foolishly extolled their self-importance.
English football's crisis was aggravated by the bewildering dearth of competent managers. Compared with
Arsène Wenger and Gérard Houllier, the Irishman was
not clever enough, especially to change tactics during a
match. The famous quip by Terry Venables – 'half-time
is when we managers earn our money' – was so relevant.
Only four managers in the Premier League could think
on their feet, Leighton believed. O'Leary was not among
that elite. Determining the fate of David O'Leary over
the following weeks would be a yardstick of the football
business, its mysteries and weaknesses.

Peter Ridsdale had identified O'Leary as a failure since
1 February 2002. At a board meeting he confided his concern about whether the Irishman was capable of
improving the club's performance. 'I doubt if he'll be the
manager next season,' he told his fellow directors. Five
days later, O'Leary presented his strategy to Ridsdale for
the remainder of the season. Olivier Dacourt, said
O'Leary, was a candidate for sale. The manager, who,
Ridsdale complained, spent too much of his week playing
golf, blamed the player for the club's failures. Two
months later, on 20 April, Leeds was defeated by Fulham.

Ridsdale was incensed and the following day, he telephoned Leighton and other directors. 'O'Leary has got to
go,' he insisted. The directors' unanimous decision, at
their next board meeting, was to dismiss the manager as
soon as possible. A few hurdles remained. O'Leary was
contracted to appear as a studio expert in the BBC's coverage of the World Cup. Ridsdale's favourite to replace
O'Leary was Martin O'Neill, the sensible manager of
Celtic. Since the two would be sitting together in the same
television studio, Ridsdale decided to avoid embarrassment and to delay the dismissal during the tournament.

Finding a replacement was a priority and there was
only one ideal candidate – Martin O'Neill – and his
appointment was vital. He was invited to visit
Ridsdale's home in Leeds secretly to discuss a contract.
Ridsdale had neither sought nor obtained the permission of Celtic's chairman, but had informed a senior
director of the Scottish team. After one more meeting
in Ridsdale's home and two more in London, Ridsdale
believed that O'Neill had accepted the job and the
terms of the contract. Since his oral acceptance was not
legally binding, Ridsdale listed the alternatives. As
reserve candidates, he contemplated Steve McClaren,
the manager of Middlesbrough, Mick McCarthy, the
manager of Ireland's national team, and Terry Venables.
The latter was Leighton's favourite.

Leeds, Leighton believed, needed someone of considerable experience with a burning hunger to prove himself,
a man renowned as the best coach in England. Terry
Venables's quip – 'half-time is when we managers earn
our money' – appealed to Leighton. Identifying Venables
as a solution to the predicament of Leeds was a remarkable twist of the virtues within the Premier League.
Venables's resurrection since August 2001 had been

public and profitable. 'Are we going to be embarrassed?' Brian Barwick, the head of ITV sport, had been asked when Venables was proposed as the principal commentator on Saturday night's *The Premiership* programme. 'No,' replied Barwick, 'Terry is part of the ITV family.' Moral judgements about footballers in Britain were easily avoided and, after ten years, memories were effortlessly expunged. Venables's appearance as the expert on British television reflected the football community's usual nonchalance towards dishonesty. Three months after the creation of the Independent Football Commission the disregard for veracity in football had not altered.

Reintroducing Venables as a manager of a Premier League club might have proved embarrassing for Ridsdale. On 11 October 2000 in Helsinki, the Leeds chairman had announced 'Terry's got too much baggage' as the reason Adam Crozier had rejected Venables's candidature as England's coach. In 2002, the 59-year-old was still disqualified by court order from acting as a company director after admitting nineteen specific instances of corrupt, dishonest and deceitful misconduct and deception, and he remained condemned by several High Court judges for giving unreliable sworn testimony. Allan Leighton and Ridsdale were undeterred by those stigmas. Similarly, the Premier League would not object to a discredited businessman's participation in a competition sponsored by Barclaycard. Football's executives could be relied upon to remain silent about the association of a dishonest businessman with a bank. In their increasing desperation to find a manager before the new season, Leighton and Ridsdale were prepared to ignore Venables's 'baggage'. 'There's no one else,' confessed Ridsdale.

Allan Leighton trusted Ridsdale's judgement, not least on financial matters, despite the value of the club's shares sliding towards just 4p. Leighton did not appear to question whether the club's increasingly perilous financial predicament was caused by the huge salaries approved by Ridsdale. In the 2002–3 season, the salaries bill at Elland Road was £53.6 million, just £16 million less than Manchester United, yet Leeds's gross income that season was £82 million while Manchester's was £140 million. Leighton also appeared to ignore Ridsdale's own expensive lifestyle. He had authorized spending £600,000 a year for a fleet of 76 company cars for 250 staff. He had paid £70,000 recruitment fees for an executive who left the club after six months. And he was leasing a tank of goldfish for £20 a month. More pertinently, he was hiring private jets to fly around Europe rather than using commercial airlines, and occupying expensive suites in hotels rather than regular rooms. To stem the drain of money, Leighton agreed that four players would be sold. Ridsdale was optimistic of finding buyers.

On 19 March 2002, he returned from Rome convinced that Lazio was prepared to pay £16 million for Dacourt. The following day he met O'Leary at the training ground. 'Good news,' he told his manager. To his surprise, O'Leary flared in anger, protesting 'Dacourt can't leave.' According to Ridsdale, unknown to him, O'Leary had flown to Turin and opened his own negotiations with Juventus to sell Dacourt. He had asked for £20 million but secured an offer of £10 million. The journey was particularly odd because O'Leary was accompanied by an agent and a solicitor. Ridsdale complained that the discussions were not revealed to him and says inexplicably that O'Leary offered to introduce Rune Hauge into the negotiations. O'Leary would convincingly deny the allegations.

In O'Leary's version, Ridsdale authorized him to negotiate with Juventus but the discussions in Turin were fruitless. O'Leary's reaction to the Lazio offer secured by Ridsdale was, he says, euphoric. Ridsdale's misfortune was that Lazio had no money, a reality which to O'Leary's surprise he ignored. Moreover, he was committed to pay £2 million in commission to agents if Lazio bought the player. Among the beneficiaries was Pini Zahavi. But since Lazio had no money and Juventus failed to make a firm offer, the sale of Dacourt and the other Leeds players – so critical to the club's finances – became paralysed until the manager dramatically misplayed his hand.

On 31 May 2002, to the directors' surprise, O'Leary asked to be present at a board meeting. He used the occasion to criticize Ridsdale and then departed unaware of his fellow directors' intentions. His dismissal was agreed upon unanimously.

O'Leary's removal from the club became easier after the Irishman criticized Ferdinand's potential sale. 'If Rio leaves,' quipped O'Leary to journalists in late June 2002, 'blame my plc board, not me.' Since O'Leary had earlier supported the sale, Allan Leighton ruled on 25 June that he should be dismissed. On 27 June 2002, O'Leary arrived at Elland Road anticipating only his imminent departure for his summer holidays. Two minutes after entering Ridsdale's office, he was fired. Ridsdale believed that the club would not need to pay £4 million in compensation to O'Leary by proving that the manager's conduct had been a breach of his contract.

Ridsdale's next chore was to appoint a replacement. To his surprise on 5 July, O'Neill withdrew his acceptance. The news sparked a flurry of telephone calls to Ridsdale. 'Is Terry on the short list?' asked Leon Angel, Venables's agent, in a breathless telephone call. His client dreamt of a last chance to restore his reputation. 'Yes,' replied Ridsdale. 'What's his telephone number?' The

following day, 6 July, Ridsdale dashed to meet Venables in
Alicante, Spain. There was no one else worth considering.
Two days later Venables signed a two year contract worth
£3.5 million. Venables, an epitome of football's skulduggery and with a questionable record as a manager, was
hailed as the saviour of a troubled club. For his part,
Venables was tempted to complete his bid to finally capture
a trophy that had been interrupted by his dismissal from
Spurs in 1993. Leeds' star players, he was convinced by
Ridsdale, gave him the final opportunity to realize a
dream.

On the same day, Ridsdale met Pini Zahavi. 'Rio wants
to leave,' said the agent. Ferdinand was at the Bellagio
Hotel in Las Vegas with Wes Brown and two other footballers. For the first time in several years, he had not
spent his holidays close to Pini Zahavi at the Hilton in
Tel Aviv. Despite the distance, Ferdinand's impatience
for a transfer to Manchester United was the substance of
repeated conversations with his agent. 'I want to keep
Rio,' Ridsdale told Pini. 'He wants to go,' Pini replied.
'Well, he's not going for £20 million,' snapped Ridsdale,
irritated by the pressure upon him to sell the club's jewel.
There were rumours that Allan Leighton had threatened
to dismiss Ridsdale if he failed to meet the deadline to
repay £15 million to the banks. Although the chairman
had earlier volunteered, 'Rio will be sold if we can get
£40 million', Ridsdale announced after meeting Pini,
'Rio's not for sale.' Ferdinand, he believed, could be persuaded to remain at Leeds while other players would be
sold. The telephone call he received from Peter Kenyon
was accordingly unwelcome. 'We'll increase the offer to
£25 million,' he said. 'Forget it,' Ridsdale replied, concealing his concern about jeopardizing his position while
also puzzled about Olivier Dacourt's obstinate refusal to

consider a transfer to Lazio. Ridsdale suspected
O'Leary's influence; the former manager, he feared, had
persuaded the player to reject Lazio and accept a transfer
to Juventus of Turin. There were reports of secret conversations between O'Leary and Alessandro Moggi, an
agent and the son of Juventus's chairman, Luciano
Moggi. O'Leary's telephone records showed a mysterious
pattern of calls to Turin and to an Italian agent in
Manchester. Amid the swirl, Ridsdale's trade of players
continued to be paralysed.

On 14 July, Ferdinand and Venables met for one hour
over breakfast at Pini Zahavi's flat in central London.
Venables's charm and persuasion caused the player to
hesitate. Two hours later, he reaffirmed his decision to
accept Sir Alex Ferguson's offer. Ferdinand's dream had
not changed. 'You see all the faces on the wall,' he said
eloquently about his memories of Old Trafford. 'People
like George Best, Denis Law and Bobby Charlton – and I
just want to be part of it. I want to play alongside Juan
Sebastian Veron, David Beckham and Roy Keane and
players like that.' Pini Zahavi passed the news to
Ridsdale. Over the past week, Ferdinand's signed letter
requesting a transfer had been tucked into the agent's
briefcase.

'I have no reason to doubt that Rio wants to stay at
Leeds United,' Ridsdale said emphatically two days later.
'He has not indicated he wants to leave and, while it is
purely hypothetical, if he were to hand in a transfer
request, it would be firmly rejected by the board.' The
following day, Pini submitted Rio's formal request for a
transfer. The request was immediately rejected by
Ridsdale: 'We've had no offers for Rio Ferdinand so it
amazes me he has a choice to make. He is going nowhere.
Where does he think he's going – into thin air?'

'We're offering £25 million,' Peter Kenyon told Ridsdale the following day. 'No way,' replied Ridsdale. 'Thirty-five million pounds or there's no deal.' Manchester United, Ridsdale knew, were desperate to sign Ferdinand, but equally Kenyon could not afford more. Events suddenly turned, characterizing the suicidal folly afflicting the football business.

On 21 July, Liverpool decided not to buy Lee Bowyer for £9 million and the sale of Dacourt collapsed. Rio's fate was sealed. Nevertheless, Leighton and Ridsdale agreed that there could be no retreat from a headline price of £30 million. The businessmen calculated that Kenyon would not call Leeds's bluff. Unlike Martin Edwards, a tough entrepreneur, Kenyon's expertise was marketing. He lacked the sensitivity for poker-style brinkmanship. His club's purchase of Juan Sebastian Veron for £28 million proved that Kenyon's judgement was clouded by Alex Ferguson's emotional demands. Similarly, on this occasion, instead of squeezing Leeds – unable to survive without the sale – to reduce the price, Kenyon threw in his hand. He accepted a solution offered by an agent. Manchester United would pay £26 million plus an additional £3.1 million if the club won a series of championships. Despite winning the poker duel, Ridsdale's announcement of the sale was mournful. 'I'm not happy as a Leeds fan because I didn't want him to leave. But when your captain says he wants to leave you have to listen.' That same day, Leeds accepted £29.1 million, a British record. The excitement masked the continuing disaster for English football: most of the money would repay bank loans rather than percolate through a sport desperate for financial support. Ridsdale was unsentimental about that scenario. In common with other Premier League chairmen, he envisaged the closure of many minor clubs and the radical shrinkage of League football.

At Old Trafford, football's perils were multiplied. Ferdinand signed a five year contract worth £18.2 million. He would be paid £70,000 a week and he retained his image rights. 'I wouldn't have come here,' explained Ferdinand after signing his contract, watched by his parents, 'if I didn't think we could win the title, and I know the rest of the lads are as hungry as ever.' Pini Zahavi smiled. Fulfilling the dreams of Ferdinand and Ferguson had made him £2 million richer. 'Locheim,' smiled Ferdinand to his agent, lifting a glass of water.

At 11 a.m. on 14 September 2002, Ferdinand returned to Elland Road with Manchester United for a League match. Serious commentators had anticipated that Leeds fans, 'spitting venom', would be rioting and lynching, and one foresaw the 'end of the beautiful game'. The mood, everyone agreed, would 'feel spiteful, vindictive and very, very ugly. Football will become the grotesque game.' In the directors' suite, the guests were eating breakfast in a mood that was unusually foreboding. Bobby Charlton's arrival was barely acknowledged. On a previous visit, Charlton's wife had been attacked by Leeds fans with scalding tea, but during his walk through the car park he had only been mobbed by autograph hunters. On the terraces, however, a banner had been unfurled bearing the inscription 'Judas', reflecting the aggressive mood. In his endearingly modest manner, the legend of England's World Cup victory in 1966 lamented the transformation of rivalry between the two clubs and cities into ugly hatred. Charlton's consolation was the expectation that, with Ferdinand's help, Manchester United would, as in the previous ten matches, win.

Across the stadium stood all the qualities and faults of English football. Lee Bowyer and Jonathan Woodgate represented the game's 'rabble'; David Beckham epitomized the wealth, celebrity and some positive attributes of English football; Rio Ferdinand, a fine footballer, represented a reckless investment vulnerable to injury; in the Sky booth, mischievously employed as a commentator, David O'Leary appeared as just another of football's forlorn casualties; sitting in his tracksuit on the edge of the pitch, Venables nervously waited to redeem himself; nearby, the grey-suited Ferguson chewed agitatedly, disturbed by the absence of Roy Keane, Manchester United's £80,000-per-week captain and the unstable 'author' of a self-incriminating autobiography emphasizing his violence; and in the centre-seat, Peter Ridsdale talked to conceal his fears. The referee's whistle at noon would reignite the competition of their dreams.

The magic of twenty-two men displaying skill, courage and stamina temporarily obscured the ills cursing the game. Their performance manifested the dreams of hundreds of thousands, most notably Alex Ferguson's. The match was a trial of the manager's skills rather than Rio Ferdinand's abilities. After forty-five minutes the result was not encouraging. The spectacle had not been rabid hatred against Ferdinand but the sight of a crumbling giant gasping to forestall the death of a legend. After a spirited start, Manchester United collapsed; the swagger was replaced by collective fright. The aura was evaporating and the single, winning goal by Leeds suggested the death of a dynasty. Ferguson's gamble had apparently misfired, mirroring the unpredictability and ills of the business.

Despite spending billions of pounds, winning worldwide acclaim for the Premier League, the heart of English football had barely changed. For twenty years, the same characters had equated money as the criteria for football's success. The idea of Terry Venables's redemption endorsed the domination by unchangeable reactionaries. Three hundred miles south, another fallen angel was enjoying his own unexpected revival. Under Harry Redknapp's managership, Portsmouth was establishing a lead at the top of the First Division. Redknapp's success contrasted with the plight of West Ham, bouncing at the bottom of the Premier League, still struggling to recover from his financial profligacy. All the ambivalence of football was represented by the resurrection of Redknapp and Venables. Their failures, waste and suspicious behaviour were ignored by their new chairmen's lust for glory. Both proved the truth of Glenn Hoddle's quip: 'If you blink, you lose the game.' The FA endorsed their appointments, their rivals acknowledged their status and the fans applauded their victories. Football remained a game without shame.

The manifestation of those flaws was the developing crisis within the FA itself. During October 2002, the Premier League chairmen had become irritated by Adam Crozier's management and style. The 38-year-old marketing expert appointed to modernize the Association less than three years earlier had alienated those who demanded a servant rather than a chief executive displaying independence, who, they complained on occasions, exercised apparently uncontrolled authority. The simmering grievances of the clubs' chairmen reached a climax. On the FA's behalf, Crozier was accused of entering into contracts with sponsors on behalf of the Premier League's star players without, it was alleged, adequately consulting the clubs. Not only did those sponsorship contracts potentially undermine the individual clubs' financial relationships with their own sponsors, but they aggravated another grievance, namely, that the star players, paid up to £100,000 per week by the clubs, were risking injuries while playing for England without any tangible benefit accruing to the clubs. The secrecy which Crozier shrouded over his negotiations and tentative agreements upset men accustomed to total control. And the notion of FA bureaucrats enjoying an increasingly expensive, unregulated lifestyle in Soho at the clubs' expense had become intolerable to those beleaguered by their own self-inflicted financial troubles.

The identities of the leading critics were not surprising. Ken Bates loathed Adam Crozier for the humiliation he felt had been heaped upon himself over Wembley's original development, a scheme which subsequently had been in large measure endorsed by Crozier himself. Peter Ridsdale was irritated by Crozier's secrecy and his decision to disperse too much of the Premier League's money to help football's grass roots and the stricken League clubs. Retrenchment and even bankruptcies caused him little concern. Richard Scudamore was angry that Crozier withheld information affecting his terrain. Other Premier League chairmen disliked the FA's attempts over the previous two years to assert its regulatory powers. Few could recall Crozier visiting their grounds to establish a close rapport. All were united by the threat to their own club's financial security; they were rightly fearful that the next Sky contract might not deliver the same fortune as previously, and bewildered about how to recover from their squandering habits. Bates and Ridsdale symbolized the financial perils facing the club chairmen. All were unwilling to embrace the FA's chief executive, whose salary had increased to over £600,000 a year and who suffered none of the burdens afflicting his paymasters. Hitting at the smooth, costly Crozier was an easy palliative and regardless of his achievements, he had lost their confidence. None of them saw any personal advantage in repairing a fragile relationship.

Their solution was the creation of a Professional Game Board to manage the professional clubs, abandoning the amateurs to their fate, and decimating the FA. Crozier saw that proposal as the deliberate destruction of the national sport and its finances. He assessed the proposers as a self-interested and transient lobby afflicted by amorality and myopia. Everything New Labour's Task Force was intended to prevent, to cure the lack of commitment by the Premier League to the long-term health of football, had occurred.

In a battle between the FA and the Premier League, Crozier might have hoped for support from Geoff Thompson, the FA's chairman who had formally appointed him, but he was disappointed. The faceless and mute symbol of the FA's traditions preferred to oblige the twenty chairmen despite the detrimental impact on 43,000 other clubs. At the crucial moment, even David Dein, Crozier's champion, remained practically silent, unwilling to confront Bates and Ridsdale. The irreversible division between rich and poor clubs was on the horizon, encouraging the grass roots to wither away, while the Premier League clubs managed their businesses free of even the semblance of control. Crozier resigned and not a single chairman of a major club publicly mourned his departure. An ugly spectacle of vanity and greed among frustrated warlords was souring the popular dream and no salvation was in sight. Sadly, those faded, aspiring grandees mirrored pertinent truths about modern Britain.

POSTSCRIPT

Football created no new heroes during the remaining months of the 2002–3 season. On the contrary, the smiling face of Harry Redknapp, the architect of West Ham's misfortunes, and the forlorn grimace of Terry Venables symbolized the wretched state of the game.

Portsmouth's dominance of the First Division guaranteed Redknapp's double triumph. While he would return to the Premier league, his adversary Terry Brown was destined for humiliation. Despite the sentiment that West Ham was too good to be relegated, the nightmare increasingly became a reality after Christmas. Plagued by injuries, West Ham's remaining players performed badly, and the fear of increasing the club's £40 million debt prevented Brown buying replacements. The prejudiced blamed Brown for dismissing Redknapp and 'ruining a club they all loved', while other fans criticized his replacement, Glenn Roeder, until he in turn was stricken by a minor stroke, the result of pressure. The forlorn hope was that Trevor Brooking, an admired director, could save the dream in the last days of the season.

Terry Venables, another aspiring dream-maker, anticipated doom on 30 January 2003. There was only £3.66 million in the club's bank account and the monthly salary bill was about £5 million. Matches at Leeds were not shown by Sky at a loss of £600,000 per match. The share price was falling towards 3.7 pence, valuing the club at just £13 million. Contrary to his assurances, Peter Ridsdale sold Jonathan Woodgate for £9 million to Newcastle, and denuded the team's defence. Without the sale, the club faced iminent insolvency. More players were offered for sale to reduce the wages bill.

The publication of *Broken Dreams* in February intensified the club's problems. The revelation that Ridsdale had employed Rune Hauge to buy Ferdinand unsettled many. The initial report that Hauge's commission was £900,000, as admitted to the author by Ridsdale, surprised Allan Leighton, the club's deputy chairman. But the subsequent revelation that Hauge had in fact received £1.75 million, astonished the non-executive director.

On Leighton's orders Leeds began an internal audit of their finances to unravel the background to the transfer. On 24 February 2003, Ridsdale proudly presented a report by the club's lawyers and Deloitte & Touche, the club's auditors, which concluded that, 'there is no evidence of any financial impropriety or lack of financial controls' with regard to Ferdinand's transfer. The conclusion was that the money paid by Ridsdale to Hauge was, 'properly authorized in accordance with Leeds United policy'.

Ridsdale, pleading that he was the victim of a smear campaign, hoped that the controversy could be forgotten. His misfortune was that the internal investigation had omitted answers to the most salient questions, casting doubt upon the chairman's version of his relationship with Hauge. Firstly, the club has failed to provide a written agreement between Leeds and Hauge which legally committed Ridsdale to pay Hauge any money; and secondly, Ridsdale could not provide any evidence which justified paying Hauge double what he had originally requested.

Further unease spread over the continuing repercussions of David O'Leary's dismissal. That rupture, with Leighton's support, had been accompanied by Ridsdale's defiant assertion that the ex-manager would not receive a penny in compensation. Not only because O'Leary had allegedly sabotaged the sale of Dacourt, but because of other unauthorized expenditure. In their bid to question O'Leary's claim for compensation, Leeds's employees had minutely examined all the former manager's telephone calls to discover any embarrassing evidence. One of the matters which they believed would undermine O'Leary's claim for compensation was a series of telephone calls to a female employee of a small airline. However, there was an innocuous explanation. Further investigation also revealed that the allegation that O'Leary had sabotaged Dacourt's sale to Lazio was without substance. Ignominiously, the chairman capitulated and Leeds agreed to pay O'Leary £4 million in compensation for his dismissal. (Dacourt had by then been sold to Roma for £3.5 million, a loss of £3.7 million since his original transfer in 2000.)

Ridsdale's humiliation coincided with the acceleration of Leeds's fortunes downwards. Ridsdale's cure was to retain Max Clifford, a colourful publicist, to promote his image, a reaction to the fans' growing hatred of him.

The pressure was unremitting. In mid-March, Leeds had won just ten matches out of thirty, and had won only one game in the last eight. With just eight more matches to play, the club was in danger of relegation and insolvency. The blame was heaped upon Venables. Some criticized him as too old at sixty to understand a Yorkshire team but the veteran retorted that he had lost too many players. The excitement at the outset, he lamented, had been 'quickly taken away with the steady sale of key players'. His misery undermined any attempt to enthuse the remaining international stars in his squad to perform.

During Thursday 20 March 2003, Venables heard rumours that he was to be fired. He asked to see Ridsdale that evening. 'I need it to come to the boil,' he explained. Without ceremony, Ridsdale fired the man he had eight months earlier hailed as a genius and saviour. Venables received £2 million in compensation for bringing the club close to relegation. His ego was seriously bruised. As a man who had got nearer to more trophies than he had won, his opinions in the television studio would inevitably command less authority.

At 9 o'clock the following morning, Ridsdale telephoned Peter Reid who had been dismissed as Sunderland's manager six months earlier. In the aftermath, Sunderland had become a confirmed victim for relegation and Bob Murray, the club's chairman, had admitted his concerns about Reid's extravagant transfers. That record did not deter Ridsdale, a desperate man. Ridsdale's telephone call, joked Reid, came 'just as I got into bed'. The offer for a man fearing oblivion was heavenly: 'When Peter called I knew it was a great opportunity and I snapped his hand off. I was desperate to get back in and now it's happened.' For the first time, Leeds offered realistic financial terms. Reid would receive £10,000 a week and a £500,000 bonus if the club remained in the Premier League. 'I've got eight games to make an impression,' confessed Reid with unusual candour. All football's experts doubted that he would keep the job permanently. That proved to be mistaken.

Allan Leighton appeared to be untroubled by the fact that Reid had been an original shareholder of Proactive, Paul Stretford's agency. None of the Leeds directors sought information about Reid's relationship with the agent. However, Stretford's practice of simultaneously representing both players and the club in transfers had caused concern at the FA and the Danish Football Association. Although Proactive's shares had fallen from 40.5p to 4.5p, Stretford appeared as undaunted by the criticism as Peter Reid and John Gregory, another client, who had been suspended as the manager of Derby on 21 March 2003 while 'serious allegations' were investigated concerning a transfer. Seven weeks later Gregory would be sacked. Nineteen months after leading Aston Villa temporarily to the top of the Premier League, Gregory's career was in free fall. His demise coincided with the crash of another falling angel.

'I'm not leaving,' Ridsdale had proclaimed after Venables's departure. Allan Leighton had decided otherwise. The misery caused by the architect of a boom to bust strategy could not be forgiven especially while pertinent questions about Rio Ferdinand's purchase remained unanswered. On 30 April, Ridsdale resigned with just one year's salary, £370,000, as compensation. Stephen Harrison, the club's finance director, also resigned. Seventeen others were made redundant. Ridsdale's obituary was that of an impassioned supporter who had bequeathed a £78.9 million debt to a desperate team.

Money rather than morality was the uniform cause of their undoing and the lessons appeared to be ignored. The deficit at Chelsea increased the club's accumulated debts to at least £97 million but Ken Bates was seemingly unconcerned. At a special shareholders meeting of Chelsea Village on 29 January 2003 to approve the issue of 15 per cent more shares (worth about £10 million to a group of anonymous investors), Bates asserted that the club's assets were worth more than £300 million although the published values were £240 million. Neither the stock exchange nor the FA were minded to query his style of management. Bates's self-confidence after winning a place in the Championship League rendered him immune to any reproach, not least from the FA, an organization in turmoil.

In the wake of Adam Crozier's dismissal, other senior FA executives were dismissed including the press spokesman and travel manager. The sentiment suggested that those responsible for the extravagances of the Crozier regime were to be punished, but no less than the 586 players who would be declared unemployed that season because their contracts were not renewed, a historic record. The FA lacked any plan to prevent that reoccurrence in the future. Even the selection of Crozier's replacement exposed the decreptitude of the regulator.

The procedure for selecting Crozier's replacement was approved by David Dein. The best head-hunters would be hired to find the ideal candidate. Unfortunately for Dein, their selection did not include his favourite but identified Mark Palios, a former professional footballer with Tranmere and an accountant at PricewaterhouseCoopers. Dein objected. He wanted either a former non-British FIFA executive or Peter Littlewood, a marketing expert employed in America by a food manufacturer to promote confectionery. Littlewood lacked experience in football or British public life. Geoff Thompson, the FA's chairman, ignored the searing experience of Adam Crozier's reign, and favoured the marketing over the financial expert. The lacklustre chairman was undaunted by the FA's own financial predicament. On the expiry of the FA's three year contract with television in 2004, it was likely that the broadcasters would pay £150 million less than the £400 million fee agreed in 2000. The FA's income was certain to fall in a critical period, just as Arsenal's was also under pressure.

Arsenal's accumulated losses in 2002–3 had risen to £42.7 million, and the new stadium, costing over £400 million, required loans of £317 million. The club was faced by the perennial problem that money spent on infrastructure would mean less cash to buy the best players to challenge Manchester United. Dein, like other Premier league executives, also feared that Sky, bidding without competition for the next licence, would offer at least £100 million less. The plight of the Premier league clubs required a financially astute custodian. Dein and Thompson were outvoted and Palios was appointed as the FA's chief executive for a lower salary than his predecessor.

Palios's task was awesome. Football's old guard remained firmly in control. David O'Leary returned to the Premier league as a manager of Aston Villa, undaunted by Doug Ellis's reputation; Sir Alex Ferguson, intent on winning the treble, ruthlessly re-organized his squad; and, in an echo of his stewardship of West Ham, Harry Redknapp mentioned his requirement of at least £20 million to transform Portsmouth into a winning side, and his expectation that many more millions would be forthcoming to replace the existing stadium for 19,000 people with a new building so that 'this club can move forward'. Survival in the Premiership, preached the sage, was 'impossible for more than a couple of seasons' in the existing facilities.

The amusing conundrum was whether the club's owner, Milan Mandaric, a Yugoslav-born American, who had already spent over £20 million since buying the club in June 1999, and suffering a rising wage bill since Redknapp took over – up from £7 million to £10 million – would risk his millions to follow the dream. Football is a sport for those able to survive a recurring but familiar nightmare. And with hindsight, few could be surprised that Ken Bates, football's most colourful aristocrat, should have chosen to escape the inevitable fate of all the sport's mavericks.

At the end of June 2003, faced with the disagreeable demand to repay the banks £23 million on 4 July, Bates chose to abandon his fight to retain the club's ownership and master Chelsea's financial quagmire by announcing the sale of the club. Without a hint of contrition or admission of failure, Bates introduced Roman Abramovich, a thirty-six-year-old Russian businessman, as the club's new owner. The Russian had been found at Bates's request by Pini Zahavi, the Israeli agent. The omens for English football were certainly mixed.

Chelsea, whose ownership under Bates had been steeped in mystery, was to be transferred to an unknown Russian whose personal wealth had mysteriously soared from virtually zero to an alleged £5.4 billion in less than twenty years. That phenomenal achievement in Russia's murky oil and aluminium industries classified Abramovich as an enigma. The combined silence of the FA, who ignored calls to enquire whether Abramovich was 'fit and proper' to own a football club, and the celebration of some fans about a source of seemingly unlimited money, exposed all the weaknesses of the national sport. Since the transaction was likely to be concluded in an off-shore tax haven, this added to the intrigue.

In the past, Ken Bates had spoken about his dream of Chelsea as England's premier club. He had transferred that dream to Roman Abramovich, a bizarre personality who even chose not to become a director of the club.

On the positive side, Abramovich promised to spend up to £100 million to turn Chelsea into a world class rival to the best teams. Zahavi was choosing players on Abramovich's behalf to satisfy the dream. The recipients of the new money were chortling. 'Chelsea were potless,' sang Barry 'Silky' Silkman, 'and now they're buying.' With even Arsenal struggling to survive financial challenges and boardroom disagreements, Chelsea was a nightmare transformed into a dream. In the normal course of football history, it was only a matter of time before the dream became a nightmare.

Acknowledgements

The inspiration for this book were two of my sons, Alexander and Oliver, both football fanatics. In researching the book, I relied on a small army of generous football professionals – journalists, officials, politicians, club chairmen, managers and agents – whose help was invaluable.

My first thanks are to Oliver Figg whose expertise, enthusiasm, energy and swift research saved me repeatedly from despair. I deeply appreciate his help.

My second thanks are to Graham Hunter, a football aficionado, who encouraged me to undertake the book and provided an astonishing list of names and themes worth pursuing. Graham's generosity and certainty of purpose were critical to motivate my interest.

I could not have started my research without the generous help of Michael Crick and David Conn, both outstanding journalists and football experts, who provided a further encyclopaedic list of topics to consider and the relevant contacts. Both deserve special thanks.

Others who were generously supportive and unstintingly helpful include Simon Banks, Oliver Butler, Hugh Dehn, Steve Downes, Rob Draper, David Hellier, Mark Hollingsworth, Matthew Holt, Mathew Horsman, Andrew Jennings, Mark Killick, Simon Kuper, Chris Lightbown, Gabriel Marrotti, Pat Masters, Kevin Mousley, Keely Storey, Rogan Taylor and Tony Yorke. Many others requested that their help should remain anonymous but I must finally thank Mihir Bose for considerable help, not least for directing me out of several dark corners.

In the course of researching the book, I interviewed over 200 people, some on several occasions. With the exception of one pompous club chairman, everyone proved to be in their own way helpful, charming and, despite my critical questions, fair. Suffice to say, I doubt if I made many new friends among those immersed in the football business but I have emerged with respect for a uniquely tough breed whose undoubted passion sustains a national phenomena enthralling millions of devoted fans every day. For many reasons, I will not individually thank all those who 'welcomed' me into their offices, football stadiums and favourite watering holes, but I doubt if either they or I will ever forget the experience!

In an unusual decision, based upon the advice of the lawyers who vetted this book, it has been decided that no interview sources will be provided or individually thanked. The reader should however be assured that every fact stated has been sourced and checked.

The legal chores were undertaken by David Hooper, an indefatigable friend, whose advice is priceless. The second vital support was provided by Michael Shaw of Curtis Brown, another veteran campaigner whose encouragement was critical to this book's birth and completion.

At Simon and Schuster, I am grateful to Helen Gummer and Cassandra Campbell. Extra thanks to Martin Bryant for editing the paperback. I also owe a debt to Carol Anderson and Piers Burnett.

I also must thank my many loyal readers. Over the past years, I have been staggered by the number of letters and telephone calls from those who appreciate my books and bother to say, 'Thank you'. Old and young, there are many people who boast a complete collection of my books and I hope that they enjoy the latest.

Finally, life is made tolerable and hugely enjoyable by my family – Nicholas, Oliver, Sophie, Alexander, and especially Veronica – whose interest in football has grown in parallel with mine over the past year. I thank them all.

Notes

INTRODUCTION

5   'make the bucks while you can': Harry Redknapp, *'Arry: An Autobiography*, (HarperCollinsWillow, 1999), p.186.

CHAPTER 1: THE SOLITARY INVESTIGATOR

25   a match in 1973 for Dunstable: *News of the World*, 19 November 1978.

26   for Queens Park Rangers: *The Times*, 5 October 1979.

26   'the law of our life': *News of the World*, 6 November 1979.

28   to allow goals through: Leo McKinstry, *Jack & Bobby*, (HarperCollinsWillow, 2002), pp.147–8.

29   £600,000 for unpaid taxes: *Sunday Mirror*, 12 October 1997.

29   sums of cash in brown envelopes: *Sunday Mirror*, 12 October 1997.

29   examination of its accounts: *Daily Telegraph*, 31 January 1995.

30   receive British citizenship: *Daily Star*, 11 August 2000.

30   the couple parted: *Daily Mail*, 26 March 1993.

30   'I only broke the rules slightly': *Mirror*, 17 May 1995.

30   to increase their value: *Independent*, 18 December 2000.

31 for 100,000 Swiss francs: *Guardian*, 28 March 1997.

31 'any single act I could think of': *The Times*, 24 December 1994.

32 jury failed to reach a verdict: *The Times*, 4 March 1997.

33 was being 'ripped off': *The Times*, 1 February 1995.

33 'men who run our national sport': *Mirror*, 24 February 1995.

CHAPTER 2: THE HERO

36 'himself and those around him': Eddie Ashby, *Bungs, Bribes and Sweet F.A.*, (Blake Publishing Ltd), pp.159.

37 'I had saved Tottenham': *ibid.*, pp.186–7.

37 'designed to deceive': 'Affadavit of Graham Richard Horne, deputy inspector of companies of the DTI, 1995, in the matter of Secretary of State for Trade and Industry and Terence Frederick Venables' (DTI Report), p.46 & 'Trial Transcript before Mr Justice Walker, 17 April 1997'.

37 'scaring the shit out of me': Ashby, *Bungs, Bribes and Sweet F.A.*, p.193.

37 'everything except football': *ibid.*, p.21.

38 'a dream come true': *ibid.*, p.130.

38 'I'm a bankrupt': *ibid.*, p.234.

38 for his Tottenham shares: *ibid.*, pp.236–7.

39 'and lose fucking money?': *ibid.*, p.323.

39 a profit on his investment: *ibid.*, p.328.

39 before Sugar's arrival: *ibid.*, p.208.

39 'the regulations of the Football League': *ibid.*, p.340.

40 'I'm a one-man-orchestra': *ibid.*, p.256.

40 impropriety in the club: *Sunday Mirror*, 12 October 1997.

41 represented by Eric Hall: Ashby, *Bungs, Bribes and Sweet F.A.*, p.285.

41 inserting stories into newspapers: The FA Premier League's Commission of Inquiry (FAPL) Report, Introduction p.20.

41 conflicts of interest to flourish: *ibid.*, p.9.

41 denied the allegation: *ibid.*, p.17.

41 'You can't survive unless you fiddle': Ashby, *Bungs, Bribes and Sweet F.A.*, p.210.

42 'would be a mammoth task': *ibid.*, p.18.

42 In the chaos: *ibid.*, p.17.

42 his own assets and loans: *ibid.*, pp.261–2.

42 'as long as we could': DTI Report, p.19.

42 finance his entertainment: Ashby, *Bungs, Bribes and Sweet F.A.*, p.370.

47 British basketball league: *New York Times*, 17 September 1982.

47 'try to do a dodgy deal': Taped interview of Richard Tessel by Tony Yorke, 1994.

48 paid each club £100,000: *ibid.*

48 'I don't deal with agents': *Sunday People*, 9 July 1989.

49 from his account in Monaco: Taped interview of Richard Tessel by Tony Yorke, 1994.

50 either the player or the club: *Today*, 20 June 1987

50 'the law on playing matters': FAPL Report, Introduction pp.5–6; *Sunday Mirror*, 19 October 1997.

50 those lodged with the FA: FAPL Report, K p.12.

51 The parcel was handed over: *Mail on Sunday*, 26 October 1997.

51 £2 million in July 1993: *Sunday Telegraph*, 19 October 1997.

51 'which weren't there already': FAPL Report, Introduction p.20.

54 'no point in taking it further': *Independent*, 10 December 2001.

54 'commission from where you could': FAPL Report, Introduction p.17.

55 during that year from the club: Tottenham Hotspur Board meeting, 7 August 1991, Second Minute, p.244.

55 would be £37,500: *Sunday People*, 26 June 1994.

55 'He's pig ignorant': Taped interview of Richard Tessel by Tony Yorke, 1994.

56 'a fuckin geezer with one leg': Ashby, *Bungs, Bribes and Sweet F.A.*, p.198.

56 'I'm a fuckin' maestro at it': *ibid.*, p.202 ; FAPL Report, Gascoigne, Introduction p.13 and Part 2.

56 income from the deal: Ashby, *Bungs, Bribes and Sweet F.A.*, p.217.

57 for fraud in totally unrelated matters: *ibid.*, p.289.

57 Roach denied receiving any money: Tottenham Hostpur Board meeting, 7 August 1991, Second Minute, p.244.

57 'like a dead body': Taped interview of Richard Tessel by Tony Yorke, 1994.

58 accumulated at least £71,000: FAPL Report, Gascoigne, Introduction p.13 and Part 2.

58 'a very sensitive area': Tottenham Hotspur Board meeting, 7 August 1991, Second Minute, p.244.

58 'to the appropriate authorities': *ibid*.

58 'any letters written': Ashby, *Bungs, Bribes and Sweet F.A.*, p.332.

58 'immediate action is taken': *ibid.*, p.333.

58 report the issue to the Football League: *ibid.*, p.333.

59 action against Scholar for 'misfeasance': *ibid.*, p.338.

59 had proved to be a failure: *ibid.*, p.478.

59 weaken his influence: Ashby, *Bungs, Bribes and Sweet F.A.*, p.303.

60 an unorthodox finance company: *ibid.*, p.305.

60 falsely claimed to own: DTI Report, pp.93–4.

60 trading while permanently insolvent: DTI Report, p.74.

60 loan of £500,000 to Venables: DTI Report, p.81.

61 the *Independent* newspaper: Ashby, *Bungs, Bribes and Sweet F.A.*, p.414.

61 'Mr Ashby's bankruptcy per se': DTI Report, p.105; Tottenham Hotspur Board meeting minute, 28 January 1993, p.693 and meeting minute 5 Sept 1992, p.533.

62 authorize a procurement fraud: FAPL Report, Introduction p.26.

62 'anything like this before': *ibid.*, p.25.

63 between himself and Clough: *ibid.*, pp.130–3.

64 'the file had disappeared': Ashby, *Bungs, Bribes and Sweet F.A.*, p.420.

66 his remaining three-year contract: Ashby, *Bungs, Bribes and Sweet F.A.*, p.647.

68 unwilling to surrender: *ibid.*, p.704.

CHAPTER 3: THE RELUCTANT INVESTIGATORS

72 'It's a forgery': *Panorama*, 'The Manager', 16 September 1993, p.756.

72 'full positive': Report by G. Jenkinson for BBC TV, 23 May 1997.

72 won £150,000 in damages: *Panorama*, p.738.

73 undisclosed 'loans' to players: *ibid.*, p.434.

73 'as repeatedly promised': Paul Kendrew, Inland Revenue, to Terry Venables, 28 November 1994.

74 four police investigations: *Panorama*, pp.774–5.

78 a vehicle for intruders: *The Times*, 15 March 1995.

78 transfers of players to the club: The FA and Premier League's Commission of Inquiry (FAPL) Report, Introduction p.20.

78 'a letter with your proposal': FAPL Report, Introduction p.20.

79 'too much money out of it': *ibid.*, Introduction p.7.

79 resold by Nottingham Forest: *ibid.*, B p.10.

79 profits from Hauge: *ibid.*, B p.19.

79 a trawler visiting Hull: *ibid.*, L p.7; *Daily Telegraph*, 20 September 1997.

81 bank account in Guernsey: FAPL Report, Introduction p.11.

83 'number of "paybacks" which are involved': *ibid.*, F p.12.

83 'introduction to the market': *ibid.*, F p.16.

84 aiding Jensen's transfer: *ibid.*, F p.20.

84 cash in a Dublin bank: *ibid.*, F p.14.

84 'George wanted a whole brewery': *Sunday Times*, 5 January 1997.

86 'any substantive questions': *Daily Telegraph*, 24 February 1995.

86 'best interests of the club': Arsenal's public statement, 21 February 1995.

86 'I have made no money from transfers': *Daily Telegraph*, 22 February 1995.

86 'benefited from any transfer': *Evening Standard*, 23 February 1995.

87 the report was published: *The Times*, 24 February 1995.

87 'We will meet that responsibility': *Daily Telegraph*, 13 July 1995.

88 'to the odd paper bag': *Observer*, 26 February 1995.

88 'direct to the selling club': FAPL Report, Introduction p.13.

89 'Do you fancy ten years in a cell?': Taped interview of Richard Tessel by Tony Yorke, 1994.

89 commissions among four people: *News of the World*, 25 November 2001.

89 'That is our business': *Mail on Sunday*, 16 April 1995.

90 'where the money went': *News of the World*, 25 November 2001.

90 Roach strongly denied: *Sunday Mirror*, 22 December 2002.

90 resolved some chicanery: *Mail on Sunday*, 18 June 1995.

90 'stories about where it went': *Guardian*, 25 October 1995.

92 'evaporated without substantiation': FAPL Report, Introduction p.2.

93 Venables refused any explanations: Taped interview of Richard Tessel by Tony Yorke, 1994.

94 refusal to 10 Downing Street: *Independent*, 1 February 1996.

98 builder denied receiving any money: FAPL Report, G pp.128–9.

99 he offered a third explanation: Terry Venables, *Venables: The Autobiography*, (Penguin, 1995), pp.87–91.

99 both were lying: FAPL Report, Introduction p.143.

99 vital ingredient of the transfer: *ibid*., pp.64, 77,85, 87, 90, 143.

99 would never be another 'bungs' inquiry: *Independent on Sunday*, 1 September 1996.

100 'mislead the Inquiry in their evidence': FAPL Report, Introduction p.141.

101 'jail me if possible': *Observer*, 21 September 1997.
101 a similar destabilizing investigation: *Observer*, 23 January 1998 and 16 September 1998.

CHAPTER 4: THE CHAIRMAN

104 'the best deal for football': Chris Horrie, *Premiership*, (Pocket, 2002), p.71.
108 produced £700,000 in profits: *Daily Express*, 12 April 1971.
109 'I am fully involved in the group': BBC Radio 5, 'Take it to the Bridge', 11 December 2000.
109 'with one absent': *Financial Times*, 25 February 1969.
111 $50 million of profits: Public Records Office, Foreign and Commonwealth Office (FCO), 12 October 1970, 44/461.
111 on 20 January 1967: FCO, 13 March 1970, 44/456.
111 source of future earnings: Public Records Office, Treasury, 317/1512.
112 'breaking the rules': *Financial Times*, 16 July 1968.
112 'living off our wits': *Financial Times*, 8 July 1964.
112 divide and rule: *Daily Mail*, 2 October 1998.
113 incensed the local population: FCO, 9 February 1970, 44/454, 44/463 and FCO, 20 February 1970, 44/461.
113 'cavalier attitude': FCO, 9 February 1970, 44/463.
113 promised tax concessions: FCO, 15 December 1970, 44/465.
114 'or he gets out altogether': FCO, 12 March 1970, 44/456.
114 compelled to abandon the islands: FCO, 7 October 1970, 44/461; FCO, 25 November 1970, 44/463.
114 'give way' without compensation: FCO, 20 February 1970, 44/461; FCO, 14 January 1970, 44/454.
114 future American investors: FCO, 20 February 1970, 44/455.
114 'social security scheme on the island': FCO, 31 January 1970, 44/459.
114 'misled by Bates': FCO, 4 August 1970, 44/459.
115 'reputation will stink': FCO, 12 October 1970, 44/461.
115 'offensive, abusive and unhelpful': FCO, 16 December 1970, 44/465.

115 'due to Mr Bates': Public Records Office, Treasury, 31 March 1971, 317/1513.

115 threatening compulsory purchase: FCO, 25 November 1970, 44/463/4.

115 'a blatant piece of theft': FCO, 16 December 1970, 44/465.

115 to seek a settlement: Public Records Office, Treasury, 25 March 1971, T317/1513.

115 $6.8 million and probably more: FCO, 19 April 1971, 44/624.

116 'It's grossly unfair': FCO, 2 June 1971, 44/627.

116 'creditors in the lurch': FCO, 25 March 1971 and 29 March 1971, 44/624.

123 driven off by his wife: *Irish Times*, 24 March 1976.

127 'His pace was too fast': *Financial Times*, 25 February 1969.

127 'make his dreams come true': *The Times*, 13 July 1997.

131 102 million shares: *Independent*, 11 November 1995.

132 'to cover the amounts owed': *Daily Express*, 25 August 1993.

CHAPTER 5: THE PASSING PURIST

138 retained a 15 per cent stake: David Conn, *The Football Business*, (Mainstream 1997), pp.34–5, 165–167.

138 flotation at £102 million: *ibid*, p.64.

138 worth £70 million: *ibid*, p.96.

139 'excessive drinking and poor leadership': HMSO, The Hillsborough Stadium Disaster, Inquiry by Lord Justice Taylor, Final Report (Cm 962, January 1990), paragraph 26.

139 'its supporter customers': *ibid*, paragraph 53.

145 listen to the fans' representatives: *Independent on Sunday*, 22 January 1995.

146 eightieth birthday party: *Mail on Sunday*, 1 February 1995.

150 'sitting next to royalty': *Daily Telegraph*, 7 July 2000.

153 properly regulate itself: *Sunday Telegraph*, 18 January 1998.

153 'fit and proper person test': Sir John Smith's report, 'Football, Its Values, Finances and Reputation', 13 January 1998, p.14.

154 nomination of an independent regulator: *ibid*, p.16.

154 'into the wastepaper basket': *Independent*, 10 December 2001.

154 'What a load of cobblers . . . A joke': Harry Redknapp, *'Arry: An Autobiography*, (HarperCollinsWillow, 1999), p.135.

158 'his vacuous posturing': *Evening Standard*, 6 July 1998.

159 'endless wrecking tactics': Adam Brown, letter to David Mellor, 22 July 1998.

CHAPTER 6: EL TEL

165 'fulfil Pompey's potential': *Portsmouth News*, 19 November 1996.

166 'the transaction as possible': *Independent*, 26 November 1998.

168 establish Oakliffe Holdings: Tom Bower, *The Paymaster*, (Simon & Schuster UK Ltd, 2001) p.104.

169 closed for safety reasons: *Portsmouth News*, 3 December 1997.

169 the near-insolvent club: *ibid*., 5 December 1997.

169 'transactions of obvious impropriety': 'Affadavit of Graham Richard Horne, deputy inspector of companies of the DTI, 1995, in the matter of Secretary of State for Trade and Industry and Terence Frederick Venables' (DTI Report), p.75.

170 guilty to the nineteen offences: *ibid*., p.89.

172 the endorsement of Alex Ferguson: *News of the World*, 15 February 1998 and 22 February 1998.

172 'only number one': *Sun*, 13 December 1997.

172 worth £100 million: *Financial Times*, 21 November 1998.

172 deterred any City support: *Sunday Express*, 15 March 1998.

173 'You're paying too much': *The Times*, 1 May 1998.

173 'I can work with him': *Mirror*, 27 February 1998.

173 'He is the authority on football': *Financial Times*, 27 November 1998.

174 received from the club's owner: *Evening Standard*, 23 November 1998.

174 receiving only £600,000: *ibid*.

176 at a client's expense: *Evening Standard*, 5 August 1999.

177 had been inaccurate: *Mail on Sunday*, 2 July 2000.

178 had been 'a mistake': *Daily Express*, 29 January 1999.

178 'a sound financial position': *Evening Standard*, 21 January 1999.

178 'I was a sucker': *Daily Mail*, 16 April 1999.

178 by a High Court judge: *Guardian*, 13 October 1999.

CHAPTER 7: FIASCOS AND DISILLUSIONMENT

181 'scheming, self-serving chairman': *Sunday Times*, 20 December 1998.

184 'nations of the world': *Independent on Sunday*, 20 December 1998.

186 would not be repeated: *Independent on Sunday*, 1 September 1996.

189 valued at £30 million: House of Commons, Culture, Media and Sport Committee, Sixth Report, Wembley National Stadium 2001–02 HC 843, Vol II, Memorandum Ev70–71.

189 'a completely transparent process': *ibid*., Vol II, Memorandum Ev73.

190 endorsement of Chris Smith: House of Commons, Culture, Media and Sport Committee, Fourth Report, Wembley National Stadium, 1 March 2000.

199 not dependent on Wembley's reconstruction: House of Commons, Culture, Media and Sport Committee, Fourth Report, Staging International Sporting Events 1998–9, 124–11, Q108. And see, House of Commons, Culture, Media and Sport Committee, Fourth Report, Wembley National Stadium, 1 March 2000, p.x.

200 'detriment of athletics': House of Commons, Culture,

Media and Sport Committee, Fourth Report, Wembley National Stadium, 1 March 2000, p.xi.

200 'like a butterfly': House of Commons, Culture, Media and Sport Committee, Fourth Report, Wembley National Stadium, 1 March 2000, p.xxviii. And see, House of Commons, Culture, Media and Sport Committee, Third Report, Staging International Sporting Events, vol I, 28 March 2001, p.xxiii.

CHAPTER 8: THE FA

203 'from top to bottom': *Daily Telegraph*, 23 June 1999.

203 he should be 'removed': *Daily Telegraph*, 25 May 1999.

208 'relationship with Adam Crozier': Richard Faulkner, letter to Kate Hoey, 5 April 2000.

209 decision to the DCMS: Adam Crozier, letter to Malcolm Clarke, 12 June 2000.

209 'over my dead body': Adam Brown, letter to James Purnell, 27 June 2000.

210 had been 'wasted': Adam Brown, letter to James Purnell, 29 June 2000.

211 from Newcastle United: Hoey, 31 July 2000; Adam Brown, letters to Kate Hoey, 31 July 2000 and 11 October 2000.

212 'thousands of football fans': Richard Faulkner, letter to Geoff Thompson, 12 July 2000.

213 'biased establishment lapdog': Richard Faulkner, letter to Tony Blair, 10 July 2000.

214 'with deep regret': John Smith, letter to Chris Smith, 3 October 2000.

217 bow to Scudamore's veto: Niall Mackenzie, letter to Chris Smith, 20 February 2001.

217 'and the entire proposal': Kate Hoey, letter to Geoff Thompson, 26 March 2001.

218 under Bates's chairmanship: House of Commons, Culture, Media and Sports Committee, Sixth Report, Wembley National Stadium 2001–02 HC 843, Memorandum Ev16.

218   the use of public money: *ibid.*, Memorandum Ev16.

219   'standards of transparency': *ibid.*, Memorandum Ev20.

219   with the contractors: *ibid.*, Memorandum Ev20.

219   about 'irregularities': *ibid.*, Vol II Memorandum Ev44.

224   The English bid was resoundingly defeated: *Sunday Telegraph*, 2 July 2000.

226   consequences of the letter: House of Commons, Culture, Media and Sports Committee, Sixth Report, Wembley National Stadium 2001–02 HC 843Vol II Ev47.

226   to above £400 million: *ibid.*, Vol II Ev48 & Ev66.

227   'value for money': *ibid.*, Vol I p.21, Vol II Ev73.

228   his 'excellent' position: *Guardian*, 16 October 2001.

229   publication on 6 May: *Mail on Sunday*, 6 May 2001.

230   'make room for new people': *Mail on Sunday*, 17 June 2001.

CHAPTER 9: THE MANAGER

232   'make the bucks while you can': Harry Redknapp, *'Arry: An Autobiography*, (HarperCollinsWillow, 1999), p.186.

232   'it doesn't last forever': *ibid.*

232   with Ron Atkinson, an idol: *Sun*, 28 April 1995.

233   'the Lampards and all them': *The Times*, 31 January 1998.

239   'I simply don't trust him': *www.soccerage.com*

242   'I have a wicked temper': *Guardian*, 7 March 1987.

242   'the "best" manager': *Sunday Times*, 16 April 1995.

242   'with my top players': Redknapp, *'Arry*, p.159.

242   talented players on the field: *Sunday Telegraph*, 10 January 1999.

243   'does not happen': *News of the World*, 17 October 1999, quoted from book by Eyal Berkovic, an Israeli journalist.

243   '"always on the booze"': *Guardian*, 7 November 1998.

243   to become 'legless': *Daily Mail*, 21 December 2001; *News of the World*, 24 June 2001.

243   'it didn't work': *The Times*, 18 January 1999.

243   'I stopped that years ago': *www.soccerage.com*

244 'I think the world of John Hartson': *Sunday Mirror*, 11 October 1998.

245 'this management game': Redknapp, *'Arry*, p.65.

245 'it is ludicrous': *News of the World*, 2 February 1997.

246 'They gut me': *Guardian*, 6 May 1995.

246 in Britain at the time: *Evening Standard*, 15 August 1996.

246 'a large part of my life': Redknapp, *'Arry*, p.136.

246 'I know what he can do': *Daily Mail*, 1 January 1997.

247 'the cheap end of the market': *Daily Mail*, 13 September 1997.

247 'players with no MOTs': Redknapp, *'Arry*, p.116.

247 'next goal is coming from': *Daily Mail*, 23 April 1997.

247 had been transferred: *Sunday Times*, 28 December 1997.

249 was his mantra: *Sunday Mirror*, 11 October 1998.

250 'obvious in this game': *The Times*, 31 January 1998.

CHAPTER 10: THE AGENT

255 tour of South Africa: Tony Yorke, *Sunday People*, 26 June 1994.

256 £138,000 was missing: *News of the World*, April 1998.

257 Kollin had appropriated the money: Erich Leimlehner file, S105227/97.

258 transfer to West Ham: *News of the World*, 1 February 1998.

261 shared with Morabito: The FA and Premier League's Commission of Inquiry (FAPL) Report, Introduction p.16.

264 'it will be the last': *Mirror*, 28 July 2001.

265 which Ferguson desired: Dennis Roach, letter to Bobby Robson, 15 November 2001.

267 sold to Charlton: *Daily Record*, 5 October 2000.

267 cost £5 to manufacture: *News of the World*, 15 March 1998 and 22 March 1998.

268 'happy to defend myself': *Daily Telegraph*, 28 July 2001.

271 double the market price: *Financial Times*, 24 January 1997.

271 'biggest money spinner': *Sunday Times*, 27 July 1997.

279 registered by FIFA: Dennis Roach, letter to FA, 15 November 2001.

281 £100 million one year later: *Football Business International*, September 2001.

281 'healthier than it has ever been': *Observer*, 2 December 2001.

285 'what happens to clubs': David Conn, *The Football Business*, (Mainstream 1997), p.175.

CHAPTER 11: TURMOIL AND TRASH

287 'stay on their feet': *Daily Star*, 20 June 1998.

289 'never dreamt it would happen': *Guardian*, 10 May 2001.

292 Veron's sale to Manchester United: *Mail on Sunday*, 17 June 2001.

294 potential conflict of interest: *Independent on Sunday*, 28 March 1999.

295 'so long as it's conducted professionally': *Observer*, 19 May 2002.

296 cost Stretford's creditors £128,000: *Sunday Express*, 29 October 2000.

296 'I don't know how or who with': *FHM*, January 1995.

296 'all parties are satisfied': *Independent on Sunday*, 3 February 2002.

297 'myself while I can': *Mirror*, 6 December 1980.

297 about two transfers: *Mirror*, 19 December 1994; *News of the World*, 2 April 1995.

299 loaned by Reid to Cologne: *Daily Mail*, 17 September 2001.

301 'what agents are involved': *Independent*, 5 May 2000.

302 diligence was flawed: *Times*, 27 April 2001.

303 had been dishonest: All England Law Reports 2001, 2A11 ER (Comm) p.828.

303 'stuck in a time warp': *Daily Express*, 28 December 2000.

303 'I don't give a damn': *Daily Telegraph*, 23 September 2000.

303 recouped £46 million: *Daily Telegraph*, 25 January 2002.

307 transfer to Middlesbrough himself: Michael Crick, *The Boss*, (Simon & Schuster UK Ltd., 2002), p.504.
308 authenticity and a frame: *Daily Telegraph*, 15 November 2001.

CHAPTER 12: THE 'DREAM-MAKER'

319 by FIFA as an agent: *Jewish Association of Business Ethics*, 7 May 2002.
323 agreed to fly to Rotterdam: *Daily Telegraph*, 31 August 2001.
331 'probably be better off': *Guardian*, 20 August 1991.
332 £6 million from Real Madrid: *Mirror*, 29 September 1999.
333 from Juventus of Italy: *Evening Standard*, 8 April 2002.
333 'orderly and dignified manner': *ibid*.
333 voicing similar doubts: *Mirror*, 9 August 1996.
339 keep £25,000 for himself: The FA and Premier League's Commission of Inquiry Report, E p.12.

CHAPTER 13: ANATOMY OF DREAMS

351 unreliable sworn testimony: *The Times*, 10 July 2002.
355 'rejected by the board': *Evening Standard*, 16 July 2002.
355 'into thin air?': *Evening Standard*, 17 July 2002.
357 'the grotesque game': *Guardian*, 14 September 2002.

Index